CHINA FRIEND ORFOE?

CHINA FRIEND OR FOE?

HUGO DE BURGH

ICON BOOKS

Published in the UK in 2006 by
Icon Books Ltd, The Old Dairy,
Brook Road, Thriplow,
Cambridge SG8 7RG
email: info@iconbooks.co.uk
www.iconbooks.co.uk

Sold in the UK, Europe, South Africa and Asia
by Faber & Faber Ltd, 3 Queen Square,
London WC1N 3AU
or their agents

Distributed in the UK, Europe, South Africa and Asia
by TBS Ltd, Frating Distribution Centre, Colchester Road
Frating Green, Colchester CO7 7DW

This edition published in Australia in 2006
by Allen & Unwin Pty Ltd,
PO Box 8500, 83 Alexander Street,
Crows Nest, NSW 2065

Distributed in Canada by
Penguin Books Canada,
90 Eglinton Avenue East, Suite 700,
Toronto, Ontario M4P 2YE

ISBN-10: 1-84046-733-9
ISBN-13: 978-1840467-33-8

Text copyright © 2006 Hugo de Burgh

Typesetting by Wayzgoose

Printed and bound in the UK by
Clays of Bungay

Contents

About the Author

Hugo de Burgh is Professor of Journalism at the University of Westminster and Director of the China Media Centre. He was first in China at the end of the Cultural Revolution. He has worked as a journalist for Scottish Television, BBC and Channel 4. His previous books include *Investigative Journalism* (2000), *The Chinese Journalist* (2003), *Making Journalists* (2005) and *China and Britain: the Potential Impact of China's Development* (2005).

Preface

This book was conceived when I heard an erudite journalist and political pundit saying on the BBC's *Start the Week* that he had never heard of the 'May 4th Movement'. It struck me then as never before just how unfortunate is the ignorance of China among people in my own country, people of the class that prides itself on having opinions worth listening to from Baghdad to Batavia. Now that China's impact upon us is getting daily greater, this is unforgivable.

This book compresses some essential information about China into concise articles, with some references to help you enlighten yourself further. The topics, of course, are those that people outside think are important about China, or that I think they want to know about, but this is a vast and complicated society and there are many others which might have been included. It is for practical people who are inquiring: those who want to know, when they see a report of some village riot, how the government officials operate, how typical this is, and what is being done. When they hear of a new scientific breakthrough, they want some context for it. You get an idea of what China's strengths and weaknesses are, so that you can make up your own mind.

I want to thank Wilf Stevenson and Gordon Brown MP, of the Smith Institute, for inviting me to work with them on the Valuing China Seminars over 2005–2006; the work done there provided the basis for this book. Peter Pugh, of Icon Books, grasped the need and refined the concept; I have greatly appreciated his, and Duncan Heath's input. At the China Media Centre, my colleagues Sally Feldman, Colin Sparks, Annette Hill, Peter Goodwin and Teite Buhr have all supported me by being understanding of my absences and by asking questions. I am grateful to them, and most particularly to Chang Yiru, whose help has been invaluable.

Introduction

The suddenness of the changes that are taking place in China astonishes. In the wealthy nations, there is awe. Are we to be surpassed? Are we to see our economies undermined? Do Chinese ambitions threaten us?

It is understandable that the questions are posed and that people imagine that a choice has to be made – friend or foe – but this book is written in part to show that they are bad questions. Having read this trailer to China, I hope that the reader will see that the real questions are more likely to be these: can the government prevent health and environmental catastrophes? Can it continue its dogged transition to more accountable government without unleashing damaging populism or military repression? Can the rest of the world manage the changes that improvements in the material lives of so many other people will force upon their countries, without blaming China and promoting conflict?

The bad questions focus on the negative; they are 'zero sum game', they derive from panic rather than reflection. If those fears themselves cause us to try to understand China better, and if they oblige the People's Republic of China (PRC) to pay attention to the international implications of what it does, then the questions are worth asking, but not if the asking of them is to incite the tension and enmity that will make impossible resolutions to the consequences of China's rise.

For consequences there are. Earlier generations thought that the economic advance of Japan would be disruptive, yet the rest of the world survived Japan's turning itself into the second economic power. What has given rise to fears in this case is not only that China is doing the same, but that the effect on us of the modernisation of the most populous nation is likely to be much greater. If present trends continue, China in time will be the most mighty **economy**, because of the numbers still waiting to add their enterprise to the

Chinese miracle. One quarter of humankind is Chinese.[1]

The impact is also potentially much greater because of simultaneous development elsewhere. The populations of East and South Asia are advancing; more and more are attaining the income expected in the wealthy countries. This is now realisable for 3.3 billion people, three times the numbers in today's wealthy countries.

Effects

China competes against established manufacturers in ever more sophisticated fields. First the companies and jobs of other textile industries are lost to rivals, then those in electronic assembly go, and so on up the 'technology ladder'.[2] So far, the alarmists in the USA, lobbying Congress to protect their manufacturing, have been checked by the big high-technology companies that are enthusiastic to sell to China. Europeans have been more interested in the benefits to consumers of China's advance, noticing that in all wealthy countries, the proportion of family income spent on consumer goods has fallen. Thanks to China, we are richer.

As competition has forced down the prices of manufactured goods, Chinese exports have increased in quantity, further expanding Chinese productive capacity and drawing more and more peasants off the land and into industry. Because of this, in the wealthy economies, the wages of unskilled workers fall and jobs are lost; governments devise more schemes both to improve education and to keep people away from the dole queue. We assume that we must race further up that technology ladder just to keep ahead, trusting in, for example, our competence at 'invisibles' and education, although we cannot be sure that we can remain competitive for long even there. To remain so, policy thinkers are asking, do we need to jettison our welfare programmes and reform our education systems?

China's need for fuel and the raw materials for its industrialisation is so huge that countries and companies are having to try to understand what influence this will have upon their own development plans.

Taken together, all this amounts to an upheaval. Whether other countries are able to adjust depends on whether their economies are complementary to, or competitive with, China.[3] Germany and the USA may be creating as many jobs as they are losing; this is not necessarily the case with Mexico, whose manufacturing is undermined by China and whose poor try harder to get over the border to the USA. Will the French, Spanish and Italian economies be able to adjust like Germany, or will they struggle like Mexico? What are the political repercussions of all this?

There are kinds of impact other than the immediately economic. It has been argued, plausibly, that there will not be enough food in the world for us all, now that China has become a net importer and that demand is rising much faster than supply.[4] Available arable land and fish stocks are both diminishing. China has become the world's biggest consumer of red meat, its grain needs are outstripping the productive capacity of even the most productive producers and, as China's population continues to increase and to consume more, the rest of the world will need to adjust, for example by eating less meat.[5] The world **environment** is affected by the scale of industrialisation and progress towards providing the same material conditions as are enjoyed in the USA.

With such disruption uppermost in many minds, there is a risk of seeing China's resurgence merely as negative. Yet we should celebrate it. That the poor may climb out of the deep well of perpetual insecurity and regular hunger, because the government has found out how to release the enterprise of the people and to make wealth-creation possible through trade, is wonderful. That they too may enjoy the material conditions already achieved in the wealthy countries is a great achievement. But as wealthy countries make way for the imports that make this advance possible, their politicians need to ensure that the creative and productive forces in their own societies can replace lost industries, so that the success of some does not lead to the impoverishment of others. The science and technology community in the USA, alarmed, is pushing for action.[6]

The challenges posed by China's advance therefore stimulate technological advance and economic development. But they may do much more. China is not merely providing toys or computers at cheaper prices; it is educating, it is creating the biggest consumer market with all the implications that has for the world, and it is thinking up new services. We are challenged to do things in different ways: to improve our education systems to keep up; to update our tourism provision for people whose standards may be higher; work out our response to environmental issues more realistically; deal with problems our politicians have avoided, from welfare reform to vocational training to job development to investment in science.

Foe?

What are the conditions under which China might come to be seen as an enemy? They tend to be conditions in the making of which others would play a larger part than the Chinese themselves. Rivalry over resources might become hostility; fearful competitors might try to cut China out of markets, so wrecking its opportunities to advance and causing political upheaval, in which circumstances it would be easy to blame 'foreigners'. Fear is sometimes expressed that the outstanding disagreements between China and its neighbours might lead to war because nationalism is so easily incited.[7] A government might either seize upon war as a distraction from economic failure or, equally, be driven to war by nationalistic fervour made uncontrollable because of slights from abroad. The most obvious flashpoint is Taiwan.

In the UK, whose politicians are still coping with the legacies of colonial policies in Ireland, and which has recently granted national parliaments to Scotland and Wales, the militancy over Taiwan and Tibet can appear very extraordinary. It seems so obvious that China's interests will best be served by respecting those territories' sense of identity. Unfortunately though, since 1949, passions have been so inflamed over these questions as to make rational discussion impossible. Otherwise reasonable Chinese people will insist to you that a war with Taiwan is inevitable and that the price of a war is worth paying to achieve 'unity'. Because the US is prepared – for the moment – to guarantee the Taiwanese right to self-determination, and because China's economy is so tied to that of the USA, the Chinese government is unlikely to repeat the kind of threatening of Taiwan that took place in 1996, unless forced to by popular emotion. But the risk remains that the government will be pushed by excitement on the streets and/or soldiers' ambition to do what it knows could be disastrous. Given both the recent history of China and the use made of that history by politicians, popular intransigence is not surprising. Until Chinese people are more comfortable with and confident about their national identity, they are likely to remain tense and to feel threatened when sympathy is expressed for self-determination for those who are not enthusiastic about being part of the PRC.

Some believe that China is to be feared in the way that Germany or Japan were by earlier generations in the 1930s.[8] They see only that China has substantial armed forces with boastful generals, a sense of grievance, an opaque political system, a poisonous environment, a chequered past, claims upon neighbouring territories and an insatiable need for raw materials with which to maintain its growth.

Yet China has ended its period of savage totalitarian rule, as bad as anything the Nazis or the Bolsheviks vented upon their subjects, and is becoming slowly but inexorably less authoritarian. It is doing what other countries failed to do – evolving out of totalitarianism without waging war. China's overriding preoccupation is with material development, which war will not advance. China is restoring some of the beliefs and attitudes which held it together before the socialist experiment, and these were rarely aggressive. Although nationalism is fierce, the policy-makers are highly educated, pragmatic, largely well-intentioned towards the world, and non-ideological. To maintain the chosen path of 'peaceful rise' and not alarm the rest of us, Chinese policy-makers know that they need to

5

address problems which not only worry others but put the whole project at risk.

Some argue that China since 1949 has been an aggressor nation, limited only by its capabilities. It annexed Tibet, instigated wars in Korea, Vietnam and India; it threatens Taiwan and has worked ceaselessly to be a military nuclear power. Equally, it can be argued that the Maoist period is now over and that the PRC government, since 1992 at least, has done everything possible to normalise relations and, moreover, that it is returning to the traditions of the Chinese past. These traditions were of restraint in strength and of belief in **softpower**, the power of cultural attraction rather than of military might. Is it the Chinese Communist Party (CCP), then, which stands in the way of China reinstating these traditions in the post-socialist era?

The main justification for CCP rule today is that it can deliver better living conditions, an advanced economy and the promise of an affluent country. Since economic development largely depends upon good relations with the US, with China the weaker partner, it behoves the CCP to do everything it can to keep those relations good, even if from time to time it will use rhetoric that seems at odds with this objective.

So anti-American nationalism is potentially damaging to the CCP and needs to be contained; but this is difficult in a society in which xenophobia has been cultivated over several generations, where the mass media is increasingly able to reflect or reinforce public opinion, and where politicians dare not be deemed less than 'patriotic'. The armed forces are thought to be much more fiercely 'patriotic' than the government, possibly because the officers have little or no experience of the complexities of managing a modern economy and its international relationships.

Seen like this, the CCP deserves the support of Western governments concerned that nationalism might involve China in international conflicts. Peter Nolan has argued that all talk among US strategists of trying to undermine the CCP in order to encourage democracy is potentially dangerous to China and to the world.[9] The Chinese have suffered enough disruption over the past century; the last thing they need is instability, let alone a revolution, when they have a government which is not only providing greater opportunity but also expanding the boundaries of the possible all the time. The consequences of turmoil would be faced not only by the Chinese but, now that China is integrating into the world economic system, by the rest of us.

Chinese perspective

Asian neighbours or economic competitors may feel uncomfortable about China's rise; China feels threatened by the major force in Asia, the USA. The disparity in economic and military power is colossal. There are no alternative centres with which China might make alliances to balance against it.[10] China is now dependent upon the USA in several different ways. It is China's largest export market and perhaps the second-largest trading partner after the EU,[11] but the USA sells relatively little to China, though the advanced goods it sells matter very much to the buyer. A high proportion of investment in China is to make exports of manufactures to the USA possible. By reducing their investment in China, Americans could cripple it. Chinese exports to the USA could be substituted from other developing economies, with severe consequences for China. Technical transfer from the US is more valuable than from any other source.[12] China receives more World Bank support than any other country, and the US influences World Bank decisions. Despite the weakness of China's position, US politicians, businesspeople and trades unionists show hostility towards China publicly and often. In trade negotiations, the US tries to pressure China on **human rights** and to motivate others to do so. US power is seen as the defender of Taiwan's separation. China tends to see particular disputes as elements of a strategic effort to impede her, whereas the US regards them as specific.[13]

All in all, the USA is regarded as viewing China as a potential rival whose rise must before long be resisted; a country which can invade Iraq on flimsy pretexts will find ways of containing China, it is assumed, helped doubtless by Western leaders such as Britain's Tony Blair, eager for association with the superpower. With such an appraisal, the PRC has to tread very carefully in its dealings with the US.

Modernity

It has often been remarked that, in historical perspective, the resurgence of China augurs the re-instatement of the world order that preceded the 18th-century European Enlightenment, in which China was pre-eminent. Then, Chinese considered their country to be the centre of the world and the source of all civilisation. Europeans admired China immensely, none more than the English. And then? The relationships between China and the rest, in particular with the English-speaking – or 'Anglophone' – world, have gone through revolutions. For the last 150 years, all the adapting has been by China; this may be changing as we find that modernity is no longer entirely defined by Anglophones.

Before 1715, the English hardly counted among the traders of South East China, but once the East India Company had opened for business in Canton that year they rapidly overtook the Portuguese and Dutch, so that soon English trade was worth that of all the other countries put together. They brought back to Europe what traders had been bringing back for generations, though in the past only for elites: silk, porcelain, tea and pretty things, the market for which was expanding as the development of business in Europe made more and more people wealthy. China's techniques and styles were copied by English craftsmen, and European opinion leaders revered what they knew of its meritocratic system of government and glorious culture. England rapidly became addicted to tea. The first tea had been imported in 1669; by 1830, 30 million tons was being bought, and the amounts kept rising.

Eighteenth-century England wanted a diplomatic relationship

with China, and wanted its merchants – who were not permitted to establish themselves permanently and who, along with their Chinese counterparts, were subject to many inconvenient restrictions – placed on a formal footing. In 1793, Lord Macartney led an embassy to the court in Peking, famous because of the Emperor's declaration that China was self-sufficient and needed nothing from any other country, except humble vassalage. The Emperor was right, for China was then the richest and most independent country; within 50 years all was changed, so that when his successors continued this isolation, they were wrong.

As the frustrations of the merchants continued, the weakness of China became more apparent. The splendour of the late 18th century gave way to reveal an Empire whose administration was ramshackle and decaying, whose forces were generations behind those of the Europeans and whose exports were increasingly being paid for in opium, spreading a habit with a corrosive effect on Chinese society.

If a country today banned alcohol and then seized the cargoes of wine traders and attacked their warehouses, we would be outraged, particularly if they were those of our fellow countrymen. Chinese officials dealt with opium in that way and aroused the fury of the British, such that they retaliated and then, when local troops had been thrashed in the Opium War, imposed the Treaty of Nanking, first of the 'Unequal Treaties' which forced China to open ports to foreign traders and to give them extra-territorial rights – freedom from Chinese law. Hong Kong was ceded. The shame of this is remembered in China, yet many good things came of it. While China suffered Civil War and socialist purges, Hong Kong, in its 135 years of British rule, became a haven for political dissidents and refugees, a Chinese intellectual centre and the model for future economic development. It was to be Britain that, in 1926, first called on the other foreign powers to give up their special privileges and worked with the Chinese government to get them abolished in 1943. Britain offered to negotiate the return of Hong Kong in the 1970s and then initiated the processes which led to its being returned to China in 1997.

Until the mid-19th century, the West copied and imported. Jesuits of the 1600s were the first Europeans to attempt to understand and learn from China, but after them the English were the foremost, adopting ceramic, japanning, paper-making and innumerable other Chinese techniques. Attached to Lord Macartney's entourage was a botanical expedition, which collected great numbers of seeds in what they began to realise was the richest temperate flora on Earth,[14] and gave England chrysanthemum, peony, primrose, tea rose, clematis, azalea, camellia and thousands of other plants and flowers. England's civil service reforms of the 19th century were inspired by Chinese example.

In the 19th century, James Legge translated the Chinese classics and Chinese merchants endowed a professorial chair for him at Oxford; after him came the producers of great dictionaries, Morrison and Giles, and many translators of literature and philosophy, headed by Arthur Waley, genius interpreter of sublime poetry. In 1908 Lawrence Binyon published the first book in a European language on Chinese painting, and in 1935 a huge Chinese art exhibition was held in London.

Yet after the Opium War the learning was really the other way. Chinese sought to understand how the West had become so powerful as to end Chinese supremacy. The educated were awakened to the need to learn, and the first way in which they formulated this was 'using the barbarians' skills to defeat the barbarians' and then, when it was clear that the mere adoption of weapons or ships was not enough, 'keeping Chinese knowledge for the essence, using foreign knowledge to get things done'. Ever since, Chinese have agonised over how or whether to retain Chineseness in the struggle to raise their country so that it is economically and politically at least the equal of the wealthy nations. At various periods they have sought to ditch everything Chinese.

The treaties forced upon China by the commercial Westerners

needed to be upheld, but by the 1840s, China no longer had administrative agencies capable of the modern regulation and tax of trade. Robert Hart built the Chinese Imperial Maritime Customs, which not only collected dues and managed ports and waterways but obliged foreign merchants to respect Chinese rights, even as it made it possible for China to comply with the treaties. Another of many British servants of the Chinese government was Charles Gordon, among those who reformed and rebuilt the army so that it was capable of suppressing the Taiping Rebellion. While there were many missionaries in China for the hundred years after the Treaty of Nanking, their achievements were less in conversion than in the introduction of modern ideas of healthcare, schooling and welfare.

Western books, from engineering to philosophy, were translated in great numbers, intellectual leaders invited to China and new universities established from the 1890s. Bertrand Russell was among the many who visited China to share ideas during the 1920s; English literature had as much influence on the literary renaissance of the first half of the 20th century as did Russian.

Large numbers of young Chinese went abroad to study – future leaders Deng Xiaoping to France, Zhou Enlai to Germany, for example – and came back determined to raise the expectations of their countrymen in every field. Many of the leading Chinese journalists of the 1930s and 40s were educated in the USA, as were engineers, scientists and medical practitioners. Officers of the armed forces were trained first by Britain, Germany and Japan, latterly by the USA, which wanted to support a unified, competent Chinese state in the first half of the 20th century, and finally by Russia.

Confidence in Confucian civilisation crumbled, particularly once the Chinese Communist Party, after 1949, had attempted to replace it wholesale with socialism, rejecting everything of the past. As faith in the CCP has collapsed since the 1970s, a greater confidence in and respect for indigenous culture has tentatively returned.

An Englishman did a great deal to change the terms of debate and to inspire those who want once more to see value in Chinese civilisation. Among many British sinologists, Joseph Needham stands out, both as the scholar who has done most to reveal the world of Chinese science and technology and their contributions to humanity, and because, in doing so, he reversed the assumption of Chinese backwardness. He showed to a world in which science is respected above all, that Confucian civilisation had achievements to its credit that were not only administrative and artistic but also scientific, and that these achievements influenced and enabled the Western advance that would challenge China. Until recently, many Chinese thought that they could be modern only if they rejected the civilisation of their ancestors. No longer, since traditional China is now understood as having contributed to making modernity. This is a profound change, with implications well beyond China.

Reflecting on the alterations that have taken place in the Chinese mentality since China and England first clashed in the mid-19th century, Wang Gongwu reasons that it is in the widespread adoption of ways of thinking scientifically, and in the organisation of business and government, that the Anglophone influence has been substantial. The first President of China, the Anglophile Sun Yatsen, initially championed 'science and democracy' for China before being won over to the ideas of socialist revolution which were to have such disastrous consequences. Today it is the executive-led political systems of Singapore and Hong Kong that are models for China's leaders. Though rejecting English politics, Chinese have admired the respect for law, civic discipline and efficiency 'even though they did not know how that respect was cultivated'.[15] In recent years, Anglophone business models have been studied with energy, but Chinese businesspeople learned much earlier (though during communism they could make use only of what they had learned outside of the PRC) how the relationships between business and government are fundamental to economic development. In traditional China, business was despised, kept on a short leash; today it is eulogised as the sharp point of national development. The story is often repeated of how, in 1995 or thereabouts, the traffic policeman on duty in Tiananmen Square was shocked to see a motor-cade advancing down the main avenue in the capital; shocked, since he had not been warned by the leadership guard, and the road had not been cleared for the high officials he assumed were arriving. Desperately, he called in for instructions. In time, it dawned on him and his colleagues that this was not an official motorcade but the wedding party of one of China's new rich.

The position of business in the Chinese social system has prob-ably changed irrevocably. The ways in which Chinese government works to protect and promote business were learned from the models provided by Britain when its government supported the determination of enterprise to get into China in the 19th century, a lesson reinforced by the modern history of Japan. Admiration for business marks a profound change in attitudes of the Chinese State, for 'never before have Chinese leaders recognised a connection between trading success and higher standards of living for all Chinese'.[16]

Friend

I find it impossible to think of China as a foe, partly because there are so many aspects of Chinese civilisation that I find attractive and life-enhancing, partly because it seems to me that enmity can be in no one's interest, least of all China's. The leaders inherited from the years of Maoism (1949–76) a mess so monstrous as to daunt Solomon: the largest population and a ruined economy; a subverted culture, millions of victims, no legal system, unkempt communities with decayed housing; a ravaged environment and feral youths, no education for ten years … and all at a time when the world around them was advancing into a high-technology and materially prosper-ous future. As you consider the difficulties, you cannot fail to admire the success of China's policy-makers and decision-takers and their courage – or foolhardiness – in shouldering the responsibilities of ruling China today. Cursed by a risible ideology, challenged by discontent within and without, given little gratitude despite achieve-ments that put other post-socialist countries to shame, they battle against difficulties that their equivalents in the West can hardly imagine, with a dogged pragmatism and duty.

This book provides an inkling of those difficulties. In preparing it, I have learned several things. First, to respect a system of government that continues to attract able people with a high sense of public service, attempting to increase accountability while managing extraordinary changes. Of course, they themselves must be scrutinised and held to account by their own citizens and by well-wishers abroad. Second, that anything that can be done to restore China's faith in its traditional identity is beneficial. Maoism has damaged **civil society** with results that hold risks for us all, and the aggressive and ultra-nationalist ideas that are, to date, those of only a minority in China, derive not from the China we admire but from a ragbag of ideas that came out of 19th-century Europe, including Darwinian selection, eugenics and 'scientific socialism'.

Third, how we react to China's advance may determine the future. Resentment at China's development is unbecoming of rich countries and it may also provoke conflicts. We should recognise that China's advance is essential: if it cannot feed its people and deal with the environment crisis, then the dangers to the rest of us are great. We are all involved.

Fourth, we will adapt to the challenge posed by China only if we know what is happening. I used to justify encouraging young Europeans to take up Chinese by the pleasure of communication with another culture, the delight which can be got from its literature, its art, its food or companionship. Or, for utilitarians, with the argument that you cannot establish long-term business relationships with people whose language you cannot speak. But there is now a more pressing need to know China and Chinese: to learn from China. As with our 17th-century ancestors, there are lessons to take back if we are to adapt to a world in which China may not be the dominant power but may dominate our thoughts.

PART ONE

Politics

CHAPTER 1

The Party

The Party provides China's leaders with a powerful weapon for keeping the country under control, yet it is weakened because of what is known of its past and widespread disenchantment with ideology. Changes are being made. Will they do?

Between November 2002 and April 2003, new leaders, with five years ahead of them, came to power. The Sixteenth Party Congress (CPC), followed by the Tenth National People's Congress (NPC), convened to endorse a 'sweeping' turnover of leadership. At the top, in the State Council, are a well known and tested executive team under Hu Jintao (President) and Wen Jiabao (Prime Minister),[1] but observers have noted that in the lower echelons the revolutionary generation of often ill-educated officials has gone. However, apart from the military – whose generals tend to be modern technocrats – provincial leaders are mostly people who are thought to be narrow and conservative in their approach, on account of their formative experiences in the Cultural Revolution (see Glossary and Key Figures).[2] The NPC – at least in terms of appointments – was a formality, in that all the State appointments could be predicted from the line-up confirmed just before the CPC months earlier. All leaders have to wear two hats, State and Party.

The Bolshevik party system was devised by a power-crazed 19th-century European for quite different circumstances, but China has been subjected to it now for over 50 years. The country first went to the polls in 1912, and, despite their limitations, it must then have looked as if China was starting down the road to Western-style democracy. Revolution intervened. The regime that Lenin's pupils would impose was much more centralised, total and intolerant than anything seen under either empire or republic.

The Chinese Communist Party (CCP) is the fount of all power. If government is the executive, the Party is the legislature, policy-maker and inspector-general all together. With a membership of 69 million, the Party as a whole cannot possibly carry out such functions. However, Lenin's party system is 'democratic centralism', which means preserving the appearance of participation while subjecting the membership to the views of the oligarchy (or in **Mao Zedong**'s day, the autocrat), as well as having the apparatus to ensure that the oligarchy's policies are enforced right down to the meanest village or work unit. Thus the people who can initiate or veto anything are in the Standing Committee of the Political Bureau (Politburo) of the Central Committee. The Politburo is the Party's executive, meeting twice a week, and its Standing Committee contains the key decision-makers, who are usually the top government leaders too. Until 1975, Mao decided who would be a member of the Politburo, but now its members, and those of the Standing Committee, are elected by secret ballot of the Central Committee.

Nominally, it is the National Party Congress that is supreme, but in reality its delegates are selected by the Central Committee, now containing 356 members. With over 2,000 members, the National Party Congress cannot be a deliberative body, but it receives the report of the Party chairman, ratifies membership of the Central Committee, approves the Constitution and is valuable for sending down messages to the membership. In 1992, Deng Xiaoping made extensive preparations to ensure that when he used the occasion of the National Party Congress to present his 'socialist market economy' policy, it would be accepted and thence disseminated throughout the Party.[3] About 40 per cent of its members are central government officials, 20 per cent are from the armed forces and 30 per cent are provincial officials. In recent years, the average age has gone down (half are over 50, half under), the educational level up, and people in business form a growing proportion.

The Politburo's powers are exerted both from the centre, and through the provinces. The Provincial Party Committees, and the equivalent committees at county level, are responsible for implementing policy decided centrally. Below this are the Party Committees for work units such as schools, enterprises (including some private ones) and villages. Every university department will have a Party leader as well as a head of department. How do they function? There is variety, as we can see from anecdotes from the media. At a national television programme, the editorial meeting (some of whose participants will be Party members) will propose ideas which will be considered at the next level of management; if that manager is unsure, he will consult the Party Committee before approving. At a regional newspaper, the Party Committee calls in the editor for a weekly meeting to discuss the last week as a guide for the future. At a local newspaper, a set of instructions are received every day from the local Propaganda (Information) Office as to what subjects must, and may not, be covered. Although media experiences cannot be generalised, these give a flavour of the various ways in which primary Party committees may operate.

At the centre, the Politburo manages at least three very powerful bodies: the Central Military Commission, the Central Commission for Discipline and Inspection and the Central Secretariat. The latter contains the immensely important Organisation Department, which decides on the appointments of all officials everywhere. It also contains the management of Policy Research, of the Party Schools and of the *People's Daily* newspaper. The Central Military Commission makes defence policy, supervises the armed forces in great detail (especially appointments) and publishes the military newspaper. The Central Commission for Discipline and Inspection is working very hard to improve 'work style', by which it means maintaining the ideals of the Party in an era of rampant corruption and nepotism. Soon after the fall of the Maoists in 1976, it outlawed the development of personality cults, issuing specific regulations on how leaders should be treated, as well as guidelines to encourage discussion, tolerance of diverse opinions and mutual respect.

These days, it investigates many thousands of corruption allegations every year, works together with journalists and whistle-blowers to expose embezzlement, and has expelled several thousand Party members, as well as turning over to justice some very high-profile crooks who were also in senior political positions. The leaders consider this work essential if the Party is to inspire any confidence.

For a crisis of confidence there certainly is. There is ever-growing appreciation of the disaster that socialist idealism has proved for China. It is difficult to know how widespread the disillusionment is, but it would seem that those who lived through the Cultural Revolution are completely sceptical, while their children can sometimes still have illusions, presumably encouraged by the school system with its requirement to internalise the orthodoxy. Among intellectuals, the growing knowledge about the behaviour of Mao Zedong, the sufferings imposed upon China by absurd policies and even the unflattering early history of the Party have all had a corrosive effect on even those whose predisposition is to be loyal.

The Taiping, Boxers and other rebels of history were indigenous, the product, as Marxists used to say, 'of social and economic forces'. Yet it can be argued that communism was a product of Russian ambitions to exert power in Asia. Russia after the 1917 Revolution first invested in the Nationalist Party of Sun Yatsen, 'the father of the Chinese Republic', providing its Bolshevik structure and influencing its anti-imperialist policies. It then agreed to support the CCP as a 'party within a party', and kept such tight control over it that it can rightly be blamed for the disasters which beset the CCP's early years. Mao Zedong broke away from the Soviet-inspired policy and attempted rural revolution, taking advantage of peasant poverty and discontent to establish his power first in the South and then, in the 1940s, in the North West. Other warlords set up principalities for themselves around China in the 1920s. Mao adopted violent methods of control and subjection learned from the Russians. To justify this, he used the vocabulary of egalitarianism, millenarianism and national salvation.

Although that is past, that past has only just begun to lose its influence. In the 1980s, there was talk, encouraged by some of the leadership, of separating Party and State in the way that is normal in most countries today, but since 1989 this has been dropped. Only recently has it seemed as if could it be said that the Party was morphing into something different – as new types of people enter it, competitive elections are introduced at the lowest level, and the two senior leaders stress their intention to respect the (State) Constitution and accept scrutiny of, and supervision by, the people's representatives. These are the responses to the new environment of market and media, and to the death of the past. The Party hopes that they will ensure its continued leadership.

CHAPTER 2

Mao Zedong

(also romanised as Mao Tse-t'ung)

In at least one village of Shanxi there is a temple to Mao, worship-ped by local peasants. In many cabs and minibuses, coaches and pedicabs, a tasselled medallion or a gilded portrait of the Great Helmsman takes the place which, in Europe, is occupied by St Christopher.

This is curious to visitors, who associate Mao with the disasters of the years of socialism and imagine that China has 'moved on' to a world where Mao's ideas are ridiculous and deference to a fallen leader is otiose. It is possible that Mao represents in the popular imagination the urge to equality which has been forgotten in the present rush to get rich. But the likelihood is that, more, Mao sym-bolises the start of China's ascent from the destructive civil and foreign wars of the hundred years from the mid-19th to mid-20th centuries, towards what is now assumed to be the assured future: China as a leading, perhaps the leading, state in the world. They know that he was a tyrant and a hypocrite, they know that he caused disasters and that they should be glad to be shot of him; but he made the world respect China, and that is that.

As a youth, Mao, the son of peasants, was a rebel and passionate for learning. He left home to continue his studies, involving himself in radical and self-education groups in his home province of Hunan, before working briefly as an assistant librarian at Peking University. A member of the Chinese Communist Party in the 1920s, when it was trying to foment uprisings in the industrial cities, he was unusual in grasping the fact that there were more peasants than industrial workers in China and that they had grievances. He established a guerrilla base, from 1931 to 1934, called the Soviet Republic of

Jiangxi, and in 1935 became de facto leader of the CCP. His basing of the CCP in the rural areas saved it. By 1938, he was referring to his work as the 'sinification' of Marxism, meaning its acculturation as well as its adaptation to conditions prevailing in China rather than Europe.[1] After the 1949 CCP victory in the Civil War he became, as well as Party Chairman, President of the new People's Republic of China (PRC), a post he lost in 1959. After that he was the progenitor of several radicalising movements which are now generally agreed to have been disasters, culminating in the Great Proletarian Cultural Revolution (GPCR). He died in 1976 and his policies were soon reversed.

In youth, Mao was influenced as much by popular literary culture as by Western ideas then intoxicating Chinese intellectuals. Typical of his contemporaries, he was influenced emotionally by the perception that Chinese frailties had been exposed and exploited by Western imperialism, and that China had been humiliated.

Much of his writing was done for the political moment; in what is more durable, he accommodated the European Enlightenment idea of history as progress, the Marxist perception of economic development, Leninist power practice and the Leninist theory of imperialism. He fused these ideas with belief in the primacy of will, best exemplified by his parable 'Old Yu moves the Mountains', in which a grandfather, derided for trying to move a mountain by transferring earth in his own buckets, responds that little by little it will be done, because 'I have sons, and grandsons …'.

In the 1950s Mao decided that the Soviet model of development was both too slow and too elitist, giving rise to a parasitic class of officials. He launched the Great Leap Forward to prove that experts and officials were not needed, if the people's revolutionary fervour were fierce enough, and predicted that their efforts would get China surpassing the Western economies in no time. It was a catastrophe. Seeking emotional commitment from the intellectuals, he failed and repressed them in the 'Hundred Flowers' period (see Glossary). For his enemies in the Party, Mao applied and intensified a system of thought reform by which individuals were bullied and tortured into recreating their own identities to conform with his ideas.

His biggest experiment was the Great Proletarian Cultural Revolution, when he called upon the young and the poor to extirpate old culture and elitism, or at least that was the reason he gave for commanding an assault upon those in positions of responsibility. Although technically not in government, his prestige was such that he was able to mobilise millions of disaffected youth to assault the older generation, burn books, wreck museums and old buildings and beat up those in authority. This got him back into power, while his colleagues lay shackled in dungeons or cleaned out pigsties, bullied by Red Guards.

In subjecting all China to his, and perhaps also his wife's, will until his death, the GPCR was successful; the costs in terms of suffering and material destruction are generally regarded as having been very great.

Few men have aroused such adulation, not only at home but among the unfortunates of the world, who were attracted by the romantic representation of Mao as the peasant risen to overthrow the exploiter and imperialist, and by his condemnation of 'old culture' as a tool of oppression. However, Mao had no proposals as to institutions which might improve the lot of the poor once those in authority had been destroyed. In this he showed himself as much bounded by the traditions of Chinese peasant millenarianism as by Lenin's limitations. Or possibly simply by his own.

A biography of Mao was published in 2005, which – in combining a great many known sources with new information from Russian archives and the memoirs of associates now able to tell their stories (and willing to do so before they died) – shattered any last illusions that readers might have had either about Mao's altruism or his patriotism.[2] Russian money is shown to have been the decisive factor in the CCP's rise to power, not social conditions. Mao himself is depicted as completely callous, prepared to sacrifice millions of lives for his own personal advancement or pet illusions. He welcomed the Japanese invasion, embroiled China in debilitating foreign wars, deprived people of food, endangered his country and subjected China to Russian exploitation, all in order to promote himself. While China starved and people were denied the smallest of pleasures, he enjoyed classical opera, stolen artworks and adolescent concubines. It was solely on account of Mao that China, according to the authors, did not develop. As if that were not enough, their research claims to prove that the Long March (see Glossary) was not the heroic enterprise it was presented as, fought against all odds, but took place with the tacit approval of the supposed enemies. This is only one of the many myths that they identify as media fabrications. The indictment could not be worse.

For a period, Mao's influence abroad was great. His Three Worlds Theory (see Glossary) captured the imagination of politicians and rebels alike; his revolutionary approach and military ideas inspired socialists on all continents. His lasting legacy is probably that the disruption he caused Chinese society and Chinese culture has made more possible China's adaptation to market economics and infiltration by the postmodern world.

CHAPTER 3

Central Government

Sceptics have been confounded: the Chinese government has reformed, maintained its authority, become more professional and more open to scrutiny. The recovery has been possible because there are early traditions to draw upon; nevertheless, it is an extraordinary achievement.

Mao Zedong's revolutionary career was based upon his authority as a Marxist-Leninist; after his conquest of China, he established state power along Soviet lines. Yet when he died, as ever, on his bedside table was *The Mirror of Government* by Sima Guang (1019–96), a record of 1,300 years of politics, written as a reference for the Chinese ruling class. This reminds us that China has an administrative tradition that has maintained continuity, while adapting to accommodate social pressures and foreign ideas, since 221 BC, when the countries composing the Chinese world were unified.[1] Today the modifications brought about by the Soviet influence, and now the pressures of modernity, seem sometimes less fundamental than that. Here I try to sketch the institutions which now make up the government.

The 'fundamental' institution is the network of People's Congresses. At the summit is the National People's Congress (NPC), a parliament of about 3,000 deputies, elected from and by the membership of Provincial and Municipal Congresses, themselves derived from lower-level congresses, and by the armed forces.

Official China is quite clear that it is 'the foremost country in the world that practises a political system fundamentally different from the Western' parliamentary democracies. China has 'multi-party cooperation and consultation led by the CCP', while the West practises 'multi-party competition'. The CCP wishes it believed that the parliamentary system was tried in China and discredited; improving the Congresses will counter Western preaching.[2]

The Congresses are legislative bodies which also (in theory) supervise the executive bodies derived from them. Thus the NPC reviews the work of the State Council. Other bodies reporting directly to the NPC are the State's Central Military Commission,[3] the Procurate and the Supreme Court. The Standing Committee of the NPC is in principle the supreme State power when the NPC is not in session. Candidates for election as Congress deputies are proposed by the Organisation Department of the CCP and the allocation of seats is determined by the Standing Committee.

At each level, there are also People's Consultative Conferences (PCC), advisory bodies representing institutions that are not necessarily represented in the Congresses, as well as professionals, academics and other specialists.[4] 'Deliberations of [PCC] advisory resolutions and reports from inspection tours often raise tough issues that officials must then address.'[5]

The State Council is the executive government, headed by the Prime Minister, with its Standing Committee as a cabinet. While it is on paper answerable to the NPC, in reality it usually controls it. Answerable to it are 29 Ministries (*bu*), each of which may contain sub-ministries, also translated as bureaux or administrations (*ju*). For example, the Ministry of Culture maintains the State Cultural Relics Administration. Then there are certain bureaux that are directly answerable to the State Council, though not full ministries, such as the State Administration for Radio, Film and Television.

In 1998, a series of reforms were started which have changed the whole nature of the administration. The State Economic and Trade Commission was set up to make economic policy and to coordinate industrial development. Ministries with the tasks of detailed management of the economy were abolished or turned into policymakers; enterprises under direct ministerial control were converted into corporations and the ministries' authority reduced.[6] The qualifications and recruitment criteria for the 10 to 12 million officials had

27

long been under fire; replacement of 'politicals'[7] by professionals gathered pace, and large numbers were to be reassigned out of government administration.

Most executive government is carried out at the level of the 30 Provinces (*sheng*) and Autonomous Regions (*zizhiqu*), or four Directly Controlled Municipalities (*zhixiashi*). Governors and Party Secretaries are central appointments, rotated regularly. Usually the Party Secretary is the most powerful; in Tibet, Inner Mongolia and Xinjiang, to make the point, the Governors are usually local (and not necessarily rotated), whereas the Party Secretary is always Chinese.

Chinese provinces are as large as European countries, often with larger populations, and with histories and languages distinct from their neighbours'. Canton Province (Guangdong, adjoining Hong Kong) has 79 million people, Xinjiang is the size of western Europe with a population of 19 million, and Sichuan has 87 million, although it also contains a separate municipality, Chongqing, with 31 million. Before the reforms of 1998, the CCP managed to stymie local initiative and force apparent uniformity through political power, but today local government is increasingly encouraged to take initiatives, yet also subjected to standard procedures and national laws. A relatively new development is the imposition of central directives which oblige conformity to international standards, such as on **intellectual property**.

Foreign observers of government have often been convinced either that China is about to disintegrate because the centre cannot control the desire of the localities to do their own thing,[8] or that China's economic growth is making the Chinese State so powerful that it poses a mighty threat to the rest of the world.[9] The first fails to take account of the centre's ability both to hold on to key powers and to renew its institutions such that it could keep its authority over the regions, while the second diminishes or ignores the problems with which the centre has to contend, and which lessen its ability to exert central power.[10]

Reforms in the 1990s made the administration more efficient, more professional, better monitored and more effectively influenced by the CCP.[11] While there is less ideological coercion, and general economic policy can be applied according to local circumstances, new legislation and regulation driven from the centre increase interference, for example over the collection of revenue, laws on quality, health and safety and the environment, plus the regulation of the financial sector. China remains essentially autocratic, with the changes driven from the top. The plans for democratisation, for reducing CCP interference and for Party and government to be more clearly distinguished (*dangzheng fenkai*) were shelved after 1989 and have not been revived.

Nevertheless, electoral reform in **rural China** demonstrates that the centre is open to change, and there are other developments with equally far-reaching implications. According to Jude Howell, 'the NPC has become much more a platform for discussion of issues than in the past, with sometimes quite big differences among delegates expressed in votes. Moreover, delegates can use their votes on work reports to show dissatisfaction. In some cases, some delegates to the NPC and to provincial congresses have voted against the work reports for the Procurate in order to protest against the government's poor handling of corruption.'[12] At the 2003 NPC, although topical sensitive issues were not discussed and the agenda was strictly controlled, many hundred amendments were proposed to the work reports, and would have to be dealt with by the responsible officials.

There have been other innovations over the past five years, 'such as soliciting public opinion on legislative items, holding legislative hearings, and establishing investigative committees on specific questions. Provincial NPCs elect candidates nominated by the Party for top civil service positions, usually unopposed. There have been occasions when the candidates supported by the Party organisations have not been elected, as in the provincial People's Congresses of Guizhou, Zhejiang, Hubei and Hainan. Also recently, provincial NPCs – such as in an experiment in Yanan – are being given functions and a greater say throughout the year, not just at the one meeting each year.'[13]

China is not about to become a multi-party democracy. The ruling class, whether politicians, business leaders or intellectuals – and regardless of their own political ideals – rarely trust 'the masses' to make judgements on anything but the most local of matters. The Party will not countenance any more dilution of central power than it is forced to concede in order to achieve its goals. Yet, in the search for allies and for understanding, the government is allowing much more open discussion and even criticism, within bounds. It recognises that scrutiny and commentary by ordinary people and journalists will help keep officials in line. These changes, together with the subversive potential of the **internet** and the determination of some courageous campaigners to get the law respected, are steadily making government both more responsive and more accountable.

CHAPTER 4

Local Government

The public service tradition is by no means dead, but those tasked with running the country have to deal with both constantly rising expectations and the unfortunate relics of a political system which is adapting only with difficulty to the runaway economy. They must do so without (as yet) the kind of legal and institutional structures that could help them.

In December 2005, reports emerged from Shanwei, a village near Hong Kong, that ten villagers had been killed by police while protesting against the expropriation of their land, with minimal compensation, for industrial development.[1] Whatever new facts emerge about this particular case, it already seems typical of hundreds if not thousands of similar incidents throughout China. One of the possible solutions – or at least palliatives – is thought to be local democracy, and because of that, as well as because of the pressures upon it, local government is one of the most intriguing aspects of today's China.

The administrative divisions are as follows: directly answerable to the centre are Provinces or Autonomous Regions (where the population is ethnically distinct), or Directly Managed Municipalities such as the city of Chongqing (*zhixiashi*). These units contain Counties (*xian*) and Cities (*shi*), and sometimes Prefectures (*diqu*) which are units of more than one county; they themselves are composed of Townships (*xiang*) or Districts (*xingzhen cun*).

Before the privatisation of **agriculture** in 1978, villages were called Production Teams, were grouped into Brigades and loosely answered to Communes. The reforms removed the Production Team layer of officialdom while leaving certain responsibilities to be carried out by the village leadership, whose most vital function is that it holds title to the land, returned to the peasants only on lease. Answerable to the former Brigade (now given its pre-1949 title of District), it collects taxes, disseminates Party policies, implements birth control regulations and organises labour for local community building works.

Local government proper starts with the District. At each level, chief executives are rotated between areas in order to prevent them building local ties; however, this system has the corollary of encouraging them to be less dedicated to their charges and to behave in ways that will enhance their own promotion prospects, or, sometimes, their families' interests. Just as government has reduced central specification of production – what must be grown, by whom and how – so it has relieved the pressure on officials, subjecting them to many fewer central controls, while calling for enterprise. It is hardly surprising that some officials have reacted by ensuring that the vast State assets they control, and their powers of patronage, are used for their own purposes.[2]

When privatisation took place in 1978, each plot allocated also had attached to it a specified tax in grain or other product; whereas under the old system, peasants had barely been aware of what Brigades took from the product of their collective work, they now had to pay taxes personally. In the recent bad years this has rank-led, and the government in 2005 abolished the grain tax. However, local officials, seeing the opportunities that their power, and the isolation and political weakness of the villages, give them, have often invented their own taxes in order either to pay for the common services they are required to supply, or, increasingly often, to pay for their own perks. They are known to levy for the slaughtering of a pig, for the right to get married, build a shed or register a birth. The kind of enrichment by local officials against which observers fulminated in the Imperial and Republican periods has returned with a ferocity unseen before the revolution obliterated all moral scruple or *noblesse oblige*. Another unresolved problem left over from socialism is the matter of land title. The peasants got back the land stolen from them, but only on lease; local officials therefore consider that they have title and can decide when to terminate a lease in order to build a factory or a profitable road, or simply to sell on to a developer at great (personal) profit. The failure properly to establish private ownership rights is the root of the issue in Shanwei, mentioned above, and many other places.

One of the great success stories of the **economy** has been the part played by the Township and Village Enterprises (TVEs) in enriching the rural areas. Once the government allowed private business again, TVEs matched entrepreneurship with under-used assets and labour, and those that brought them together were usually local officials who could use the profits to improve local services, to enhance their own power and to make themselves independent of their nominal superiors, or at least to spread favours so that they need not fear interference. Of course colluding networks of officials, frustrating central policy and looking after each other's interests, existed before reform, but the harshness of ideologically driven discipline then gave them pause; moreover, the much greater wealth now available provides many more corrupt opportunities. This is now a well recognised phenomenon which is regularly discussed in the media and to which the central government has sought to apply some measures.[3]

The need for Party and government to be seen as even-handed and as competent in dealing with abuse grows, as expectations rise and as the large numbers who have not benefited from the economic miracle are forced by desperation to express their disgruntlement. Demonstrations are now commonplace, and are often suppressed with violence. The protesters may be pensioners who have not received what they are owed;[4] householders and farmers cheated out of their property; laid-off State employees; abused migrants; environmentalists. 'Over the past two decades, letters, complaints and petitions received by courts at all levels have risen almost 500 times. In 2004 alone, more than 3.76 million people took part in 74,000 protests.'[5]

The government considers that these are consequences of the inadequacy of existing methods of mediation, of control of officials, and of public accountability. Thus, over the past few years, many reforms have improved the quality of administration, although these have stopped short of separating the Party from government, with all the opportunities that their effective fusion provides for interference on 'political' grounds. Initiatives have included administrative investigation and intervention, encouraging journalists to reveal corruption, an acceptance of the growing countervailing influence of businesspeople,[6] the introduction of responsibility contracts and training of officials to develop a more consumer-orientated 'work style'.

Responsibility contracts stipulate clearly what economic and social targets officials are expected to meet, and how they must behave. There are well known cases of officials being held to account in accordance with these contracts. As to 'work style', 'practical, local innovations are being made, such as obliging police to meet complainants face-to-face; government trying to become more service-oriented in such matters as relocating offices for the disabled to ground floors; encouragement of public dialogues; and greater consultation, though mainly of the intellectual and professional elites.'[7]

Most remarked on is the introduction of competitive elections at the village level. As early as 1987, a series of regulations stipulated that elected village assemblies were to be introduced, with elected executive committees, and that the leaders should have fixed three-year terms of office. The ideas behind the innovation were to allow energetic locals to challenge entrenched, corrupt authority; to get popular people into positions of trust in order to reduce cynicism; and to introduce some accountability through making the village books public, through having officials report back to the assemblies, and by making it possible to eject failed leaders at the end of their terms. No new parties were to be allowed, nor collusion between villages, and where able people emerged as leaders they would be invited to join the Party, thus bringing in new blood and associating the Party with popular initiatives. It has taken a very long time for most provinces to undertake these reforms and even where they have been put through, local officials have often conspired to reduce their potential impact by packing the elections with supporters or making sure that supposedly multi-candidate elections are not really so. Elsewhere, though, since ultimate power usually resides with the Party Secretary rather than the executive, some areas have gone on to introduce elections for Party officials too. In a few places, the experiment has been extended to Townships and to urban neighbourhood committees.

In summary, local government is becoming more accountable, policies are discussed more widely and officials are provided with opportunities to become more professional and responsive. When UK Prime Minister Blair talked about China's unstoppable march towards democracy on a visit in 2005, he was exaggerating. Very sensibly, it can be argued, changes are coming slowly, giving both enthusiasts and opponents opportunities to adjust. But the Party's monopoly of power has been breached, and a measure of electoral democracy introduced, the mere start of which is changing perceptions of the possible.

CHAPTER 5

Nationalism

Other people's nationalism is always more noticeable than our own, and there is a risk that outsiders will mistake touchy pride for active hostility. There may be bitterness against the outside world in China, but that is tempered by the overriding desire to be part of that world, and to concentrate on the practical issues requiring attention.

'You foreigners want democracy in China? Look at the anti-Japanese demonstrations: do you want that kind of anger allowed to vote? For every Supergirl waiting to be elected [referring to the pop talent contest], there's a mad man who'll win millions of votes for bombing Japan ...'

No, that wasn't a cab driver, but a leading professor. Perhaps he was tailoring his words to a foreign audience. After all, the sight of Chinese crowds cursing Japan or the USA is a scary sight.

In 1999, the US accidentally bombed the Chinese embassy in Belgrade, killing several. An orgy of fury hit the city streets. Students paraded the 'Demon of Liberty', showing how much the 1980s admiration for the US had been replaced by contempt. In 2001, a Chinese and a US plane collided and the Chinese pilot died. Rage erupted. When the US government issued its regrets, the Chinese government hid them.

From a football match in 2004, sporadically in 2005 and through into 2006, demonstrators chanted 'Japanese invaders must die' and 'the war is not yet over', as they smashed Japanese cars and premises in protest at a textbook issued to Japanese schools which allegedly glosses over Japan's 1937 invasion of China. They were also protesting against Japan's bid for a permanent seat on the UN Security Council.

Observers who dismiss these protests as manipulation by government are as wrong as those who declare that they are proof of the danger posed to the world by China's flawed nationalism. All over Greater China (see Glossary) the same sentiments are expressed, from Vancouver to Manchester, São Paulo to Hong Kong. The media reflects, even in the face of government disapproval.[1] It is more realistic to say that they represent popular feeling that is comprehensible in the light of history, at least in the light of history as people have been taught it.

By tradition, China thought of itself as the centre of world civilisation; thus, defeat by foreign powers in the 19th century, and subjection to their rules and demands for territory or resources, were seen as humiliating violations. As awareness of China's relative under-development grew, pride in Confucian civilisation gave way to an angry resentment against both that civilisation – blamed for China's inability to compete – and against 'the West' (including Japan). Under Mao, the Party was presented as the best expression of the nation, and socialism as the ideology realised most perfectly in China. But the Mao years are now widely seen as failures, all the more so because his claims of world leadership and domestic success were so absurd.

So what now is there to be proud of? For some it may be culture, but this is confusing at a time when economic achievements seem to be coming about as fast as culture can be jettisoned. After all, if you have to change everything in order to advance, all that is left is what cannot be changed, i.e. race and geography, the mere fact of being in a particular location and having shared a common history.

Thanks to the Party, it is the modern history of China that is best known. Hong Kong was ceded to Britain after the Opium War of 1841, but how you interpret this is what matters. The importing of opium into China by British merchants was unsavoury, but the market was Chinese. In reality, the disputes over trade were less about opium as such than about the unwillingness of Manchu officials to manage trade in ways that were practicable to both foreign and Chinese merchants. Yet the last few generations of Chinese have understood that Hong Kong was ceded to Britain after a war to force China to allow drug addiction. The lesson that seems to be being taught is that wicked things come about when foreigners are allowed to trade; the Chinese that are celebrated in monuments and history books are not the merchants but the patriots who resisted foreign business. Thus the scene is set for blaming foreigners, rather than the government, if things go wrong with today's Open Door policy. And thus China is recorded as the victim of malevolence, which is not the whole story, but is convenient.

Of course, during the 20th century China *was* the victim of malevolence, in particular the Japanese invasion and Russian encroachments. Other Western powers were keen to establish trading bases and often behaved as arrogantly and greedily as they did in many other parts of the world; but the Chinese experience was no more rotten than that of many other countries. In fact, innumerable foreigners, admiring of China, in the hundred years before 1949, contributed hugely to the development of China's schools, universities, welfare institutions and government. Unfortunately these contributions have been forgotten as historical memory has been poisoned.

It has been thought necessary to condense modern history into a simple myth of 'foreigners bad, Party good'. Edward Friedman and other scholars have characterised the CCP story of how it saved China from both foreign imperialism and internal traitors – and how it remains the only possible salvation for all Chinese people everywhere – as the 'northern narrative', because it suits the people who sit in the capital, though it's hardly relevant to the rest of China.[2] It is not a narrative that is common to Chinese communities outside the PRC, where until recently there was more sympathy for the Nationalist view than the CCP's. Nowadays, though, it is difficult for those Chinese outside the PRC not to be influenced by it. After all, it is under the Party that China is now growing economically at such a dramatic rate, and it is easy to forget that the Party was also in command during the wasted years. And the Party constantly reminds us that it is the guarantor of stability, wealth and the growth of the Chinese power in the world that will ensure that China is never-more humiliated. There is an element of social Darwinism in this too: the patriots are competitive, and see themselves in a struggle for survival.

There *are* other ways of being a good Chinese. As early as the 1930s, there were those who objected to 'education on national humiliation', as well as the assumption that the present is always superior to the past, the Western to the Chinese, both of which are implicit in the curious official nationalism that wants to be proud of China yet not proud of those aspects of China that are generally most admired. As early as the 1930s, the dangers of the 'May 4th Outlook' (see Glossary), the urge to modernity at all costs and rejection of Chinese tradition as inferior, were evident. There was a view that China should look within itself for sources of change and development.[3] It is possible that, today, particularly in the South, something of this may be returning. The 'northern narrative' may seem irrelevant to increasingly cosmopolitan, outward-looking southerners who anyway have very different ways of being Chinese to those of the capital.

But when people take to the streets, or anti-foreign headlines scream from the press, they reflect the myth of the 'northern narra-tive' which has been promoted in school, through the media, at official functions, in a multitude of ways that are impossible for people in pluralist democracies to imagine.[4] These are the ideas that inform the emotions of nationalism. Intellectuals naturally con-tribute their books. While *Behind the Demonisation of China* was in part a reaction to US misrepresentations, it was, like *China Can Say No*, also an expression of outraged nationalism.[5]

Circumstances have not helped to dilute them. The **geopolitics** of China's borders render it, in the eyes of its leaders, uniquely vul-nerable. Fear of Japan and Japanese rearmament is real. Taiwan is not seen as the rest of the world sees it, as an outpost of democracy and enlightenment in the Chinese world, but as a potential base for Japanese operations and a sore kept open only thanks to the protection of the US. According to the Chinese view, the USA, the mightiest economic and military power the world has ever known, considers China a potential enemy and wants to put it down, contain it. It was the USA which prevented the CCP from completing its conquest of China, by holding the Taiwan Strait in 1950. Today, US support for Taiwan is another manifestation of its will to subvert and divide China, as are the sympathies expressed by Americans for the independence movements. By extension, the concern for **human rights** is actually realpolitik, a way of diminishing China in the world and fomenting disorder. The guru of the Falungong (see Glossary), like the inspirations for, or leaders of, many Christian organisations in China, resides in the USA.

And there is evidence to back up what might otherwise seem to be Chinese paranoia. In the 1990s, the Taiwan issue became inflamed when first the US appeared to be withdrawing support for Taiwan and then reconsidered and increased arms supplies. Under President Clinton, perceived in the US as soft on China, Congress repeatedly attacked it on human rights, intellectual property, interference in US politics, and spying.[6] In 1999, Congress received the Cox Report, fruit of American neuroses as much as real assessment, claiming that China is engaged in multiple espionage attempts.[7] Numberless US commentators talk of China as military enemy or economic threat, 'violent and primitive', 'a tyranny' subject to 'psychopathological' nationalism,[8] and receive coverage in China. Factual books such as *The Coming Conflict with China* or *Red Dragon Rising* and lurid novels like *Dragonstrike* or *Dragonfire*, predicting monstrous wars with China a villain, are all taken as indications of hostility.[9] Educated Chinese note how astonishingly ignorant their Anglophone equivalents are of China; modern Chinese can operate effectively in both worlds and both languages – how many Americans can? Even quite ordinary Chinese know infinitely more about the West than the average Westerner knows about China; Westerners are thought to have failed to discard the prejudices of their grandparents. (Returning from a recent visit, I talked to an English engineer who told me of his astonishment at the swanky hotels, high rises and spanking new labs in one unimportant Chinese town. 'My colleagues think like I did three weeks ago', he said; 'I thought they lived on sampans.')

Chinese nationalists point too to how much China has sought to meet the West on its terms, to be fully engaged: the World Trade Organization, the Comprehensive Test Ban Treaty, the Nuclear Non-Proliferation Treaty, the Chemical and Biological Weapons Convention. 'Look at our economies', they say: 'we are mutually interdependent. The nationalism that you see on the streets is a natural reaction to the hostility of the US and Japan. But China is still a very poor country. It needs', they say, echoing a view of Deng Xiaoping, 'a hundred years of peace if it is to achieve prosperity for its people.' In other words, concerns about nationalism are misplaced – they reflect the ignorance and the irrational fears of the beholder rather than a realistic assessment of the situation.

The invasion of Iraq convinced China, as nothing else, that the USA was a danger to world peace and a potential threat, even as it recognises that the Chinese and US economies are now interdependent. The USA, and perhaps its allies, may fear Chinese nationalism; yet Chinese say that the nationalism that has realised itself, with force outside its own borders, is not the Chinese but the American. Since the tragedy of the Twin Towers, US aggressive nationalism has appeared to be orchestrated by its government, pulling behind it an often reluctant people, whereas in China the reverse is the case: the government can seem surpassed, perhaps unnerved, by the nationalism of the streets.

CHAPTER 6

Armed Forces

The implications for the world of the military modernisation of China are potentially great; the People's Liberation Army seems intent upon preparing for an attack on Taiwan, and it is not clear whether the government can limit its freedom of action.

The People's Liberation Army (PLA) is the largest of three armed forces, the others being the Militia and the Chinese People's Armed Police Force (CPAPF). Extraordinary though it may seem, the PLA, which consists of the Army, Navy, Air Force and 2nd Artillery Force (missiles and nuclear weaponry), answers not to the State but to the CCP, and is controlled by the Central Military Commission, whose Chairman is usually one of the two or three most powerful leaders. The Militia, whose members hold civilian jobs, is divided into primary (ex-armed forces personnel and younger members) and secondary (all other males 18–35) divisions. Militia units are organised in villages, towns, urban sub-districts, large enterprises and institutions, and provide specified days of training per year, often based at county centres. The CPAPF was set up in April 1983 as an armed defence force deployed in police duties on borders, government premises, national construction works, and other high-security tasks.

   In order to explain the importance attached to its armed forces, official Chinese publications[1] remind us that China in the 19th and early 20th centuries was maltreated by stronger powers. China from 1841 found foreigners' laws being imposed on the country, punishment attacks inflicted on the State, and extraterritoriality established (the system by which foreigners lived in enclaves subject only to their own laws, though on Chinese soil); in the 1930s, the USSR ate away at China's frontiers and dominated border areas; Japan invaded. This is part of the modern identity that the CCP has been so active in forging. More than this, there are claims that every nation has a 'strategic cultural tradition' operating like a genetic code, such that you can fruitfully compare Japanese emperor-orientated militarism with China's non-belligerent tradition, and contrast the peaceful voyages of 14th-century Admiral Zheng He with Europeans' voyages of conquest. However, the aggressiveness of the PRC under Mao, which invaded Tibet and started wars in Korea, and against India and Vietnam, is not explained. The question for the rest of the world is: If China operates according to a 'strategic cultural tradition', is it a Confucian one or a Stalinist–Maoist one? Publicly, the State emphasises that military expenditure will damage the prospects for economic development, yet its investments are huge. Perhaps, though, China's strategic position makes this understandable.

The PRC has frontiers 136,700 miles long, and its coastline measures 111,850 miles. At least two very large areas are culturally distinct and contain liberation movements which, if not a serious threat to China, are nevertheless a nuisance. The PRC is contiguous with fourteen countries, with three of which – India, Vietnam and the USSR – it has had military clashes in the last 50 years. The Republic of China (ROC), the remains of the pre-communist state, sits in Taiwan, just a few miles from the coast. Although it has successfully settled territorial and maritime disputes with several countries over the last decade, those outstanding involve Japan, India and Russia in particular. There are disputes adjacent, though not involving Chinese territory, over Kashmir and the Kurile Islands; the Central Asian neighbours are plagued by instability. Moreover, China's recent economic development has involved not only a massive increase in exports but also a growing dependence upon imports of raw materials. This is the context within which we must see the growth of Chinese military power.

After 1978, the PLA, as with other institutions, began to modernise in accordance with the requirements – as the generals understood them – of the modern world, rejecting the doctrine of Mao, which held that vast numbers of guerrillas were more valuable than technology.[2] Earlier convinced that the US was decadent as a military power, subdued by its Vietnam failure, the High Command was astonished by what the first Gulf War revealed to them of American military superiority. In 1996, when the US sent aircraft carriers to the South China Sea while the PRC was firing missiles at targets just short of Taiwan, it was further shaken by the demonstration that the US could, and well might, intervene should the PRC attack the Republic of China. The US involvement in the Balkans in 1999 convinced them that America was capable of intervention anywhere to defend its interests and influence. There then grew up the fear that the US was indeed bent upon global domination, and even that it might consider China's own colonies appropriate for intervention. By the end of the 1990s, the policy advisers believed that the PRC is threatened by an aggressive USA and a hostile ROC, while Japan and India are also potential enemies. The PLA's response was a very careful study of the Balkan and Afghan campaigns.

While the Twin Towers reduced China's fear of US interest in helping the independence movement in (Muslim) Turkestan, subsequent moves by the US to establish itself as influential in several Central Asian countries, as well as the invasion of Iraq, have served to convince many Chinese, not just Chinese generals, that the US is a dangerously belligerent power and may well turn its attention to curtailing China's rise.

In the last fifteen years, China has made great progress in modernising its forces, with investments rising 15 per cent a year.[3] There has been radical overhaul of doctrine, of command and control organisation, and of procurement. The objectives appear not to be to challenge the US in an all-out conflict but, first, to convert the overmanned and under-trained PLA of the past into a nimble, high-tech force with a well-trained core of officers and NCOs able to operate in conditions of technologically advanced warfare, and second, to develop the capability to damage any US attempts to defend Taiwan from Chinese attack, such that the US staff has to ponder carefully the costs of such a mission. To this end, China has equipped itself with cruise and other anti-ship missiles designed to pierce the electronic defences of US vessels.[4] The Chinese Navy now has two Sovremenny-class guided missile destroyers and has ordered from Russia six more, equipped with Sunburn missiles able to skim 4½ feet above the water at a speed of Mach 2.5 to evade radar. It is buying eight Kilo-class diesel submarines that carry Club anti-ship missiles with a range of 145 miles. 'These systems will present significant challenges in the event of a US naval force response to a Taiwan crisis', Vice Admiral Lowell E. Jacoby, director of the Defense Intelligence Agency, told the Senate Armed Services Committee in a testimony on 17 March 2005.[5] China's fleet of fighter planes is being greatly increased, and will soon number over 2,500 aircraft. An improved nuclear deterrent against the United States has been developed, a nuclear submarine carrying missiles with a 5,000-mile range, soon to be supplemented by those with an 8,000-mile range.[6]

Western military experts believe that, notwithstanding these advances, China probably does not have the capacity to succeed in an attack on the ROC, let alone challenge the USA.[7] Expenditure is not everything, but the differences in defence budgets are telling. China spends $56 billion a year. The UK spends 20 per cent more and Russia 20 per cent less. The USA spends nearly eight times what China does, and NATO and the US together spend eleven times China's total.[8] Moreover, experts consider both that the gap between its capabilities and those of the US have gone on widening because of the Chinese problem of bureaucracy and the US technological lead,[9] and that there are institutional and cultural barriers to greater progress.

Nevertheless, the USA takes China's military modernisation seriously. One camp believes that Chinese suspicion and hostility can be contained or reduced by openness, exchanges and dialogue. The other, epitomised by Secretary Rumsfeld, points to the failure of the PLA to reciprocate with the kind of transparency that is now general elsewhere in the military world, refusing to acknowledge the existence of installations, let alone to countenance the kind of access to them that the US has permitted on its part.[10] Yet, in some earnest of its willingness to engage, since 1998 the PLA has been, or is still, involved in thirteen UN peacekeeping missions, operating in Afghanistan, Bosnia, East Timor and Congo, among others. In 2003, it carried out joint naval exercises for the first time, with Pakistan, and has done the same with India and France since; and in 2004, it established a joint anti-terrorism organisation with Russia, Kazakhstan, Tajikistan and Kyrgyzstan. The US government's hostility, in 2005, to the idea that the EU should sell arms to China is further evidence of its suspicion, as is a codicil to the National Defense Authorization Act of 2001 which set limits on what China might obtain from US military suppliers.

As to the PLA at home, the fact that ex-President Jiang Zemin held on to the Chairmanship of the Central Military Commission beyond his presidential term caused disquiet, because it confuses the chain of command.[11] Already the fact that the armed forces are answerable to the Party, not the State, provides potential for trouble, for example in a crisis over Taiwan if there are differences of opinion between generals and government. Given that, much more so than in the past, generals and civil leaders are very different in formation and instincts, this is possible.

CHAPTER 7

Softpower

Compared to the USA, China is still poor and militarily weak; yet it is extending its influence through public diplomacy and cultural outreach.

When President Hu Jintao visited London in late 2005, admirers of Chinese civilisation could have been forgiven a wry smile at the sight of the leader of the Party which has done so much to destroy culture opening the Three Emperors Exhibition. Whether the Party now really defends that culture, or whether it is seen merely as a weapon in the pursuit of power, is open to question. What is clear, though, is that it now knows the meaning of softpower.

The concept is a simple one: that the way a country is perceived in the world depends upon many factors, only some of which are necessarily material or military. Perceptions strongly influence a country's relations with its neighbours and its business dealings, so that positive perceptions are a kind of power. Softpower. We all know about German efficiency and the dependability of its machinery; such a brand image gives Germany advantages. Italy is perceived as the heart of European culture, a country which has maintained its artistry in its beautiful natural settings. In connection with this, Italy's designs, foods and clothing in particular are respected everywhere. As China has become a great, perhaps the greatest, trading nation, it has begun to seek a comparable image.

The process is dated from 1994, the 'China Culture Year' in France. Several government departments are now involved in the projection of Chinese culture abroad as part of a public diplomacy strategy, and leading intellectuals are helping government think it through.[1]

The national news agency New China is trying to build its status as an international supplier of news, particularly in the developing world, where it often provides free or heavily subsidised feeds to impoverished news organisations. It provides a public news service in Chinese, English, Spanish, Arabic, French and Russian.[2]

More ambitious is the English language channel, CCTV 9, available by satellite in most parts of the world, as well as online at www.cctv-9.com/2005. It is part of the Sky package in the UK, and is carried by DirecTV in the USA. The audiences for this channel are very small indeed but the Chinese government continues to invest in its news and cultural documentaries, and has recently launched Spanish- and French-language channels.[3]

Part of the price of allowing Rupert Murdoch's Star TV to extend its landing rights in South China was that DirecTV agreed to carry the Jadeworld service, which includes CCTV 4, on its US feed.[4] This is aimed at expatriate Chinese, important participants in China's economic rise, as investors, networkers and suppliers of trained personnel. Today they are moving their allegiance from Taiwan to the PRC, just at the time that their confidence in expressing their Chineseness in their host societies has grown immensely. In many Asian countries they comprise powerful business networks.

Cultural outreach is provided by the Confucius Institutes, an equivalent of the British Council or Goethe Instituten. Several hundred are to be set up to teach Chinese and to showcase culture. In South East Asia, where opinion polls show that people look forward to the withdrawal of US influence and the rise of China, many young people are learning Chinese.

China's **geopolitics** for Asia are designed to reassure its neighbours that China is a valuable trading partner, without military ambitions. The Free Trade Agreement, investments in Asian economies, cooperation over health projects, tourism and wooing of business leaders are all transforming China's position. Chinese consumer brand names, film stars and pop bands help.

China's outreach extends beyond Asia. The China Africa Cooperation Forum of 2000 has been followed by Chinese aid, including health, technical and education projects. Of the Africans who study in China, over 1,500 receive full Chinese scholarships, furthering existing ties with Chinese institutions. China's non-judgemental approach is preferred by African leaders, sick of being told by the West how to reform their countries.

Australia is going through a China infatuation, helped doubtless by China's importance to Australia as a customer for its minerals and natural gas. Chinese is the second most spoken language and is now on the curriculum of most schools, and educators are opening campuses in China. Chinese culture is increasingly integrated into Australian schooling, logical now that there are 70,000 Chinese students, many of whom will stay. China's energy future is looking nuclear and Australia has the world's largest uranium reserves, so the unquestioning admiration of China may be useful when it comes to discussing uranium sales.

All over the world, millions of young people are involved in Chinese martial arts; others consume Chinese films, art exhibitions and medicine. Advertising agency Ogilvy and Mather is busy 'nation branding' China, both to enhance tourism and investment and in preparation for the Olympics.

There are contradictions in the projection of Chinese softpower, though these are hardly as glaring as those of the USA, with its image badly tarnished by the Iraq occupation. In China's case, the most obvious contradiction is between the desire to be seen as peace-loving and non-belligerent, and the constant threats to attack Taiwan. To non-Chinese, the idea of using force against a peaceful, successful and prosperous little island smacks of the brute. Outsiders can see no true reason for even contemplating such behaviour, except jealousy. Originally, Taiwan's economic success showed up the CCP's failure; today it is its political success.

Then there is the problem of what China is in fact projecting when it sets up Confucius Institutes. Confucius may once more be seen as the essence of China, but despite the CCP rather than because of it. Tens of thousands of temples and physical expressions of Confucianism were destroyed in the name of social-ist progress and are now being destroyed in the name of market progress. The idea of the clean slate suits profiteers just as it suited Mao. The family life out of which came the Confucian order is under pressure from industrialisation, increasingly feverish mobility, forced urbanisation, the One Child Policy, and the elimination of social housing catering to larger family units. Several generations of Chinese have been brought up without much schooling at all, and probably had little of the tenets of the sage passed down.

So is Confucius a coherent symbol for today's China? And does the projection of softpower need coherence, anyway? China is attracting respect because of its economic rise and because the USA is today less attractive as a model than it was for previous generations. Few people are yet asking the question 'What does China stand for?', because they know there is as yet no answer. China's leaders are too driven by the immediate problems of their country to be able to resolve that, but it is comforting to those nerv-ous of the military power to see that the symbols deployed in the projection of softpower are those of the civilisation that preceded the revolution.

CHAPTER 8

Tibet and East Turkestan

*Under the CCP, Chinese policies in these areas have both dam-
aged China's standing and caused instability; a courageous leader
would put this right. It may not be too late.*

Were Spain to invade the Netherlands, a country which Spaniards
once ruled as part of the Holy Roman Empire; give all political
power and economic opportunity to Spaniards; and smash up most
of the several thousand Dutch churches and other cultural centres
while locking up, torturing and killing the Dutch who objected, then
I suspect that the Chinese government would today join the rest of
us in disapproving. Even if Spain were then to try to atone by allowing some Dutch cultural life, but still refuse even to discuss the
Dutch having any say in their own affairs, let alone stop mass immigration of Spanish lowlife, we would still regard this as barbarous
colonialism.

The tragedy is that, unlike in this analogy, the Chinese government could have had friendly relations with Tibet, run its foreign
policy and not drawn upon itself the contempt of the world, had they
not sought to impose their ideology. Chinese repression created
Tibetan resistance, which gave rise to world admiration for the
Tibetan liberation struggle. And it was all so unnecessary.

In October 1950, Chinese armies crossed the frontier into Tibet.
In fact, there were already Tibetans under Chinese rule, because
many of them live in what is loosely known as Eastern Tibet. They
had until 1949 lived unmolested under a relaxed Chinese administration. The CCP incorporated Eastern Tibet into the Chinese
provinces.

However, the area ruled by the Dalai Lama, Tibet proper,[1]
remained independent, with its own administration. Since 1950,

China has been given to saying that Tibet has 'always been part of China', and Tibetans have declared that 'Tibet has always been a sovereign state', neither of which statements is true. Tibet was part of both Mongol and Manchu empires, just as were China and Mongolia; in the distant past, Tibet has at times even been a more powerful state than China. The Tibetans at various times acknowledged the leading status of the Emperor in China, as indeed did the Vietnamese, Koreans and assorted others.

Today, when generally it is believed that people of a particular race or culture should have the right to determine how they live, and not be ruled by foreigners, these historical debates are rather irrelevant anyway. The Tibetans in 1949 had no ill will towards the Chinese. The CCP destroyed that.

In Eastern Tibet it introduced 'class struggle', the activities carried out in China itself by which it destroyed potential resistance and created a constituency of supporters. It nominated target groups who would be savagely attacked, denied normal rights and have their property distributed to others. These others would then both perpetuate the oppression of the target groups, did they survive, and fervently support the CCP as the guarantor of their ownership of the stolen property. That was how it was supposed to work. But in Eastern Tibet the targets and the proposed beneficiaries saw themselves as Tibetans oppressed by foreigners and united against them. This was the first ignition of Tibetan consciousness, which before had hardly existed.

In Tibet proper, the government was left alone and no attempt was made to interfere with Tibetan society. But the disturbances in Eastern Tibet could not but affect other Tibetans, and the struggle spilled over until, in 1959, there was a revolt against the Chinese presence. Chinese troops poured over the border, the Tibetan army was swept aside, the Tibetan government was abolished and its members fled over into India and exile. The harsh subjection familiar to Eastern Tibet was now extended to Tibetans everywhere.

Since then, the liberation struggle has never ceased, although, being a very unequal battle – with on the one hand heavily armed and completely unrestrained troops prepared to kill or maim any person or destroy any building, and on the other unarmed civilians desperate to save their culture and dignity – it has varied in intensity.[2]

In the Chinese Cultural Revolution, the fight was very bitter. Thugs, inflamed by racism and loathing for any expression of religion, came over the border to enjoy an orgy of violence and destruction, ruining or pulling down several thousand temples and monasteries, as well as causing incalculable suffering during intense fighting.

Hundreds of thousands of Tibetans fled, at great risk. After the Red Guards had gone, savage military rule kept order until the 1980s, when, affected by the changed political climate in China itself, Tibetans began to speak out against the immigration of large numbers of colonisers and the continued repression of their language and religion. Monasteries began to function again. Tibetan could be used in education, at least in cultural studies.

As in Poland under the Soviets, religion had become the focus of, and identified with, the survival of moral values and culture. Tibet had been a theocracy, ruled by its priests; their rule might have given way naturally in time but, because of the Chinese, everyone united around the Church and the monks sustained, where they did not actually lead, the resistance. Daily there were clashes between the races on the streets as Tibetans saw more and more of their country being taken over.

In 1989, martial law was declared in Tibet, which resulted in yet more refugees fleeing to India, where the government in exile of the Dalai Lama continued to beg the world to get the Chinese – not to grant independence, very few expect that – to allow Tibet to be Tibetan.[3] In recent years, as China has sought to integrate into, and gain the approval of, the world, conditions have improved. Culture has been revived and there is now developing a secular, modern cultural life in Tibetan. Its use in education is restricted, and the policy is clearly to make it impossible for Tibetans not to use Chinese, while flooding Tibet with Chinese immigrants. Nevertheless, the better conditions in China appear to have relaxed tensions somewhat.

Some Tibetans still seek to get their children out into the Tibetan school system in exile, and most appear to revere the Dalai Lama as the symbol of alternative authority and of survival. The wrongs done to the Tibetans need to be righted, but only a very strong and courageous Chinese leader could do so, since the CCP has indoctrinated most Chinese to the extent that they can see no problem. But why should he bother? Perhaps because it would be better for China not to be seen as uncivilised; perhaps because it would be convenient to have peace.

Peace would be useful in Xinjiang, or Doğu (East) Turkestan as its inhabitants call it, too. In 1990, I met in London a businesswoman from its capital, Urumchi, who was being feted in China, and in the *Financial Times*, as a marvellous example of how a Turk and a Muslim – and a woman! – could succeed as an entrepreneur. The next time I heard of Rabıya Kadır was through Amnesty International, which was campaigning for her release from prison for talking of more independence for her homeland.

Kadır's homeland is a vast area of Central Asia whose principalities, like Tibet, had on-off relationships with the empires that ruled from Peking. The indigenous majority are Turks speaking a dialect called Uighur, but there are sizeable minorities speaking other Turkic dialects, such as Kazakh and Kirghiz. When the CCP came to power, the area became the East Turkestan Republic. In 1949, leading members of the government mysteriously died on their way to discuss the future with CCP representatives, and troops invaded. One of the ministers, Isa Yusuf Alptekin, fled and set up a government in exile in Istanbul; some leading Turks threw in their lot with the Chinese, handing over their wealth in return for lofty positions in government or representative institutions. Although there were resentments over language use in particular – the dominant language was Turkish and is now Chinese – occupation forces minimised opposition by executing or terrifying those of the educated people as had not fled,[4] so that hostility really erupted only with the attack on Islam during the Cultural Revolution. It has been continuing ever since as the Turks have come to realise the determination of China to change the character of their country through colonisation.[5] The government in exile still sits in Istanbul and there are East Turkestani communities in several Muslim countries and in Germany, but little attention is paid to their campaigns for the rights of their compatriots. The rise of Islamic terrorism elsewhere has given the Chinese government the opportunity to brand the anti-colonial struggle as fundamentalist, suggesting that it is fighting the same anti-terrorism war as the West, which, at least initially, was not so.

Under the last dynasty, law was indigenous and administration tolerant, 'mild and humane'.[6] By contrast, either because the reserves of oil and minerals in Turkestan are too important to be left to the indigenous people, or out of that socialist urge to dominate and change everything, the CCP has not yet attempted to allow the natives to govern themselves.

PART TWO

Business

CHAPTER 9

Economy

In 2005, China's economy was reported to be 20 per cent bigger than had been realised, outstripping the UK and making it the fourth biggest economy in the world. But, if all goes well, China has only just begun.

Recently, a British chief executive, woken in the early hours by arc lights, looked out of his hotel window in Shanghai and saw building workers labouring through the night, seven days a week, for $5 a week. He felt his heart sink, and asked: 'How can we compete with that?'[1] This is an economy of peasants freed from their chains. Like the Calabrians and Turks who relocated to Stuttgart and Torino after the Second World War, the rural migrants work crazily. With their labour and much ingenuity, China has become a leading force in many sectors from nothing, and very fast. The most obvious examples are mobile phones (local suppliers in the world's biggest mobile market are fast squeezing out the rest) and the DVD, which in less than five years has gone from being local eccentricity to global standard, with China producing 60 per cent of DVD players.[2]

Gross Domestic Product (GDP) doubled in the nine years to 2004, and grew 9.5 per cent in 2003–04. Because of the exceptional openness, as well as on account of cheap labour, China has become the world's largest recipient of foreign direct investment.[3] Substantially integrated with the world economy, in 2004 China replaced the USA as the main trading partner of Japan and South Korea. It has the fastest-growing economy and is expected to have surpassed Japan by 2020, re-establishing the centrality of China in Asia, and to have surpassed the USA by 2039.[4] What astonishes foreign observers is just how rapidly these advances have been achieved; what scares them are the potential effects, should China's **trade** growth continue. How has all this happened?

Until the late 1970s, China was becoming progressively more under-developed economically and culturally, thanks to the State control of the economy and social regimentation enforced by Mao and his heirs. Once they had been cleared away in the late 1970s, farmers were allowed to work for themselves rather than for collectives, foreign investment was encouraged in Special Economic Zones, local authorities were freed to sort out their local economies, and price controls were gradually eliminated. This was Deng Xiaoping's policy of the Four Modernisations (see Glossary), and it caused wealth to increase rapidly in the 1980s. The main executive was Zhao Ziyang, who was to fall because of his sympathy for those student protestors eliminated in the 1989 Tiananmen massacre. A hiatus followed as the left tried to reassert control.

In winter 1991–92, Deng Xiaoping, prohibited by the capital's media from calling for freeing up the market, made his Southern Progress to lecture reform-minded provincial leaders on the need for free enterprise. They seized their chance, fully realising the Special Economic Zones and impelling China on a course that has involved rapidly reducing the State's direct involvement in the economy, bringing back the stock market, joining the World Trade Organization, privatising housing and making institutions conform to international standards.

The Chinese economic miracle is normally attributed, first to the step-by-step, pragmatic government policies which made possible rapid productivity growth, and second to massive investment, both from foreign sources (about half being overseas Chinese) and domestic savings, which are among the highest in the world.[5] There is a relatively unexplored third factor, the cultural one, which may explain why the first two were successful.[6]

Those government policies included abolition of price regulations, reduction of internal tariffs and multiple exchange rates, and relinquishment of the export trading monopoly. The dismantling of the nationalised industries or State Operated Enterprises (SOEs) has been an enormous undertaking, fraught with dangers. In Xian, I went to a government garment and protective wear factory to buy some traditional Chinese shoes. The factory itself was as big as a mighty public hospital, behind guarded gates bearing a red star and an exhortation to serve the people. Although hundreds still lived in the dormitories in the grounds, the factory itself was dead, awaiting demolition. In the street outside there remained 40 or so shops selling its products, or the products of the spin-off workshops which had derived from it and still exist. Nearly 4,000 major State enterprises such as this have been closed in a massive programme of marketisation[7] which has put tens of millions on **welfare** or released them for private enterprise. In new enterprises, employment contracts are 'flexible'. Private enterprise now produces well over half of GDP and an overwhelming share of exports; private companies create most of the new jobs and are infinitely more productive and profitable.[8]

Prohibitions on private involvement in certain sectors of the economy have progressively been removed; in 2005, public utilities, financial services and infrastructure were thus freed up. New laws and regulations, in such areas as company and competition law, have been in line with international practice. In 2004, the role of the private sector and private property were acknowledged in revisions to the Constitution.

The cumulative results of these changes have included an overall improvement in living standards; it is generally thought that 400 million people have been lifted out of poverty.[9] Government revenues have greatly increased, making possible investments in infrastructure.

Infrastructure development is now integrating China with the rest of the industrialised world. Fifty thousand miles of three-lane highway were under construction in 2005, the size of the entire US interstate network; whereas these works took 40 years in the US, China plans their completion in five.[10] Twenty-six Chinese cities are installing underground railways. There are 30 nuclear power stations on order.

China thinks big. Visiting new leisure complexes, university campuses or science parks, you are very soon made aware of this. Entrepreneurs and officials have thrown themselves into ambitious projects that often dwarf those that were their models in the West. In Shanghai, you will find the world's tallest hotel, the biggest shop, the highest TV tower, the fastest train. The **Three Gorges** hydroelectric project is the most titanic such operation the world has ever seen, five times the size of the Hoover Dam in the USA, submerging tens of thousands of communities.

Can the advance continue? External observers agree in their suggestions as to what China needs to do if it is to maintain its trajectory.[11] There is much scope for further progress by China first imitating advanced technology, benefiting from technology transfers, and then by developing its own innovations; both require – and are getting – impressive investments in both R&D and in **science and technology** education. The government is also keen to develop the service sector and is taking action to increase domestic demand, or consumption.

Despite the phasing out of SOEs, there are still too many requiring subsidies which could be put to more productive use, and needing the trade protection which hampers innovation. The banks have been obliged to lend to SOEs for political reasons, such that a very high proportion of their loans are 'unperforming' and they themselves, but for government support, would be bankrupt; furthermore, like the widespread practice of loaning on the basis of personal connections rather than commercial analysis, this restricts the amount of capital available for efficient enterprises.

Energy problems are familiar to visitors who find themselves using torches in hotels. Less well known are the shortages of water and inadequate transportation. Infrastructure cannot keep up with demand. Development has produced losers as well as winners and there is much discontent from the unemployed, the bankrupted, those whose assets have been stolen and those in localities left behind. The **health** services cannot cope, in particular with the HIV/AIDS epidemic. Degradation of the **environment** is very serious.

Most intractable is the absence of the rule of **law**, which encourages corruption, embezzlement and expropriation. This is linked to the difficulties faced by the government in getting laws and regulations implemented. Absolute recognition of private ownership[12] would be helpful.

These are big problems to sort out in the period of the Eleventh Five-Year Plan, formally approved on 5 March 2006,[13] with its emphasis on sustainable, all-round and high-technology-based development. Yet, in their pragmatic, careful and gradual approach, policy-makers have already achieved the unimaginable in their reforms of both government and market conditions. They may well be able to continue with the same verve.

CHAPTER 10

Trade

So far, very large numbers of people around the world have been made richer thanks to China's rise, and there are further impacts to come; these will be positive only if their economies can adapt. How China trade will affect you depends on where you live and of what class you are.

Reforms of the economy have transformed China trade such that, though in 1979 its exports were worth $14 billion, by 2004 they amounted to $593 billion.[1] That year, China overtook Japan and became the world's third biggest trader after the USA and Germany; the pace of growth suggests that China will overtake the USA by 2010. There is fear of the effect of Chinese exports upon domestic jobs, of China's need for raw material upon prices and of China's productivity upon other developing countries. There is fear of the scale of China's impact.

In the 1980s and 90s, China's exports consisted mainly of clothing, footwear and other light manufactures. It pushed both South Korea and Taiwan out of the shoe market, replaced Mexico as textile supplier to the USA and is competing keenly in the US market with Bangladesh, Vietnam and Cambodia. To offset their losses in that and other markets where Chinese competition has won, some South Asian countries have developed more skill-intensive industries and sought to increase exports to China itself. Countries with flexible economies have quickly adapted to the production of higher-order goods. In advanced economies where manufacture had already shrunk, a further reminder was offered of the need to adapt, to specialise and become more skill-intensive.[2]

Since then, there has been rapid increase in exports of office machinery, electronic goods, telecommunications, travel goods and furniture. China has shown that it can 'climb the technology ladder' very fast. Unskilled industrial workers of other countries, particularly where the educational institutions do not assist them to adapt, are the main losers.

Furthermore, the arrangements made with foreign firms for the sharing of technology, combined with the phenomenal copying ability of Chinese designers and technicians, make it highly likely that China will score more and more successes. In the mobile phone market, it is possible that local products will soon have superseded those foreign firms from which they have learned so much.

There are at least three beneficial effects upon trading partners of China's export explosion. The first is that over 50 per cent of Chinese exports are those of foreign-funded enterprises in China, set up there in search of low-paid workers, attractive conditions and educated personnel.

The second is that consumers back home benefit as the prices of clothing, furniture and electronic goods tumble. Consumers in the USA and Europe are becoming richer, in that they spend an ever smaller proportion of their incomes on such goods.

Thirdly, China is a creator of jobs abroad as much as it is their nemesis. Most of what China earns from exports is being spent on imports. Most of what it imports is what it needs in order to produce exports: raw materials, components and manufacturing machinery. Thus Germany, for example, maker of much of this kind of machinery, has a substantial surplus trade with China, as do suppliers of oil, tin and zinc.

The demand for raw materials seriously profits other economies – one small, sleepy Chinese town has in five years set up 200 sawmills and 500 floorboard manufactories working with imported timber from several countries.[3] The Middle East and African countries gain from the voracious need for energy. Australia is enjoying a mining boom, to the extent that new mines are being opened and new port facilities built for China trade.[4]

The commodities boom that was caused by Japan's industrialisation was driven by a population of 150 million. China, India and Russia together involve a demand more like 3 billion, and of the three, the biggest appetite is China's.[5] Already, Chinese demand in many international markets has become the dominant price-setter, or at least a big swing factor.[6]

Thus in China trade, the losers are developing countries with plenteous labour, which compete in the same export markets or for component assembly contracts, and which are forced to match the 'China price'; and countries competing with China for the same raw materials, for they are faced with much higher prices.

In general, the impact of China trade is going to be big because of the openness of its economy, because of its large population and because of the numbers of poor people queuing up to get low-paid industrial jobs. The economy is remarkably open: trade amounts to 75 per cent of China's GDP whereas in the USA and Japan it is 30 per cent or less. Investment by foreign firms is 36 per cent of GDP in China, compared to 2 per cent in Japan.[7]

The idea of reaching 1.3 billion consumers has fired the imagination of world business ever since Deng Xiaoping inaugurated the 'Open Door' policy or *kaifang*. But penetration of the Chinese consumer market is only just beginning, both because the Chinese have been too poor to buy foreign goods and because the difficulties which membership of the WTO is intended to sweep away are only gradually being addressed.

Chinese growth depends upon exports; a big internal market, the size of which has mattered so much to the USA during its rise, is only now becoming a focus of policy for China,[8] as the government realises its importance both to social stability and to exports. For although only a small proportion of the Chinese population are consumers, nevertheless the size of even this domestic market is having a profound effect on the world. It enables Chinese business to gear up for huge quantities and then export surplus capacity, contributing, along with cheap labour and high skills, to the phenomenon of the 'China price', which buyers demand that competitors match – or fail.[9]

The first coming effect of China trade is therefore that, as the consumer market develops, it may be less significant as a source of profits for foreign businesses than as an immense domestic market in which local companies can grow sufficiently rich and experienced to launch themselves into world competition with anything from washing machines to cars. The USA's greatest advantage in becoming an economic power has been the accidental one of its size; China has the same advantage, many times over.

The second effect will be on demand. Even if average incomes in China remain low, there will be enough wealthy people to influence the economies of other countries; soon 200 million people will have **jobs** making them 'middle class', with income sufficient to interest many sales departments. China will stimulate production as this number grows and seeks sophisticated goods from advanced economies.

Chinese consumers are already becoming powerful in that it is their lack or their tastes that determine whether it is profitable to make certain products; we can foresee a time when what we consume may be dictated by the preferences of the biggest bloc of consumers in the world. And of course China's economy will be bigger than the USA's when its per capita income doubles.

Thirdly, there is an almost unlimited supply of cheap labour, such that wages will be held down for at least twenty years.[10] And that labour is both low-skill and, increasingly, skilled. Investment in education will soon pay off for many millions. With these advantages, China will be able to turn itself to almost any kind of business or service.

The main charge made against China trade is that it causes deindustrialisation elsewhere. Most authorities acquit China of this charge, and, anyway, see it not as a negative phenomenon but 'a natural consequence of further growth in advanced economies' in which 'North–South trade has played very little role'.[11] And, as we have seen, flexible economies do not necessarily need to fear change, provided they can prepare their new generations to

67

respond. Countries in direct competition with China, lacking that flexibility, will suffer. In the advanced economies, certain categories of people are vulnerable as the rewards for lower skills go down, while the more affluent benefit as returns on capital and higher-order skills improve. In general, the development of China as a great trading nation may provide the spur to further development all over the world. There are wider implications of this for **geopolitics** and the **environment**.

CHAPTER 11

Money

Nowhere is the prediction of China as a vast market for foreign wares more likely to be true than in financial services; partly it is the weaknesses of Chinese banking that are to blame for these opportunities. External forces oblige reform of both financing and of the fiscal system, for the contradictions inherent in both threaten China's progress.

The contrasts between the optimists and the pessimists are at their starkest in the arcane yet fundamental world of finance. The pessimists predict that China's banking system is so tawdry that it will bring down the whole economy once its fraudulence is rumbled. In this corner, there camp some sinologists who find it difficult to believe that the culture of corruption nurtured in the socialist years can possibly change, and democratisers who argue that, as long as politics is illiberal, a trustworthy financial system cannot emerge.

So far the optimists have the running. They include the government, the international financial services empires, salivating on the sidelines, and European governments urgent to sell China services to make up for all that lost manufacturing.

From a Chinese point of view there are two issues to be resolved: whether the government can create a modern fiscal environment, i.e. get its taxation and regulation intentions implemented; and whether the banks are capable of reform. To some foreigners it may be acceptable for China not to achieve these objectives, since there might be more business for international companies if the domestic financial services industry remains weak.

China is a fabulous market for international financial services companies for several reasons. People save a very much higher proportion of their income than in the Anglophone world (UK: 5 per cent, China: 40 per cent); they put more of their money in banks and cash deposits than others (UK: 20 per cent, China: 60 per cent),[1] partly because the stock and bond markets are viewed with suspicion; there is very limited welfare; the middle class is expanding fast; a consequence of the population policy is that very soon one child will need to care, alone, for at least two older people and insurance will become highly desirable; and the government is determined that the private sector will have a leading role in the provision of social security.[2]

The pessimists notice, however, that political interference, bad loans, incompetent management and corruption plague the banks. Not that the international financial community seems too worried. Two years ago the China Construction Bank (CCB) was technically insolvent and five years ago its Chairman had been arrested for bribery. Today, thanks to foreign investment, CCB is more valuable than Barclays, AE or Deutsche Bank.[3]

CCB is one of the top four State-owned banks. The People's Bank of China sits atop the financial system as the regulatory authority, after which come the Bank of China (BOC), CCB, Industrial and Commercial Bank (ICBC) and Agricultural Bank. Thereafter, there are policy banks (for infrastructure projects) and then joint stock commercial banks. Eighty-eight foreign banks are permitted to do *renminbi* ('people's currency' or RMB) business, though many others have representative offices.

It often used to be said rather cruelly that those European countries most unbothered about Brussels' interference in their affairs were those which had no faith that things might be improved by their home politicians. The rules of the EU would force reform. Although the PRC government has established the China Banking Regulatory Commission (2003),[4] and invested heavily in trying to clean up the banks by buying out their bad loans; although it has imposed better accounting and regulatory standards, bad loans continue to be made, loans are not monitored and information about them is not transparent. Whatever the rules, it is widely known that local branches tend to be heavily influenced by personal, local connections, and are only marginally susceptible to pressure from above. CCB's Chairman admitted that 90 per cent of his risk managers – in 14,250 branches – were unqualified.[5] As a result, bank profits are pitiful.

Although foreign banks such as HSBC (with its buying of BOC shares), Royal Bank of Scotland and others are aware of this, they are presumably so impressed by the branch network and client list as to have convinced themselves that a combination of government pressure and foreign expertise can change the culture. The opportunities for them are dazzling. Currently credit cards are used by only 2 million people;[6] most transactions are in cash. Many banks see this as a growth area.[7] Online banking has 12 million clients of ICBC online alone. Ten non-Chinese banks have launched internet banking, which they are permitted to offer to individual customers from 2006. Online shopping was worth $507.5 million in 2005.

When not admiring their own prescience, Western financial operations are most concerned at how political priorities override economic decisions. Despite the booming economy, the equity market is in a bad way, partly because the top companies prefer listing abroad, partly because of the incompetence or dishonesty of brokers, and mostly because for several years the government obliged the market to absorb overpriced shares in State firms.[8] This is a waste, because troves of private savings sit unproductively in banks, which don't deserve them, or are blowing up the property bubble, while enterprises need funds. And it might be easier to reform the banks were they not so awash with savings.

Since outsiders can buy no more than 25 per cent of Chinese banks, the Western new owners of bits of them are condemned to be without much influence, unless this changes. Meanwhile they have to live with the fact that senior banking appointments are made through the Party.

So in the financial system, the main concern is of too much

political power; in the fiscal, it is its absence which is problematic. After 1978, the government found itself unable to extract adequate taxation, and in 1994 attempted to introduce a rule-based fiscal system. The principal introductions were that tax rates would from now on be centrally standardised; central and shared taxes would be collected by central agencies and local taxes locally, all according to centrally-determined formulae. Although in theory all local discretion in providing tax breaks was disallowed, a permissive transitional period was required in order to sweeten the pill for the richer provinces, which were going to lose out from the reforms; this unfortunately has permitted some bad practices to continue, such as unauthorised exemptions and overlooked tax evasions. There are other unresolved difficulties. The central government has not bound itself not to alter the rules, so that the provinces have little incentive to abide by them if they know that changes of direction may come arbitrarily. There is no clear allocation of expenditure responsibilities, thus plenty of scope for conflict, and there is no formal system of fiscal transfers, for dealing with extra budgetary funds, which are sometimes very substantial.[9] As in other areas of administration, law enforcement is inadequate.

Does this matter to the average citizen, does it affect the financial services industry? In the short term, only insofar as government fiscal weakness is indicative of a general difficulty in assuring economic stability.

CHAPTER 12

World Trade Organization

If the world needed proof that China really wanted to be part of it, then entry into the WTO provided that.

The accession, in 2001, of China to the World Trade Organization was the biggest step away from China's past that the government could take. It has been the hope of reformers in China that being obliged to comply with WTO conditions would force their country to adapt its economic system to international norms, and of much of the rest of the world that cooperation with China over many matters – from the environment to the proliferation of weaponry to the control of diseases, terrorism and criminality – would be more feasible.

This is because the WTO not only obliges its members to grant to all other members the conditions provided to domestic producers or service providers and to afford to all WTO members the most favourable treatment afforded any other country, but because it requires government and business to be rule-based, transparent and non-discriminating.

The implications for China's own enterprises are many, including the ending of export subsidies and special tax zones, more regulation and international competition in the domestic market. These innovations may improve their own performance but may also drive them out of business. The advantages, much stressed by the very partial media,[1] include many more markets abroad for Chinese goods, and knowledge transfer from foreign companies, not only of technology but of management and financing expertise.

Average tariff barriers are down from 41 per cent in 1992 to 6 per cent since 2001, i.e. the government is making it as easy as it possibly can for importers to succeed, and giving China 'the lowest tariff protection of any developing country'.[2] China is the most open economy in the world, at least in principle, keeping restrictions only on certain critical raw materials[3] and on the media.[4] But not only does membership involve abolition or reduction of tariff and non-tariff barriers to trade, it requires the reform of deep-rooted practices of favouritism or local protection, hidden accounting or unpublished regulations. To develop understanding of these far-reaching WTO requirements, innumerable Chinese officials, business managers and lawyers have been sent on training courses.

China has agreed to publish a journal giving advance warning of legal and regulatory measures affecting all kinds of trade and foreign exchange so that interested parties can comment before implementation, and has agreed that measures not made public and easily available to other WTO members will not be enforced. This is intended to undermine the custom of having regulations with restricted circulation (*neibu guize*). Dissemination of this kind is not yet thorough and there is not yet one source of advance information, rather the enquirer needs to access many websites and even then may not get the full picture. The trade ministry, MOFTEC, has set up the China WTO Notification Enquiry Centre, which provides authoritative responses to challenges to regulations within 30 to 45 days. Where measures are found, as a result of the challenges, to be non-compliant, they are to be amended or rescinded.[5] It is as yet unclear how such decisions will be executed or whether plaintiffs will be satisfied.

Since the 2001 agreement, wholly-owned foreign retail enterprises and foreign insurance companies have been established in China and, from 2006, foreign banks have had all restrictions lifted. The penetration of China by foreign manufacturers has been very fast, with whole sectors such as car-making already dominated by them. Imports have grown phenomenally. Wheat imports from the USA[6] increased by 2,000 per cent in the first year; cotton and soybeans have increased by several hundred per cent, and manufactured goods such as semiconductors, medical and optical equipment and construction and transport equipment have also been imported in massively larger quantities, such that China is the US's second- or third-largest trading partner.[7]

Despite US success in the China market, perceived threats loomed large in the 2005 US election campaign, with the opposition accusing President Bush of being soft on China, of allowing US jobs to be eliminated by cheap imports, and of allowing discrimination against US goods. But President Bush's team did achieve accords with China which improved US companies' positions in markets as diverse as biotechnology and postal services. It persuaded China to abort its plan to develop a wireless encryption standard different to that of the US.[8] The US had recourse to the WTO complaints procedures when claiming that Chinese subsidies to domestic semiconductor producers breached WTO rules, and China caved in before proceedings started. The US has also used the WTO to resolve disputes over agricultural quotas.

The WTO allows members a 'safeguard' measure, whereby they can place tariffs to prevent dumping of large quantities of underpriced goods; the US has deployed the measure three times to curtail Chinese imports of textiles. Forty-six per cent of textile imports into the US are from China. A similar feat was attempted in the EU. More such actions can be expected following elimination of the world quota system for textiles. Early in 2005, Congress toyed with a bill that would impose a 27.5 per cent tariff on Chinese goods unless the PRC adjusted its currency – which it did.

Although the benefits to China have included free access to world markets, a voice in the world forum on trade, and external pressure upon Chinese business to reform, the disadvantages have also been notable, though little discussed by the Chinese media. The intensifying elimination of the State enterprises have put millions out of work; businesses, such as the vehicle industry, may prove unable to compete; Chinese farmers – their practices outdated, every spare grain wrested from them in taxes, and their ability to resist vicissitude minimal – are beginning to suffer from cheap imports of food and are forced to send their children to work in the sweatshops of the East. As always, the poor suffer most.

Foreign firms may not find business as easy as they had hoped. At least one book by a disenchanted investor[9] has vividly described failing to cope where the rule of law is a mirage and rights derive only from personal power; where accounts and agreements could not be trusted and where there were no effective ways of resolving disputes; where the legislation of the centre can mean nothing on the ground. But he was reporting of his experiences in the 1990s. When I bought a trinket for my daughter in a backstreet workshop, I chatted to the teenager behind the counter about the hot issue of intellectual property. Miss Hu said to me, glowing with pride: 'Now China is in the WTO we obey the rules just as foreigners do, otherwise we will be shamed and there could be wars.' If Miss Hu grasped the point, so may many others.

CHAPTER 13

Science and Technology

The speed with which China has advanced in several fields is due to the systematic way in which government has gone about organising research and development, as well as to the incentives of the market. Popular enthusiasm for science has merged into an attachment to a scientific approach to life in general that is a marked feature of China today.

'What's our town like? Oh, it's not modern; come and see it in a few years when it has been rebuilt.' 'You don't smoke? ... You're right, it is not scientific to smoke, I am ashamed.' Such curious exchanges are part and parcel of travelling around China, where anything good is described as 'modern' or 'scientific' and anything to be condemned is 'backward' (as in: 'My grandmother is backward, she thinks it is unhealthy for children to watch TV', or 'We must extirpate Falungong, it is not scientific'.).

In the 1980s, in reaction against the irrational fervour of the Mao years, itself built on the faith in the communist Utopia and economic determinism which were the core beliefs of the Party, Deng Xiaoping called upon people to 'seek truth from facts'. Empiricism then became the weapon used to belittle the faith-based approach to development that had earlier done so much harm. The study of science and the organisation of that study had been wrecked almost as comprehensively as education.

Before the European Enlightenment, China was the most technologically advanced country in the world. In the mid-18th century, Europe was developing fast and China was in reverse. By the 1870s, it was sending students abroad to learn science, conscious that its decadence in science and technology was having economic, political and military repercussions. Under the Republic (1911–49),

77

research institutes were set up, as well as many universities, often with foreign help. From 1949, science and technology were further developed with Russian assistance, almost totally military.[1] Although military scientists were protected during the Cultural Revolution (1966–76), most research stagnated.

Since 1985, the achievements have been substantial, not least in awareness and education, such that observers talk seriously of China overtaking advanced countries in the near future. And that is despite the fact that US spending on research, for example, is 200 times what China can afford.[2] China was in 2004 labelled 'the first cloning superpower'.[3] This and other successes have been possible on account of the reformation of the frameworks for science and technology, research management, investment and the widespread diffusion of scientific and technical knowledge.

An indication of the importance attached to the field of science is that the Prime Minister chairs a Leading Group representing the main interests, and under which is the Ministry of Science and Technology. There are Committees of Science and Technology at all administrative levels, whose tasks are to monitor development in their provinces, cities, counties, etc., and propose plans. The overall objectives of policy are to 'revitalise the country through science and education', raise the level, reform the framework, innovate, enhance competitiveness.[4]

The principal framework plans have been the 863, the 973, the 'Torch' and the 'Spark'. The 863 (March 1986, Deng Xiaoping's plan) identified key fields in which China might become a world leader. It fostered high-tech industries and personnel in IT, biology, agricultural technology, new materials, automation, energy and environment. The 973 emphasised the building of research facilities and nurturing of personnel. One hundred and thirty-two projects were launched between 1997 and 2002, some of which were initiated by EU and Chinese scientists together.

Other plans, coming under the over-arching framework of the national 'Tenth Five-Year Plan', are those for Key Laboratories

(164 in 2002), Nationally Important Science Projects, Technology Research Centres and Key International Projects. The China Education and Scientific Research Net (CERNET) is the basic platform for science research and cyber-education. Under the Torch plan, scientific research is converted into commercial applications (well over 20,000 to date); science development zones and incubator centres are set up and management systems made appropriate to high-technology development. Emphasised areas include new energy sources and energy-saving technology. The Spark plan involves the demonstration of advanced technologies, particularly in the countryside, through setting up technology zones, 'backbone industries', demonstration projects (120,000+) and training bases (5,000+), as well as forming 70 million technicians. There is also the Plan for Popularising National Achievements in Science and Technology.

The government has invested in the **universities**. Fifty-nine per cent of undergraduates study science and engineering, compared to 32 per cent in the USA and 36 per cent in the UK.[5] Universities aside, the State owns well over 4,000 research institutions, headed by the Academy of Sciences (CAS), which has 60,000 professional scientists and has translated many hundreds of scientific works from European languages and Japanese. The Academy of Social Sciences (CASS) was split off from CAS in 1977 in order to free the natural scientists from the Party's propaganda and ideology system and put them directly under the State Council, effectively insulated from politicisation.[6] Parallel to CAS are the Academy of Agricultural Sciences (CAAS), Engineering, Forestry (CAF), Medical Sciences and Environmental Sciences. All these academies have their own research laboratories, as do 1,396 higher education institutions, with 181,000 researchers.

Reforms in 1985 decentralised decision-making and intensified links with industry. Since then, China has recorded some substantial achievements, such as the first remote sensing satellite ground station; the Shenguang High-Power Laser Device; a 2.16-metre optical telescope; the first physical mapping of the rice genome; carbon nano-tube arrays; and 1 per cent of the sequencing work for the International Human Genome, among other international projects. 'The composition of the Ba-y-Cu-O Superconductor was published for the first time in the world, indicating that China was in the world's front rank of the superconductivity research.'[7]

CAS has initiated six high-tech parks, and a further 80 institutes, of which 30 are intended to become internationally eminent, are planned. It has over 200 commercial enterprises, mainly in information technology, new materials, electronic-mechanical integration and bio-medicine, and in addition, over 1,800 joint ventures or other kinds of partnerships with firms. Abroad, its best-known creation is Lenovo, the multinational which in 2004 bought IBM's PC division. Others of its enterprises have succeeded in producing: very high-resolution scanning radiometers for the Fengyun meteorological satellites; the first underwater robot; an intelligent English–Chinese machine translation system and the world's first pocket English–Chinese electronic dictionary; a new cardio-vascular drug, Diao Xinxuekang; new types of polymer engineering plastics; heat-shrinkable polymer materials; and Linux operational system software.[8]

By 2010, CAS is planned to have developed into the National Innovation Centre for Natural Science and High Technology, which aims to be a world leader in research, science education and knowledge-pooling.

Aside from directly controlled research institutes, and CAS, the government also supports R&D centres in private enterprises, such as the Haier Research Institute, which cooperates with partners in Japan, the USA and Germany. There are reported to be 700 multinational R&D centres, up from 50 in 1997.[9] Many State research institutes have been transformed into commercial enterprises – for example, the research operations of the old Ministry of Metallurgical Industries were reborn as Antai Science and Technology. Foreign enterprises which want contracts from China must share their technology, as in the current building of nuclear reactors. Technology transfer is 'a major source of advanced technology for the PRC'.[10]

Commercial applications are enabled in other ways. The telecommunications giant Huawei was born out of an army enterprise in 1988; in 2005, it was competing in international markets with Cisco, considering acquisition attempts for major international competitors and turning out 2,300 patent applications. Its success abroad is, according to critics, due to the favourable treatment it receives from government, which enables it to undercut competitors' bids by 70 per cent. The advantages enjoyed include State R&D funding ($9 million in 2003–05), tax concessions, easy and massive credit facilities and export credits. As to the latter, the China Development Bank recently extended $200 million to Nigeria in order to buy from Huawei.[11]

According to an authoritative report,[12] in micro-electronics, China could at its present rate of progress catch up with the state of the art by 2008; in computers, it can assemble as well as the most advanced countries, but mainly from imported parts; it is progressing very rapidly in telecommunications equipment; in biotechnology and chemistry, its research capabilities are strong but commercial application weak; in the nuclear field, it has been dependent upon imports until recently and will manufacture most of the components for the current foreign-led power plant projects; aviation is backward but this may soon change, since Chinese firms have entered into co-production arrangements with Western manufacturers, leading to rapid advances; and satellite capabilities are 'limited'. Necessity, in China as elsewhere, is the mother of invention. China's ever more urgent need for energy has turned its scientists towards pioneering both liquefaction plants (converting coal to petroleum) and pebble-bed (purportedly 'meltdown proof') reactors.

Deng Xiaoping's exhortation to be scientific has taken an extraordinary grip on China. As the scientific world was startled when China put a man in space in 2003, so was it in 2005 when

Chinese cryptographers exposed the US government's encryption code SHA-1.[13] There is a general enthusiasm for science and technology, evident from the media coverage, school curriculum and science study centres for children. Most Chinese ministers since the mid-1980s have been qualified scientists or engineers. So it is not surprising that the government has paid great attention to the establishment of an institutional and regulatory framework for science and technology, their research, application and popularisation. The commitment to science goes deep. Writing about the way CCP leaders think about the world, Susan Greenhalgh has described 'the larger culture of scientism – a widespread belief in modern science as a totalistic body of thought, the prime source of truth and an all powerful solution to China's problems'.[14] Science, in other words, is almost a religion.

CHAPTER 14

Intellectual Property

One of the biggest sources of friction between China and the more advanced economies is its cavalier attitude towards intellectual property. But this may be changing.

The Valentino suit goes well with the Lauren shirt; strap on your Rolex, adjust your Ray Bans and stow her Hermès scarf and Gucci handbag in the four-wheeler … all those odds and ends will have cost you 5 per cent of their price outside China. The car, at least until recently, might well have been a rip-off, and the medicines you use, the DVDs you watch and your electronic goods and their software are in the same category. It's really handy to live in China.

Yet even the minuscule prices charged for pirated versions of goods designed outside China are beyond the pockets of most Chinese. And this is the rub. If these pirate editions were not so low-priced, not even the middle classes could use and get to know these products. Intelligent foreign companies such as Microsoft have understood this and, instead of just railing against China, have continued to work there, reasoning that piracy is a necessary phase but that it will, in time, be in China's interests to end it.

In markets now, you will see pasted up large notices under official seals with, in between the Chinese text, the logos of a host of well known companies from Prada to Burberry, Ray Ban to Calvin Klein. These are warnings that no goods marked with these company labels may be sold here, on pain of arrest. For reasons of international relations, the PRC government has undertaken many measures to protect intellectual property rights (IPR), such that it is increasingly risky to sell pirate goods publicly, and tourists have to worry about customs searches.

China has signed the Berne Convention for the Protection of

Literary and Artistic Works and the World Trade Organization's TRIPS Agreement on Trade-Related Aspects of Intellectual Property Rights. In doing this, it agreed that foreign rights be protected in China. To avert sanctions, it also signed understandings with the USA in 1992 and 1994 and, in response to US threats to retaliate on account of losses of a billion dollars annually because of piracy, the PRC has enacted stringent laws against theft of intellectual property and stepped up enforcement.

When China established the State Intellectual Property Office (SIPO) in 1998, it was intended to merge all aspects of intellectual property – copyright, trademarks, patents and domain names – under one authority. But there are many other agencies involved. For patent, trademark and domain name rights to be enforceable in China, they have to have been registered with the correct Chinese authority. Copyrights do not have to be registered with the National Copyright Agency, and copyright is extended under the international copyright conventions or bilateral agreements to which China is party.

Patent protection is granted under a 'first to file' system, lasts twenty years and covers food, beverages and flavourings as well as pharmaceuticals and chemicals. Filing is through approved local agents and with SIPO head office; provincial and municipal SIPO offices are responsible for enforcement.

Trademarks are protected by the Trademark Office, a division of the State Administration for Industry and Commerce (SAIC), also under a first to file system, but the Office has deterred abuse by cancelling trademarks registered unfairly.[1] SAIC's Fair Trade Office is responsible for the protection of unregistered trademarks and company names. Domain names are registered with the China Internet Network Information Centre, of the Ministry of Information. Authority to resolve disputes lies with the China International Economic and Trade Commission.

The concept of intellectual property is probably now widely understood; certainly it is discussed in the media. There are still major disagreements, such as that over Pfizer's Viagra. In 2004, SIPO revoked the company's patent on a technicality; it is appealing.[2] There remains, too, as in many other areas of the administration of justice, the problem of enforcement. Central agencies are not adequately resourced and local ones are often complicit with pirates, especially since government and enterprise are so closely connected. Investigation is problematic because of lack of skills and funding, as well as the cleverness of the violators.

There are two complaints channels: the administrative, handled by SIPO and/or the other government offices involved; and the judicial. There are conflicts of jurisdiction. If you go down the law route, you find that divisions of provincial and municipal courts have been tasked to adjudicate intellectual property disputes and specialist IP courts have even been established throughout the PRC. The courts hear complaints, make decisions and recommend penalties. 'Possible penalties (specified in Article 51 of the 1991 law) include fines of 10,000 RMB to 100,000 RMB, civil damages equivalent to two to five times the value of the infringing copies, and two to seven years of prison depending on the specific case. The second of these penalties is more in line with international standards, allowing both for recovery of real damages and for deterrence.'[3]

Going to law to protect copyright entails expense and is unpredictable. Moreover, Chinese computer software protection regulations and the copyright law are considered flawed because they regard unwitting copying as not culpable and because they allow pirating for non-commercial purposes.

IPR is a controversial issue worldwide, because protection appears to benefit the rich countries at the expense of those attempting to develop their own industries. A British government study found that too much patent protection damaged, rather than encouraged, trade. Poor countries cannot be customers if the prices of goods are kept high in order to reward the originator (and allow future investment), and nor can they learn by copying, thus risking being locked into under-development.

So poorer countries want to get the richer to limit their protective demands, but they do not oppose the concept altogether. Why? First, patents are also valuable to countries developing their own competencies, of which China is the major example. One of China's biggest biotechnology companies, Kexing, is busy launching several patented drugs because it has ambitions to be a global supplier and knows that the fruits of its R&D need protection if it is to be rewarded.[4] Because, by agreement, patents registered in the USA before 1993 are not universally protected within China, it has, legally, been able to make and sell drugs at home, such as a widely-used medicine for hepatitis B, that are the property of big pharmaceutical companies abroad.

Second, Chinese enterprises, from film producers to electronics manufacturers to clothes designers and musicians, see the domestic pirates as their enemies as much as they are the enemies of foreign enterprises.

Although the problem is truly vast at present – with the USA claiming that 'the piracy rate remains one of the highest in the world (over 90 per cent) and [that] US companies lose over one billion dollars in legitimate business each year to piracy. On average, 20 per cent of all consumer products in the Chinese market are counterfeit'[5] – the indications are that China will get the problem under control, not simply because of the proliferation of agencies or the threats of its trade partners, but because there are voluble interests in China itself that want to see intellectual property safe.

CHAPTER 15

Jobs

The opportunities to better yourself have never been greater: but the likelihood of failing to do so is made more acute by the injustices of the system – the lack of worker rights and representatives, the excessive power of local officials and the failures of mediation and justice.

Ling works in a graphic design studio. She is aged 26 and came from Xian to Shenzhen two years ago, about 1,500 miles from the home to which she returns once a year. She works six days a week, twelve hours a day, in a room with 100 others.[1] Her frustrations are that the factory (and her accommodation) are miles from anywhere, there are few ways to advance and the boss makes them work extra time without increase on her 800 RMB per month. However, she will not move jobs because the boss is decent and she receives her pay properly, and these are great advantages in the wilds of Shenzhen where management can be unjust and brutal, while conditions may be unhealthy or unsafe.[2] Bai is a security guard on 450 RMB, on duty all day and night seven days a week. His wife and children are 700 miles away and he is afraid his family is forgetting him, but proud that he supports them. Their smallholding could not. Yi is seventeen and came from a village in Hunan eighteen months ago. She worked in a department store but was cheated of her wages, 450 RMB a month, so left. After a succession of temporary shop jobs and bad experiences with dishonest employers, she and three other Hunanese teenagers set up a business. They employ a couple of middle-aged ladies as 'representatives' to work the streets offering their services ('young, beautiful, will do anything you want') and a couple of cab drivers to take them to appointments. They receive 400 RMB a trick and keep 250 RMB. In Yi's case, of that, 200 RMB goes back to her parents. Zhang, 61, was laid off from a big State enterprise five years ago. His compensation is about 1,500 RMB a year, which he supplements with odd labouring jobs at 25 RMB a day. Whereas all his services from lighting to medicines to schooling used to be provided, he now has to find cash for all these for himself and his parents out of casual jobs. His wife packs toys in cartons to pay for their daughter's schooling.

These are some of the stories I have collected while travelling, and they bring home how hard life is in a country where there is no protection for the vulnerable. Of course the stories are not those of my students, with good qualifications and worthwhile networks. There is a gulf between the minority in the relatively high-paying professional world and the majority struggling to get by, although with illness or misfortune it is no longer difficult to slip downwards. In the recent past, socialist society allowed virtually no social mobility, but the compensation was security. Coming to terms with the dynamic, free-enterprise world of today's China is proving unnerving for both winners and losers.

Over-40s in China will often explain that they did not choose their career, it was simply assigned them. For before the 1980s, you might have an element of choice only in that, if you were lucky enough to go to a decent school, your capacity for study might give you an opportunity to go on to further or higher education. Yet, after that, you would, just like the schoolfriend you had left behind some years before, wait to be told where you might live and what job you might do for the rest of your life. The only employer was a State or collective operation, which also determined your access to food rations, residency, health and schooling services; remuneration was fixed by government, movement was restricted and a change of job almost impossible. It was a very unequal society in which most people were at the bottom but officials ascended through a steep hierarchy of ranks until they reached the luxury of splendid courtyard homes, many servants and free access to anything they might want.

The consequences of this system that were most glaringly damaging to the economy by 1978 were over-manning, low productivity and the lack of either innovation or growth. The Four Modernisations (see Glossary) brought back private business to **rural China**, and non-agricultural rural enterprises were freed from the collectives. They were permitted to recruit labour directly and according to whatever employment conditions their managers desired. New businesses began to spring up, and again jobs could be had on short contract, bonus or piece rate conditions.

The second stage of reform involved permitting the State Owned Enterprises (SOEs) to lay off nearly 60 million surplus workers who supposedly had lifetime jobs, eliminating food rations and social services. Although people lost the security of the old system, more jobs were created in both cities and countryside until about 1996. From then until 2002, the cities shed surplus labour faster than new jobs were created – many of the new jobs were informal and irregular, and there have been large numbers unemployed for long periods.[3] In the same period, opportunities improved in the rural areas, where enterprises continued to be set up and migration got under way once the economic, if not the legal, impediments had been removed.[4] Recently, rapid technological change has eliminated more urban manufacturing jobs, but services are recruiting more. Complementing the 'de-industrialisation' of the cities, the rural areas are creating more industrial jobs, such that they now account for more formal industrial jobs than the cities, calling into question the State policy of urbanisation. Agriculture remains the leading employer.

China is famous for its low labour costs. Although wages are notoriously difficult to compare, because of the complexity of accounting for purchasing power, hidden subsidies and misreporting, average compensation (i.e. wages plus remuneration in kind) in manufacturing is reckoned to amount to 3 per cent of the equivalent in the US and other developed countries; even more remarkable is that compensation in Mexico and Brazil is four times that of

China, and in the non-industrialised countries of Asia, main competitors for manufacture and assembly, it is ten times higher.[5]

The 30 million employees of manufacturing enterprises had average reported earnings of just over 11,000 RMB in 2004. Of these, those in electronics, pharmaceuticals and other high-skill sectors earned more (13,000 RMB), whereas those in textiles took less (7,000 RMB), as did those in food, paper and wood products (9,000 RMB). The benefit for laid-off State enterprise workers amounted to 2,213 RMB a year. In addition, at least in theory, employers contribute to funds for pensions, medical insurance, unemployment insurance, maternity leave and housing. Not surprisingly, tax avoidance and parallel book-keeping are rife.[6]

For those who have regular employment (there are no data for those in irregular employment), wages have been rising as technological development requires higher-order skills, but this brings with it a widening gap between skilled and unskilled. Zhang, a technician in a factory in Central China, earns 5,000 RMB a month, ten times the ordinary workers in the factory, and probably qualifies as 'middle class'. But in the Eastern cities to be middle class you need to earn 10,000 RMB as minimum; you are well established if you earn as much as 40,000 RMB. At present, there are thought to be about 50 million in those categories. It is predicted that 200 million will be added by 2011 and there will be over 400 million in 2016.[7] 'Middle class' means having stable income, being able to buy homes and cars, and paying for private school fees and holidays. To make the middle classes more accessible, the government is working to bring down the cost of housing and the major consumer goods that help define middle-classness.

And then there is the small minority of officials, managers and substantial entrepreneurs who can afford an item of luxury clothing – Louis Vuitton, Burberry, Gucci, Cartier all have shops in the major cities – that costs, say, twelve to fifteen times an average annual salary.[8] According to Goldman Sachs, Chinese will be buying 29 per cent of the world's luxury goods within ten years.[9]

The government has plans to narrow the gulf between rich and poor, concerned that the 'trickle down effect', anticipated when reform started to benefit the East and certain categories of people, is not happening. But perhaps it should be more concerned about the injustices perpetrated upon the poor which make it impossible for them to reach upwards. The example of the USA has shown that people are not necessarily jealous of and angry against the rich, as long as they believe that they have a chance to get there too.

CHAPTER 16

Tourism

Tourism's greatest benefit to China may be not so much that it creates jobs, but that it halts the destruction of the cultural heritage and keeps attention focused on the environment. Meanwhile, the world is only just waking up to the possibility that tens of millions of Chinese are potential tourists for them, and that, once those visitors have got over the first joy of merely 'going', they will need to be shown what there is to appreciate abroad.

Standing in the Colosseum one morning, thinking of Emperor Nero, it was quite a surprise to find myself surrounded by bejewelled Chinese girls in mourning clothes, accompanied by gallants in what Europeans normally associate with dinner dances, i.e. black bow ties and shiny lapels. As soon as I started finding out who they were, I was incorporated into the photographs of the fourteen wedding couples from Zhejiang, who were celebrating nuptials in the Eternal City. What the brides were wearing were European wedding dresses, which happen to be of the Chinese mourning colour, white. Traditionally, Chinese brides wear red.

In 1978, there were no Chinese tourists abroad; now there are over 30 million and the World Tourism Organization expects that to go up to 100 million by 2020. They deposit collateral with their government against their return and they may travel only to approved destinations, of which the UK became one in 2005, and in groups organised by approved agencies. Unlike Chinese students abroad, who, if they wish, can get to know European cultures and people, these groups usually consist of those who speak only Chinese languages, and who zoom from such sites of minor significance as Tower Bridge, Mannekin Pis or the Tour Eiffel taking snaps and girding up for the next (Chinese) meal or shopping spree at Hermès or Burberry. In 2005, a London guidebook was for the first time available in Chinese, and in 2006, Lonely Planet announced they would shortly be translating their library into Chinese.[1]

'Doing Europe' might, at its most extensive, involve a day or two in Rome, Paris, Madrid, London, Berlin and Prague. Merely making such a list reminds us that, despite the terrible wars that devastated Europe in the 20th century, we have much more of our heritage left than does China. The equivalent 'doing China', despite all its differences of **regions and languages**, would include Peking (Beijing), Shanghai, Canton, Xian and Hangzhou. What other cities have more than one or two obscure relics to remind us that they were once more than American suburbs? Adding on Lhasa and Kaşgar would be rather like tacking on Kiev and the western shore of Istanbul to your European itinerary – OK, they are related, but hardly mainstream to western Europe.

Although China is becoming rich enough to preserve its heritage, so much wilful destruction was carried out in the first 50 years of CCP rule as to make most irrecoverable.[2] Just as bad, a contemptuous mentality developed among those with power such that the destruction continues, propelled now not by socialist loathing of the past, but by developers' greed and planners' ignorance. The capital was inherited intact in 1949 as the world's greatest medieval walled city, whereupon the new government smashed away at its centre to build a parade ground and tore down – with great difficulty – its walls. Many of its 14th-century streets and houses remained in 1980, but are subsequently being flattened to make way for buildings which are rarely impressive. The conservation battles now being fought by non-governmental organisations (NGOs; see **Civil Society**) are too late, the forces committed against them too strong and too unprincipled.

So what is there to see in China? A glance at the Great Wall is an exhilarating moment, particularly if you can hike along its lesser-known tracts; the scale of the Forbidden City, the natural beauty of

Guilin, the tomb guards of the First Emperor and the stone Buddhas of Longmen ... these are some of the delights available to the foreign tourist, even if the barriers of language and knowledge cut her off from most of Chinese culture. Enough great monuments have survived to please the brief visitor; it is only those who know what is missing that feel dissatisfied. Thanks to tourism, city councils, such as those of Xian and Qufu, are suddenly trying to save what they can and even to oblige builders to respect cultural norms near the great sites. There are fabulous museums, individual monuments, scenery and even the spectacular tempo of modern Chinese cities such as Wuhan and Shanghai to experience. Some smaller places, too poor to destroy their heritage, such as Pingyao (Shanxi), Yixian (Anhui) or Zhouzhuang (Zhejiang) provide amazing cameos of how Chinese life was lived everywhere just 50 years ago. Purpose-built tourism facilities, providing spectacle and story, are emerging fast, and combine with eco-tourism and ethnic minority tourism to make up for the paucity of original Chinese townscapes.

In Shenzhen I went to an Ethnic Minority Experience Garden, where we boated down a tropical river past the huts of the 'local' fisherfolk; lunched in the bamboo house of another minority, joined in Turkic dancing, clapped a display of Mongolian horsemanship, took tea in a Tibetan house ... well, it could have gone on for ever, since there are 56 'minorities'. Up and down China now are these kinds of theme parks, often with complete reproductions of the Potala Palace or the Great Wall (part). *Son et lumière* on Chinese history is available at the Tang Village – an enormous and luxurious compound – followed by, for those who want it, a rock concert.

In 1978, there were no tourist arrivals; in 2004, there were 41 million.[3] Of these, 64 per cent are Asians, with Japanese and Koreans making up well over half. Twenty-three per cent come from Europe, of which over half are Russian and 11 per cent from the UK. Only 9 per cent of all tourism comes from the USA. The market is worth 7 per cent of China's GDP and is rising. The World Tourism Organization forecasts that China will be the leading tourism destination by 2020, receiving 167 million visitors.[4]

Not surprisingly, the government is stimulating investment in speciality tourism too – health tourism (acupuncture, massage, *qigong*, operations), sports tourism (especially climbing and martial arts), agro-tourism, cuisine tourism, folklore, ecological and art tourism; tourism by train, boat or bicycle. Hotels and other visitor facilities are increasingly expected to respect local norms and traditions in style. The capital's University of Tourism, one among 845 specialist tourism schools (many others have courses in tourism), seeks to adapt the best modern practice.[5] With foreign travel still too expensive for most Chinese, domestic tourism dwarfs international, with 930 million home tourists in 2004. This has been government-inspired: with more tourism, domestic consumption increases, and three week-long public holidays – at Spring Festival, May Day and National Day – have been introduced to get people to spend more.

Business opportunities abound. Although over half of tourist hotels are State operations, many foreign hotel groups of luxury, mid-market and budget types operate via franchise, joint venture, management contract and other arrangements. Big Chinese hotel groups are in the making, but from December 2005, it became possible for foreigners to own 100 per cent of hotels and restaurants.[6]

The only really bad meal I have ever had in China was when entertaining another Englishman in one of the capital's grandest hotels. To add humiliation to disgust, it cost about ten times the price of a really good dinner in a local dive. Perhaps it was a mistake to eat Chinese food in somewhere with a French manager, no matter how charming. But at least it made me see what most foreign tourists probably experience – they never know just how good Chinese eating can be. This will change. As Chinese culture enters the mainstream, rather than being buttoned up into Chinatowns, tourists' expectations rise. And meanwhile, mindful that Chinese tourists to their countries can provide growing economic benefits,

Europeans have to show that they have more to offer than whistle-stop shopping tours, and to educate this vast number of potential customers as to what they can experience abroad.

PART THREE

Culture

CHAPTER 17

History

There are two things to know about Chinese history. First, that the Chinese is the longest-lasting civilisation; and second, that this matters.

'Empires wax and wane; states cleave asunder and coalesce.' Thus begins the first English translation of China's greatest historical novel, the *Tale of Three Kingdoms*,[1] set in 220–280 AD. Then, China was divided, a situation deplored by historians as problematic and unnatural. For one of the great ideals of Chinese civilisation has been unity: of government, of culture, of family, of thought. And it is believed that the greatest achievements and advances have been made during periods of stability and unity.

Tradition holds that the first dynasty was founded in 2100 BC. From 770–221 BC, the area of today's Central China was divided into several kingdoms before being unified in 221 BC, shortly before Hannibal crossed the Alps in his wars with imperial Rome. The 'First Emperor', as the unifier styled himself, standardised the written language, currency, measurements and roads. He also, like Mao in recent times, attempted to destroy thought. He is mostly associated in the West with his Terracotta Army, the thousands of life-size figures that fill one of the underground guard chambers to the network of edifices which comprise his, as yet unexcavated, tomb. The figures themselves and their placing demonstrate advanced skills of artistry and organisation.

The First Emperor's administrative legacy was to form the basis of the Chinese State until 1911. By his time, the core beliefs that were to dominate the future had already been developed by Confucius (551–479 BC, a contemporary of Pericles) and his successors. Today again, as in pre-communist times, Confucius' birthplace in Qufu is a place of pilgrimage, and people (say that they) refer to his *Analects* for inspiration. For Confucianism, the longest-lasting of all political philosophies, the ruler was the link between heaven and earth, whose moral duty it was to promote the harmony and prosperity of the world and to set an example of good behaviour and reciprocity between generations and people of different social conditions. He must strive for unity and shared culture, as must the official in his region or the family head. Good government depends upon consent, not force. Confucianism emphasises the value of education in developing moral values, in self-improvement and in advancing people on merit. Officials were appointed after competitive examination, a system emulated by imperial Britain some 2,000 years after its adoption in China.

Until the 19th century, educated Europeans were greatly in awe of China, whose empire was stupendously rich and magnificent, whose products were of great sophistication and whose rule was believed to be more benign and well regulated than those of the warring Europeans. Once the West had superseded China in technological competence and military efficacy, the respect evaporated and practical people looked upon China with pity, scholars with regret. Regret because they saw in decline the extraordinary creativity of this, the longest-lasting human civilisation, from which Europe had copied many scientific and technical achievements.

By tradition, Chinese believed in a cyclical theory of history, with a tendency for each cycle to be rather less acceptable than the last, the assumption being that the further we get from the legendary past, the more difficult it is to emulate its successes. The only factual basis for this idea is that a dynasty was usually founded by a tough, often low-class, outsider. He would be succeeded by competents for a few generations until inevitable feuds, among the extended families of the emperor and his women, and courtiers, dissipated administrative attention and the lazy life of the palace brought into office debauched or weak emperors. By this time, administration would have broken down and, with the 'Mandate of

Heaven' lost, peasant rebellion or nomad invasion would destroy the dynasty, which would be replaced.

The main dynasties can be characterised by their great achievements. The First Emperor was followed by the Han Dynasty (206 BC–189 AD) which expanded China, traded with Rome and established the foundations for literature and the arts. After a period of disunion, the Sui and Tang Dynasties (581–907) brought about the 'Golden Age' in which China for a period ruled Tibet and Turkestan, reformed internal government and made possible a great flourishing of sciences and technology. The world's oldest Academy of Letters was founded by Emperor Xuancong (712–756 AD). China's greatest poets lived under the Tang, and Buddhism and Taoism took root.

After a further period of division, the Song Dynasty (960–1279), celebrated for its porcelain as well as for moveable printer's type, the compass and other inventions, incorporated what is now South China. The following Mongol or Yuan Dynasty (1279–1368) tolerated all religions and encouraged external trade. Drama and novels in vernacular Chinese flourished in this period, shortly before their development in England.

The Ming (1368–1644) consolidated the achievement of its predecessors and is often thought of as the greatest of the dynasties; China was indubitably the most successful world power in this period, during which the voyages of exploration by Zheng He were launched. In 1644, the Manchus, a border tribe, overthrew the Ming and replaced it with the Qing. Unlike the Mongols, who had resisted assimilation, the Qing emperors were enthusiastic admirers and proponents of Chinese culture; their influence extended well into South East Asia, Central Asia and Korea. Three of China's most scholarly and able emperors were of the 18th-century Qing. By the 19th century, not only was the administration weakened in the time-honoured way, but a new force was on the scene, a Europe determined to trade and competing to dominate the world; and hand-in-hand with its military and political leaders were missionary traders and enterprising missionaries. The Taiping, a huge peasant rebellion influenced by Christian ideas, broke out in 1851 and was not put down until 1864.

The British forced China to cede the territory of Hong Kong in 1842 and other countries soon made similar demands which the Chinese military, outclassed and corrupt, could not resist. There followed a humiliating period, in which European and Japanese troops could invade China at will to punish infractions of agreements they had imposed, and before long they managed much of China's political and financial affairs.

The Qing Dynasty was overthrown in 1911 and replaced by the Republic. In the 1920s, its energies were greatly taken up with attempting to gain control of the country, whose regional rulers jockeyed for power, then in resisting Japanese invaders (1937–45) as well as fighting a crippling war against communist subversion. In the Second World War, China was the sworn ally of the US and UK against the Axis powers, and its status in the West went up immeasurably as China was seen doggedly to resist the Japanese onslaught. Under Chiang Kai-shek's Nationalist government, the Republic managed to get extraterritoriality – by which foreigners lived in enclaves subject to their own laws – abolished in January 1943.

The Republic lost the Civil War in 1949, though it still exists on the island of Taiwan, to which the remnants of its army and government fled while the CCP consolidated its hold, declaring a new State, the People's Republic of China (PRC), on 1 October 1949. 'China Shakes the World' was, according to the title of a famous book,[2] the outcome. The Cold War, the US policy of containment of communism and its involvement in the Korean and Vietnam wars can all be seen as deriving from that moment, although it might be more true to say that the world shook China, since its options were limited by the international suspicion surrounding it. Meanwhile, in 1950 the Red Army took over East Turkestan, restoring its Chinese name of Xinjiang, and asserted authority over Tibet. In doing so, they were carrying out their declared mission of consolidating the Qing Dynasty borders. In 1997, the British returned Hong Kong, and Portugal gave back Macau in 1999. The vicissitudes of life in the first 50 years of the PRC are described elsewhere.

Until foreigners challenged, defeated and humiliated their country, most Chinese believed that China was the only civilisation. Today it is common to find that people consider China surrounded by enemies, selectively interpreting the history of the past 200 years in order to present their country as unique, not so much as civilisation, but as victim. Observers argue that this is a very important component of modern Chinese identity, of **nationalism**, and a political factor of great power.

For history is taken seriously. According to the sinologist who wrote a book on this theme, 'history plays a role comparable to that of religious texts in other cultures ... the religion of the Chinese ruling classes is the Chinese state, and it is through history that the object of devotion is to be understood.'[3] Not only are the ruling classes affected: in the gardens of a temple in Hangzhou there are some statues of 'bad' ministers of the 12th century.[4] A modern sign admonishes: 'It is forbidden to spit or throw refuse at these statues.'

CHAPTER 18

Arts and Literature

The impression you get in China today is of a headlong rush to build, to create businesses, to make money. Do modern Chinese have time for art any more, except as something to import as a sign of sophistication, or else as something to sell to foreigners?

In the courtyard of an old house in Xian we met some students making and selling *xun*. These look rather like small oval melons, except that they are glazed earthenware and have two little holes at one end. When we had sat down and accepted to sip cups of green tea, one of the students taught me to blow through the holes to make music, for the *xun* is a kind of flute.

Everywhere in China you come across pockets of the diverse and immensely rich culture – of music, the plastic arts, calligraphy, theatre, shadow puppetry, story-telling or whatever – that the foreign travellers used to dilate upon in wonder when they visited in the early years of the 20th century. But today there are, it seems, but pockets.

The young students with their *xun* prove that culture is not just for the old, but to be honest, their contemporaries are more likely to be in a club sweating into their thongs to the sound of the electronic production of some dance music company in Los Angeles. The Cultural Revolution ripped traditional culture out of the lives of several generations; the government has been too preoccupied to shore it up, and commercial interests have provided globalised substitutes for mass consumption. In clothing, music and appreciation of the arts, things Chinese are for the elite.

Between 1949 and 1979, the arts were expected to serve the Party. Nationalised, the colleges, galleries and foundations were organised into a Soviet-style system rendering all practitioners

State employees in hierarchies of seniority and remuneration. At the pinnacle was the national centre, in the case of the plastic arts, the Central Academy of Fine Art, where I met Han Xin in 1982 as he finished his oil portrait of an Irish girl. Until that time, like all artists, he had practised socialist realism, with the limited range of themes allowed. His illustrations for patriotic children's books were particularly talented and he gained some important commissions, such as a famous portrait of Chairman Mao with his successor, Hua, and murals for the capital's airport. No sooner was he able than he left for the USA, where his painting portfolio to date was irrelevant until he had entered the Western system, won prizes and obtained scholarships to Giverny and New York. He has evolved a style which blends both Chinese techniques and Western themes. He is particularly successful in the USA, but his is a story typical of many of his generation of artists, who have sought to combine Chinese and Western traditions.

Back at home, the art of the 1980s was scarred by the experiences of the preceding years of turmoil and suffering; 'scar literature' and 'scar art' evoked and sentimentalised them. Then the Stars Group (see Glossary) began experimenting with new forms and themes, inspired by all the Western artists of whose experience they had been denied. After 1992, not only did this flower into a plethora of approaches, tagged as Pop Art, Cynical Realism, Contemporary Avant Garde and shock art, but multimedia, performance and installation art arrived too. The Chinese art market has become big business, with specialist galleries and exhibitions throughout the world. Much of the art plays with traditional Chinese motifs, interpreting or applying them in new ways, often intertwined with images from commercial art. Today, genuine traditional Chinese painting is again studied to a high standard in the art colleges, but few people have the scholarship to appreciate it.

Literature had a glorious period under the Republic, when its writers drew upon both the Chinese and European fiction traditions, especially Russian. Among them, Shen Congwen, with his sensitive and illuminating stories of ordinary people, has often been compared to Turgenev. In the 1950s, Zhang Ailing (Eileen Chang) exposed the misery imposed by socialism in a spare style demonstrating a profound empathy with others and a revulsion against the moral and material cruelties. Although popular outside the PRC, she was not published there until the 1990s. Instead, socialist realism – or socialist illusionism – dominated such publishing as there was, tales of iron heroes battling for the motherland.

The reaction in the 1980s was to recall the past with bitterness (scar literature) and to enjoy the sentiments that had been occluded for so long. Wang Shuo's *Yearnings*, a melodramatic tale of love recovered after the political blight, was adapted into a 50-part TV soap opera in 1989. But soon the tone of Chinese writing had changed to one of disillusionment, even nihilism. Wang Shuo depicted the ludicrous situations people got into as they attempted to succeed in the new market society or even the black market, living as 'hooligans'.

China is today the world's major publisher of books and virtually every genre is being attempted. 'Net fiction' (example: *My First Intimacy*) is concerned with encounters through, and conversations on, the internet; 'Prettywomen' literature describes the supposed experiences of predatory females experimenting with drugs and unconventional relationships (*Candy*); girly novels purport to be by teenagers and describe (usually unrequited) passions in lengthy dialogue, often including adolescent slang (*Whoever's Cool You Fall for Him*). There is fiction as moral commentary, often later turned into television serials or films, as with the powerful *Divorce, Chinese Style* (2004), described in **Family Life**, or *Qiaoqi Don't Weep* (2005), about a graduate far from home who, spurned by her boyfriend and unemployed, sinks into the murky world of the bar-girls. The historical account – describing recent history and family history, in an attempt to understand the present – has gone through several phases. Perhaps the most famous is Wan Anyi's *Song of Unending Bitterness* (1996), the life of the winner of a

1940s beauty competition. A recent such novel to attract attention is *Cottonhead* (2006) by Tie Ning, previously known for erotic women's fiction, which tells of the Xiang family's survival in a small town over 50 years, and of the efforts of individuals to retain moral integrity. *Wolf Totem* (2005) deals with man's relationships with nature and is set in the Mongolian grasslands.

The most popular adult fiction genres are detective-romance or martial arts (tales of derring-do set in the past), but they are all outsold by writers of children's fiction and teenager romances. Although the prevalence of business manuals, personal development guides and parenting handbooks in bookshops might suggest that they are the top sellers, the most commercially successful writer in China is Guo Jingming, who writes teenager tearjerkers.[1]

In traditional Chinese high culture, fiction had a lowly position. What mattered were poetry, calligraphy, painting, history and philosophy. Chinese civilisation has the biggest repository of writing of any. Today historical novels and spin-off TV programmes and films are still popular, and all schoolchildren learn some poetry, but even calligraphy is given little attention in many schools. Soap operas set in Chinese history and the immensely popular martial arts novels are possibly the principal means by which historical culture is passed on through the generations.

In 2006, the Three Emperors Exhibition in London recalled a time when the empire was both the world leader and cosmopolitan, but relatively few people enjoy such treats. It is probably through the successes of modern Chinese cinema that the rest of the world knows of Chinese art. Paintings, porcelains, jade carvings, architecture, costumes and music have all come to us in the succession of films with historical settings which have been celebrated internationally. The first Chinese long feature was released in 1921. A sophisticated film industry developed until the early 1950s, when politics began to exert a malign effect. From the 1960s, the Hong Kong and Taiwan film industries dominated Greater China. Within the PRC, the first generation of film-makers (cultural reformists, before 1949) were succeeded by the second generation (socialist realists), the third and fourth generations celebrating the State's myths of China, and the fifth generation which has been identified, more abroad even than at home, with getting to grips with issues in Chinese society and using panoramas of Chinese history and traditional life, rendered through artistic and technical mastery, to do so. Chen Kaige's *Yellow Earth* (1984) pictured peasant life and projected a vision of the interdependence of nature and man; Zhang Yimou's *Red Sorghum* (1987) dealt with passion in the context of rural life and social pressures; Chen's *Farewell my Concubine*, telling the story of two opera singers, posed the question of how people have survived the upheavals through which China went in the 20th century.[2] The sixth generation has had different preoccupations, often urban 'realism' and disillusion. Representative are Zhang Yun's *Beijing Bastards* (1993), telling the story of a rock band kicked out of its squat, and Wang Xiaoshuai's *The Drifters* (2003), about an illegal immigrant to the US who finds it difficult to fit in when he gets home. Other recent films have dealt with a poor migrant boy's longing for a bicycle; a city family's desperation to return to Shanghai after their daughter is courted by a peasant; the affection an old man and his son have for a doomed public bathhouse while around them the capital changes; and the rough life of coal miners in the North East. Zhang Yimou's 2005 film, *Hero*, takes a very different turn. Set in the Warring States period (475–221 BC), it rejoices in glorious martial arts and is thought to convey a message of nationalist assertion.

The principal popular art forms are opera and folk music. It is not clear what is happening to them, although it is thought that the Cultural Revolution had a devastating effect, cutting off several generations from the many different regional variations of both, and that this estrangement is being increased through the penetration of commercial pop music. The leading opera companies receive some subsidies, as do schools of acting and music, both Western and Chinese classical, in each province. Many manifestations of traditional music are small-scale, such as the meetings of aficionados in the gardens and tea-houses of Hangzhou or in small suburban theatres in Shanghai.

Peking Opera is surviving as a 'national treasure', brought out for international acclaim. But there is genuine local affection for it, with clubs devoted to its perpetuation, fan clubs and television productions. Music-hall comedians in the *xiangshen* (cross talk) style are very popular, as are *Errenzhuan* shows, smutty and very lively double acts from Shandong. For these you usually take dinner as you watch.

In the last 75 years, Chinese culture has gone from traditional society, in which the arts were central to life, to the narrow buffoonery of socialist realism, to the parched combat-zone of the Cultural Revolution. Will anything distinct, reflecting and reinforcing China's particular takes on the world, survive globalisation and mass consumption? Probably not without conscious effort; but Chinese sense of identity is sufficiently vital that that effort may yet be made.

CHAPTER 19

Culture of Food

Mao tried to destroy almost every aspect of Chinese culture bar food; but now the transnationals are getting going on that.

I never leave one grain of rice in my bowl. When first I stayed in a Chinese family, it was made clear to the teenager that frugality is a virtue and that each grain of rice is respected as the result of someone's labour. In Europe, I had been dimly aware of the beliefs that revolve around the table – that adults consider the balance of a meal's ingredients and that the way in which a meal is consumed is as important as what is eaten – but these were more explicit in China, perhaps only because, for me, they were slightly different.

By tradition, there are five main premises underlying eating. One is that food is to be approached with a certain reverence; the consumption of food is an opportunity, perhaps the most important opportunity, for sharing and enjoying the company of others, first of all your own family, whose harmony and affection will be improved by eating together, but thereafter friends and work associates. Meals themselves are the product of reflection about what is healthy and appropriate and of the application of wisdom about balance; cuisine is an art, and knowledge of food and its preparation something to which everyone aspires; the regulation of diet is medicinal.

Balance is maintained by regulating the proportions of *fan* (staple) and *cai* (meat and vegetable) in a meal, as well as, where money permits, by balancing the variety of *cai*. The *fan* cooker and the *cai* cooker ('wok') are not interchangeable.[1] Staples in the South means mainly rice, while Northerners eat wheat and millet in forms as varied as many different types of noodles, bread and pancakes. *Cai* comprises a multitude of dishes, which can be as simple as cabbage topped with a little oyster oil or as complex as braised trotter with vegetables, slithers of chicken in fish sauce or fish steamed in chilli peppers. A simple family meal today will probably include two vegetable and two meat or fish dishes plus staple, washed down with tea and finished with fruit. Since fresh ingredients are essential, little is prepared in advance; someone has to shop every day, hence the great number of markets. Visitors to Fudan and other university campuses are sometimes surprised to see that they contain markets to which small producers bring live fowl, fresh vegetables, fruit and living seafoods. In winter, there will be preserved foods – steeped, salted, smoked and pickled everything. Because of lactose intolerance, there are few dairy products south of Mongolia, but beancurd and soya milk are protein-rich equivalents. Each of the main festivals has its special dish, from Mooncakes at Mid-Autumn to Sweet Dumplings at the Lantern, buns of rice and nuts wrapped in leaves for the Dragon Boat, and porridge with dried fruit and nuts at the Winter Festival.

Consumers are demanding, so that restaurants and foodstalls come and go quickly if they cannot keep up standards. They are sophisticated in their understanding of regional and local cooking. Virtually every village has its special dish or dishes, situated within one of the twelve or so principal schools of regional cuisine, of which the most famous are Shanghai (much seafood), Sichuan (chilli hot), Muslim (stews, hotpots and much mutton), Canton (delicacy and unending variety) and Peking (roasts, breads and dumplings).

Knowledge about the cuisines and the ability to discriminate, to order well or to control the preparation of different dishes has long comprised a set of skills required of the educated and been celebrated in literature and painting. As ordinary Chinese grow up, they imbibe knowledge about food from the older generations, and are mature when, among other things, they can share the food talk that crosses boundaries of class and gender and age.

An illustration of the culture of food adapted to modern life is the food courts, which pit suppliers against each other to attract customers wandering from a Hunan to a Hong Kong to a Shanxi to a

Chaozhou specialist, questioning each on their preparations, after the best and tastiest meal deal. Several university student canteens have food courts.

But if the anthropologists are right, the culture of food, arguably the one area of Chinese culture not wrecked since 1949, is being undermined. Since the 1980s, 'business enterprises ... have employed aggressive marketing strategies in the hope of inculcating in young people as early as possible [new] eating habits that will last for a lifetime'.[2] This, where the families of urban children are much better off than a generation ago, has had a number of results. Children press their parents to allow them to go to 'American' fast food outlets and to let them buy new products such as sweets, biscuits, chocolate, soft drinks and ice cream, unknown to the traditional diet. Children have pocket money and indulge newly-created tastes,[3] reinforced by peer pressure, also manipulated by advertising.

Until recently, children ate as adults, though, as in Mediterranean countries, they would often be given the best and most healthy parts. 'Children's food' appeared as a special category only in the 1980s. The traditional balanced diet is giving way to high cholesterol intake. There is now a problem of obesity among urban children, something inconceivable before marketisation.[4]

There may be other social effects. 'The process by which children learn about food has been taken over' by commercialisation, i.e. cultural transmission from the older generation is being replaced by self-interested seduction by some shareholders on the other side of the world. Images of the way food is consumed conflict with the idea that food is shared in fellowship.[5] Consumption comes to be about fashion, not nutrition or shared family experience.

Why do children like to go to McDonald's, KFC and Pizza Hut? It is argued that they feel empowered, that whereas at home the family decides for them, at the fast food outlets they are liberated from parental choices and grandparents' exhortations to eat 'properly'.[6] If so, this is another 'cultural interference', but I suspect that fast food outlets are attractive less out of a sense of rebellion but rather, in a society which is unlike the Anglosphere in that good-quality, inexpensive food is readily available outside the home, on account of the exotic ambience. They are regarded as 'different', 'scientific' and 'modern' and, thanks to advertising, associated with things 'advanced'.[7]

One student talked to me after a bruising battle with his little brother, whom he had refused to take to McDonald's. 'Fast food', he said, 'is eaten in a different way. It is not just that the taste and appearance are unpleasant when you have been brought up on fresh food and a balanced diet, but that the approach to life which its consumption implies is objectionable. The speed suggests both plenty and the insignificance of eating, as if it were just about filling the stomach. The serving in disposable containers is anti-environment and irresponsible, as well as opposed to our traditions of frugality. There is no thought of health in the menus of the fast food outlets and the rudimentary nature of the preparation diminishes the efforts put into wholesome family food by parents and grandparents.' He paused before declaring: 'It is a big assault on our country, much more dangerous than what the imperialists tried in the last century.'

I once saw a proposal for an advertising campaign for the Middle East and North Africa, which was to denigrate traditional coffee-drinkers as elderly, disabled clots in order to compare them with zestful, sexy and modern drinkers of instant coffee. It seems as if the transnationals are today engaged in something similar in China – the undermining of arguably the greatest and most imaginative food culture on earth.

CHAPTER 20

Religion

China may be experiencing a religious revival, despite half a century of crusades for secularism. And Confucius is rediscovered as perhaps China's greatest gift to a world in which religion has caused as much suffering as solace.

At the Lama Temple, many little children are learning how to pray, instructed usually by grandparents. As they bob up and down, others come and kneel, teenagers and twenty-somethings mainly. The official with me, fresh from a Masters at the London School of Economics, is shocked. Is it really possible that China is experiencing a religious revival?

Several religions and many sects and cults have long co-existed. Until the CCP, and since 202 BC, the official, ruling-class faith or 'way' was Confucianism, the ethical and social teachings of Confucius and his interpreter Mencius (371–289 BC), which spun off rituals that involved commemorating one's forebears rather than worshipping extraterrestrial gods.

An alternative 'way' is Taoism, advancing the virtue of passivity, rejection of worldly ambition and the escape to nature. It developed in the 6th century BC. Buddhism, with its emphases on meditation, following the example of the Buddha and overcoming personal desires, entered China at the start of the Christian era and became widespread in the 3rd century AD. Islam came to Canton through Arab traders, but today is most established in the westernmost provinces, since the Islamicisation of Central Asia. Christianity first arrived in China in the 17th century, but did not gain any popular following until the missionaries of the 19th.

Up to 1949, Confucianism underpinned Chinese social life. As well as the shrines of particular families, every community and hamlet had networks of voluntary bodies, schools and welfare institutions inspired by the Confucian ethic of social responsibility. Complementing the Confucian emphasis on 'works' – being good by being practical – the other 'ways' spawned a variety of different, often local, modes of worship. Temples were shared by several gods; a general of yore, a Buddha, Jesus Christ and great scholars might have been featured. The resident priest would organise collective worship, give moral teaching and provide divination services. All cities boasted large foundations and temples, and there are at least ten nationally famous holy mountains, which traditionally had large Buddhist or Taoist monastery complexes associated.

The main Muslim communities were more or less autonomous, guarded by their own warlords, even if nominally allegiant to the State. The Christian sects established many colleges, schools and missions, some 4 million adherents and a few influential and wealthy Chinese who combined Christianity with their traditional beliefs. After 1949, the CCP, adopting the Soviet hostility to religion, attacked it with constant abuse, and by confiscating assets, persecuting adherents and destroying places of worship.

What survived has been carefully controlled. It can be argued that the government has good reasons for this. From time to time religion has inspired mass movements; several civil wars in Chinese history have been based on Buddhist or Taoist cults, and the most recent was the Taiping, a form of Christianity whose armies dominated half of 19th-century China for three decades. The Tibetans, in their struggle for recognition, are as moved by their faith as the Poles of the 1980s were by theirs; the Christian churches are associated with subversion by hostile foreign powers, and now there is the spectre of Muslim terrorism to add to government worries.

Nevertheless, the government is proud of the greater freedom afforded to religion since the 1980s, and points to Article 36 of the Constitution, which stipulates: 'Citizens of the People's Republic of China enjoy freedom of religious belief.'[1] Over 10,000 Buddhist temples and monasteries have been rebuilt and there has been a proliferation of Christian sects. Until recently it was thought that the gradual relaxation of controls would continue, at least for the mainstream faiths if not for Falungong (see below). However, critics claim that the government has become more oppressive recently. As testimony before the US Congress' House Committee on International Relations put it:

> China's government, through a series of Party policies and government regulations, including the March 1, 2005 'Regulations on Religious Affairs', sharply curtails both freedom of religious belief and the freedom to express one's belief. Religious activities that are banned include publishing and distributing texts, selecting leaders, raising funds and managing finances, organizing training, inviting guests, independently scheduling meetings and choosing venues, and communicating freely with other organizations. In China today, all such activities are subject to regulatory state interference and even imprisonment and severe mistreatment of offending believers and practitioners.[2]

On 25 April 1999, the government began to persecute a then little-known 'way' called Falungong, when 10,000 of its followers assembled in the capital to protest against a dismissive press article. This movement of practitioners of exercises traditionally associated with Taoism and of believers in a mixture of ideas both Christian and Buddhist, had until then been tolerated to the extent that many people in responsible positions had been happy to be associated with it, even though its leader was based in the USA. It was the demonstration that Falungong could mobilise so many people, without the security services being aware of its operations, that shocked the government into repression. A very high proportion of the practitioners were women and older people, and at first the authorities behaved reasonably. Intransigence riled the authorities and treatment became brutal. Many Falungong adherents appear to have died in custody.[3]

It is possible that the renewal of religion is a phenomenon of the poor, the marginalised and the unemployed, those who are not benefiting from the economic revival. The CCP leadership finds the very idea of religion incomprehensible: President Jiang Zemin expressed his incredulity to US President Clinton that in 'modern civilisation' people could have a religion such as Tibetan Buddhism.[4] Yet there are now thought to be about 250 million practising Taoists, 100 million Buddhists and around 30 million Christians.[5] There may be more Christians than dare admit to being so; there is thought to be a large number of evangelical sects such as the True Jesus Church, Little Flock, Spread the Gospel, Principal God Cult and Jesus Family, of which an important appeal is the egalitarianism. The opinion-forming classes may be rediscovering Confucianism, with its strict hierarchies. Family shrines, in which the tablets of many generations of ancestors are venerated, are reappearing. There is constant reference in conversation and the media to Confucian terms such as filial piety and moral behaviour; intellectuals revisit their Confucian heritage and policy-makers refer to it approvingly.

As a faith, Confucianism has the incomparable advantage, in a society in which empiricism is almost a religion, of not requiring its adherents to believe in metaphysical and miraculous things, whether the ascent to heaven of the Prophet, virgin birth or reincarnation. The Master thought that, as we know so little about our fellow men, it is a waste of effort to speculate about gods. Confucius acknowledges the possibility of an outside agency, God or heaven, but relegates it to the unknowable and requires of us that we worship him by respecting his works – the environment, society, the cultural evidence of our climb out of barbarism and the attempt to create civilised life. Most of all, Confucianism is an ethical system that creates a sense of obligation to others. At its worst, it upholds stagnated and unfair power relations; at its best, it emphasises justice, humanity and the benefits to society as a whole of our behaving morally and dutifully in whatever small sphere we inhabit, particularly in the family, which it holds to be the fount of all sense of purpose and the prototype of all human relations. Confucianism is tolerant of other faiths, with which it can co-exist, accepting the variety of peoples' needs for meaning and for life beyond the present.

CHAPTER 21

Family Life

Although generalisation is risky and the data is conflicting, it seems that the Revolution took a terrible toll of the core institution of Chinese society, of civil society and of social institutions – the family. And now there are new pressures on traditional ideas of family life.

When an English friend married a Shanghai girl, he was besotted by her looks, stylish clothes, cosmopolitanism and familiarity with all that is high-tech and most modern. The first intimation that marriage to Yingzi was more than just romance came at the wedding itself, when several hundred relatives promised to visit his rather stiff parents upon their return to Gloucestershire; the second was when he realised that her parents and brother had moved in to his home.

By tradition, marriage is very much more than a romantic coupling. It is a family event which brings two groups together to share networks and resources, to bring about the continuation of the spirit of the older generation, which gives purpose to life. Foreign anthropologists have accordingly investigated that family as if it were an economic enterprise, or a political institution or a manifestation of curious cultural traits.[1] However, though all three of these aspects of family life have been mercilessly attacked since 1949, although choices for the individual are greater, and despite excited reports in the Western media about nymphomaniac female novelists who eschew family life and are pioneering liberation, most women in China marry and the divorce rate is low.[2]

The ideal family, with several generations living harmoniously in a succession of interconnecting courtyard homes, of rich and poor, young and old, acting in harmony for the common good, may always have been merely an ideal, but it continues to influence.

And, curiously, although city people are less likely to live in homes physically organised for multiple-couple use, since life expectancy is greater and there is increasingly an abundance of small apartments, families try to arrange to live in the same block or close enough to eat together, as in the traditional ideal.

In fact, my friend did lose his in-laws after a few months, but only to the floor below, since he and Yingzi helped them buy the next flat to become available in the block, allowing his parents-in-law to supervise the cleaner, prepare the meals and ensure a friendly welcome upon their return from work.

This seems like a happy modern adaptation of traditional values, and because of greater longevity there may be more three-generation households than ever before, but it would be wrong to imply that circumstances have not changed. Socialism undermined the family, in order to break the loyalty of the individual to any but the State. The functions previously performed by the family were those of other civic institutions in Europe: education, religious instruction, welfare, recreation and economic activity were all managed by the family until the CCP destroyed those institutions. The 1950 marriage law empowered the young in their selection of mate, and simplified divorce. There were political campaigns against the power of family heads, familism generally and the traditional festivals, folk customs and ceremonies. According to administrative whim, families were broken up, solidarity undermined and the sense of mutual obligation and social responsibility, powerful in traditional Confucian society, dissipated; collectivisation broke the link between family and property; desperate straits in the countryside have increased mobility and made keeping in touch with family hard for millions; the One Child Policy means that fewer children have siblings or even aunts and uncles; couples expect more privacy than the traditional collective living arrangements allow.[3] Thus it is not surprising that the traditional family is under strain. Certainly commentators think so, enthusiastically announcing that 50 per cent of professional women are single and view marriage with indifference,[4] that fewer people return home for New Year, that nuclear families are the modern couples' preference, that the influence of parents has dwindled, that divorce is on the increase.

In the cult novel *Divorce, Chinese Style*, and the telefilm that magnified its reach, the hard-done-by protagonist finally contemplates divorce only after his wife has harried him into opting for a much more stressful job, berated him for being exhausted, humiliated him in front of colleagues, alienated him by her unending complaints and encouraged her young brother to beat him up for alleged infidelities. Never once does the husband question his duties towards her or her parents, who, as do most Chinese grandparents, spend as much time (at least) looking after his son as do the parents.

When that boy gets to marriageable age, his grandparents will probably investigate the various matrimonial agencies that are taking the place of matchmakers, and accompany him to his appointments there; they may patrol the public parks looking for similar grandparents holding photographs and resumés of eligible daughters; they may make inquiries through their former colleagues and kin. They will usually be his closest friends after his own parents, and may in effect be substitute parents in the case of many professional families, in which both parents are absent far away studying and working for long periods, when they often leave the child to be brought up by the older generation.

Virtually all children remain at home until marriage, excepting the tiny elite who go away to university, and because they marry so much later than their forebears, daughters today stay at home much longer than before and develop a closer relationship with their blood families. In the past, they were encouraged to invest all in their marriage family; one of the consequences of this was that, in a society without public **welfare**, their parents desperately needed a son in order to survive in old age. If a modern daughter and son-in-law remain close, that need may be not so desperate and, furthermore, if there is only one child there is less likelihood of a new household being created. However, it is thought that today's couples feel greater loyalty to each other than to the wider family, in particular the groom's family, than was the case in the past. And notwithstanding doomsayers, for the country as a whole, divorce is still a rarity.[5]

Over 50 years ago, it could be remarked that individual, family, kinship and culture were all 'under the ancestor's shadow', but this is no longer so. 'Coming out of the ancestors' shadow is the principal change in the private lives of villagers in Xiajia village', studied by Yan Yunxiang.[6] There is less sense of intergenerational reciprocity, less automatic respect for the older, more romantic love, more freedom for women to decide their own paths. But the 'uncivil individual' has appeared. As the State has loosened its grip on family life, it has not only been replaced by traditional culture but by the competing influences of the market economy and of consumerism. Traditional family culture was too ruined to be restored when the State retreated. As Wittgenstein put it, 'to restore a broken culture' is like trying 'to repair a torn spider's web with our fingers'.[7]

The lack of traditional restraints on behaviour, the cynicism which the revolution brought about, the crass materialism that has replaced it, seem to have given rise to some predatory and callous individuals.[8] Nevertheless, the idea of family life is still powerful, as are traditional ideas of reciprocity and responsibility to the old and to children.

CHAPTER 22

Media

The Party will keep control. But journalists and their managers do influence the processes upon which they report.

'The man was an athlete yet, as he jumped from a first floor window, he managed to land on his head. Or else he was manacled, beaten and then flung out dead by the policemen commanded to cow him, who were then protected by the Prosecutor. You decide.'

So concludes the presenter of China's most famous investigative TV show, *News Probe*, in a programme called 'Death in Custody'. Not quite the image of the Chinese media that Westerners tend to have. But true.

Government people, immersed in the history of the Chinese Communist Party, know that control of the media has been very important in its rise to, and consolidation of, power. So 2005 measures tightening up control of, and limiting foreign investors' involvement in, the media are not really very surprising.

Until recently the media were used, in the Chinese phrase, 'as the throat and tongue of the Party', effectively to promote the Party's ideas. Since 1992, the situation has become more complicated. Commercialisation and digitalisation have brought a riot of new ideas, formats and approaches, and the media are broadening horizons and, doubtless, changing attitudes and ambitions. In entertainment and consumer information and trivia, the Party has minimal interest. Even where the Party seeks to keep tightest control, news and current affairs, there are public debates and discussions of issues. And the media matter.

1.16 billion people have access to television; the numbers of newspapers, periodicals and radio sets per head are getting close to US ratios. Over the past twenty years, growth has been spectacular, with the number of newspaper titles growing fifteen-fold and book publishing exploding.

Taken together, China Central Television plus some 3,000 other television stations, along with their satellite and ground network systems, make up the largest television system in the world. China is a major market for pay TV; it is forecast to have 128 million sub-scribers by 2010.[1]

The national radio station is China Public Broadcasting. It has eight channels and broadcasts through satellite 156 hours a day. The national overseas broadcasting station, China Radio Inter-national, is beamed worldwide in 43 languages and broadcasts 290 hours per day. It is the third largest such provider in the world.[2]

Just one of the many educational media, the China Agricultural Broadcasting and Television School, with its annual enrolment of 900,000 and 26,000 centres, is possibly the world's largest distance-learning operation.[3]

Conventional media can be divided into three types: first, the core Party and government organs, such as the *People's Daily* or New China News Agency; second, those still closely controlled by the Party and State, but not the core, such as the *China Economic Times*; and finally, those that are technically 'fringe' and completely dependent upon the market, yet may – as with the influential *Caijing*, a bi-weekly journal, or the *Xin Jing Bao* – be leading media. The fringe media are not as closely watched as their counterparts in the other categories of media and therefore have more leeway.[4]

Government organs still retain ultimate ownership of probably all media operations and can shut them down at will. Where con-tent is relatively non-political, it is commercially driven.[5] News is subject to heavy political influence. Media coverage of the 2005 tsunami disaster minimised the role of the USA, when it in fact pro-vided the most massive aid; coverage of the failed Chinese bid to buy a US oil company was restricted before the 2005 presidential summit.[6] Although the **internet** has made it more difficult, the authorities still make many topics out of bounds. In December

2005, the editor of *Beijing News* was sacked, probably because the newspaper revealed that six farmers had been killed in a crackdown on rural protests in Dingzhou, Hebei, six months earlier. In protest at the sacking, 100 journalists went on strike.[7] In January 2006, reports on many blogs were ensuring that the incident was becoming known all over China.

One of the most interesting developments has been investigative journalism. Investigative journalists of both TV and newspapers use techniques familiar to viewers of BBC *Panorama* or *60 Minutes* to expose corruption, abuse of power, exploitation and expropriation. Their stories make very popular journalism but they also perform a political function. Media power to examine and expose helps the Party get its policies implemented or just recognised far from the capital. So investigative journalists function by identifying abuses and highlighting problems.

Even when articles and programmes are spiked, they are still distributed to officials through a restricted circulation system. The journalists who carry out this work are in a very privileged position. They are an intermediary between government and governed in a society in which they are almost the only such intermediary.

Before the triumph of the Communist Party in 1949, there was a vigorous press, which was varied and could be independent of politics.[8] So present developments can be seen as the press trying to re-establish professionalism. But the media have not succeeded in having their rights and responsibilities clarified in law, and journalists are often subject to intimidation and worse. On the other hand, journalists are widely regarded by ordinary people as a special kind of official, people to be lobbied because they have access to authority and can solve problems, and the official who is an honest and disinterested critic of vested interests is a well-established figure in Chinese history. Investigative journalists are more likely to see themselves in this tradition than as subversives or Westernisers, even when they are knowledgeable about foreign examples.

The WTO does not oblige China to open its media to foreign

influences, but the government has four main strategies for collaboration. It encourages training arrangements that raise industry standards, and it permits programmes and programme formats to be acquired.[9] The third strategy is cultural extension, the projection of **softpower** abroad.

The fourth strategy is of collaboration with foreign companies to produce material to attract large Chinese audiences. The programming that gets the biggest revenues is produced in Chinese societies, and mostly inside China. The preferred method is through joint ventures, of which Phoenix Television is the best known. Others include:[10] Clear Channel Communications, with its joint venture to produce outdoor advertising; Bertelsmann, which has book clubs and book stores; Time Warner, which manages cinemas; and Hearst, which has both trade magazines and consumer titles such as the Chinese version of *Cosmopolitan*.

For provincial media, alliances with Western media corporations were, until new controls were introduced in 2005, seen as a source of programming and expertise. For example, Shanghai Media Group entered an alliance with CNBC to run a specialist financial channel, China Business Network.[11]

To enter the Chinese market, you accept government terms. News Corporation's Star operation makes heavy losses and has only a toehold in South China. It has had to accept political conditions such as not using BBC material.

In periodical publishing, British leaders such as Haymarket find that their initiatives are contingent upon working through a Chinese organisation permitted to operate licences, in effect rented out by a political institution authorised to publish. The initial public offering by Baidu.com (China's Google) was complicated by restrictions on foreign ownership. Investors were actually being offered (non-voting) shares in a Cayman Islands holding company, which owns a Virgin Islands company, which has contractual agreements with a company controlled by the two founders of Baidu.com.[12]

In summary, the Chinese media exhibit many of the features of any modern media system, always on a vast scale. Yet ultimate State ownership, Party influence and journalism traditions make for very particular characteristics.

CHAPTER 23

Sports

China has been participating in international sports only for about twenty years, yet has moved fast to achieve so much at the last two Olympics. Many see that the immense efforts that China is putting into the 2008 Olympics, by developing its athletes and through the spectacular plans for the event itself, will not only establish China in the same league as the USA for sport, but transform the very stature of the Olympics and, at the same time, announce that China has arrived as a power in the world.

A few miles from the Shaolin Temple, we stopped the car to watch about a thousand boys doing warm-up exercises on a parade ground before a palatial school. From the guys in grey tracksuits we came to ones in blue, then fields of green, yellow, brown and red … we must have passed 30 martial arts colleges before we arrived at the principal shrine to China's most famous sport. In the temple complex there is a great demonstration hall, where adepts in monks' robes show off their speed and dexterity in battles with bare hands, spears, sabres, maces and flails.

So far these ancient arts have not been tamed, with the possible exception of Taekwondo,[1] by being transformed into competitor sports such as judo. The young foreigners who are taking the monks' instructions in the courtyards of the temple itself are not after money, but enlightenment, or at least skill. Nevertheless, China is burning with Olympic fever, and when you as a foreigner stand in line at a bus stop or squat on your train bunk, if it's not which soccer team you follow, it's likely to be the Olympics that you are asked about.

It's hardly surprising. At the Athens Olympics, following the achievement of 63 medals at Sydney, many expected China to do even better. However, the coaches appear to have reduced their chances somewhat by deciding to enter younger performers who can be expected to reach their prime in 2008. Nevertheless, golds were won in weightlifting, swimming, running track, shooting, canoeing, tennis, windsurfing, volleyball and diving, and China did well in sports in which it was hardly registered ten years ago: judo, hockey and fencing.[2]

Though only in the last two decades have they started to be seriously taken on, Western sports were introduced to China 150 years ago. Before then, China's main equivalents were martial arts and *qigong* (breathing exercises), although the Manchu ruling class had polo, hunting, falconry, wrestling and archery. As trade grew in the latter half of the 19th century, the cantonments of foreign traders brought yachting, golf, cricket, bowls and croquet for themselves, which were picked up by wealthy Chinese associates. Missionaries, and especially the YMCA and YWCA through their schools and youth clubs, imported basketball, athletics, gym, tennis and ping pong. As the armed forces began to modernise, physical education (PE) was introduced into military academies.

There was hostility to these foreign activities. The elite disliked the competitive and violent aspects of the sports, since exercises traditionally had been about health and relaxation and were linked to religious notions of developing spirituality rather than physical prowess or winning. They also saw these energetic pursuits as vulgar.

When a popular movement arose against foreigners in the last years of the 19th century, it was closely connected to traditional sporting practices. The 'Boxers' (*Yihetuan*) were adepts at martial arts. Most villages had a hall where these could be practised, and itinerant monks would instruct in them, for martial arts had grown out of the monastic tradition and all the leading adepts were religious. As Susan Brownell puts it, 'muscular Buddhism preceded muscular Christianity by at least 1,200 years'.[3] The societies of practitioners were often disposed towards 'restorationism', that is, the overthrow of the Manchus and restoration of the Ming Dynasty to the throne. Xenophobia was an easy step further.

By 1905, Western-style PE was a required subject of the school curriculum, though whether in practice this affected many youngsters is open to doubt.[4] With the establishment of the Republic after 1911, the Nationalist Party (Kuomintang or KMT), influenced both by Soviet example and by European eugenic theories, advocated military-style physical training in schools. In 1928, the *Guoshu* movement introduced martial arts into schools as compulsory; sports facilities were built in many cities, the *Journal of Physical Education and Hygiene of China* was established and, in 1930, China held its first all-China sports meeting in Hangzhou. China took part in the Far Eastern Olympics regularly, and in 1932, the first Chinese delegation participated in the world Olympic Games. However, the Japanese invasion and the Civil War, followed by the CCP terror, limited progress.

Once the CCP had established control, it set up a Soviet-style organisation of sport, nationalising or incorporating those bodies it did not abolish, and in principle developing sport such that China could compete in the various sporting tournaments of the communist world.

It was in the 1980s that China began to develop the sports consciousness that is associated with modern societies. The National Sports Commission produced a strategy to both try to develop a fitness culture in the country as a whole and to orientate sport towards participation in the Olympics. Aside from martial arts, which, as China's national sports, were not to be tampered with, where sports did not belong in the Olympic fold they would be sidelined.[5] The quadrennial National Games were arranged to prepare for the Olympics, and investments were made in the development of specified elite sports in which, it was believed, China might succeed. The sense of this was evident at the 1984 Olympics, at which the PRC took away fifteen gold medals, although performance was subsequently disappointing until 1996, when it took fourth place.

By 1993, when China was bidding to host the 2000 Olympics, knowledge about, and fascination for, the Games was widespread. By the Sydney Games, China was proved a rising force, taking 32 gold, seventeen silver and fourteen bronze medals. When in 2001 China won the right to host in 2008, the government set aside $200 million for further athlete training.[6]

Most universities have sports departments, there is a specialist sports university, and there are sports tracks in the Normal (or teacher training) Universities, Institutes of Physical Education and Sports Technical Institutes.[7] Every province now has an Institute of Sports Science, the principal role of which is to assist the provincial teams to compete in the National Games.[8] Training for the 17,000 athletes in the Sports Technical Schools is often very rigorous indeed; Matthew Pinsent, UK gold medallist and Olympic spokesman, was reported to have been shocked at the severity of the training regime to which young gymnasts are subjected in one institution.[9]

Although central funding for many sporting activities ceased in the late 1980s, the provinces and localities are expected to invest in sport, and such central funding as remains is to be more carefully targeted, by, for example, financing an infrastructure for soccer. Professional soccer started in 1993 and is now the most popular spectator sport. Sports awareness is widespread, and there are newspapers entirely devoted to football and golf.

In a little park near London's Tower Bridge, a young woman can often be seen at 6.30 in the morning, whirling a tasselled scimitar and battling invisible enemies with stylised martial arts movements. The same sight can be seen in parks all over the Chinese world; of a Shanghai morning on any patch of grass or temple courtyard, you will see several hundred people practising callisthenics. But the curiosity is that they tend to be the well-over-50s. University campuses aside, young people are rarely to be seen. The fitness culture has not developed as had been hoped. In 1995, a National Fitness Promotion Programme was introduced. Two years of planning were followed by two years of propaganda and awareness promotion, and two years building the facilities and getting schools to act upon their awareness; now we are in the later phases of the process, raising the levels of activity. All over the capital, you will see little wayside exercise machines and climbing frames, but they seem little used and it appears that initiatives are almost all confined to the cities, and even in many of those they are as yet sparse.

Given the huge population, the fact that China has not succeeded in disseminating fitness culture generally does not hold back its rapid progress in Olympic sports. Large investments are certainly being made. The main stadium will be the biggest ever, the pool the most expensive, and Peking is being ripped apart to make it as grandiose as possible, a suitable backdrop to the ultra-modern Olympics that the PRC government wants to show the world. Pressure from the government for China to become a power in world sport has stacked up notable achievements already; more is possible. It may be coming. Thoughtful UK observer Dennis Whitby returned from meeting Chinese coaches with 'an impression of teamwork, of a steady but relentless push towards excellence that involves everyone'.[10]

PART FOUR

Context

CHAPTER 24

Geopolitics

China is recognised as a rising power. It is establishing itself as an important factor for most countries. Yet this does not amount to a challenge to US dominance, because it is constrained by its poverty, domestic discontent, geopolitical vulnerability, dependence upon foreign resources, and its leaders' beliefs about China's history and its relations with foreign powers over the past 150 years. How the world reacts to China's rise may do more to determine its influence than China's rise itself.

Caught at an embassy party, a Western military attaché may fume at the challenges posed by China's forces, its alliances or its burgeoning economic influence. But a Chinese counterpart will tell you that his country's talk about 'peaceful rise' is not just a slogan to calm the anxious, but an essential strategy for a country beset with many dangers.

China shares borders with fourteen countries. Since 1949, it has fought wars in Vietnam, India and Korea and skirmishes with Russia. There are difficulties with Cambodia, Thailand and Burma over water resources. The Central Asian states are newly independent, multi-ethnic and open to influence from Islamic fundamentalism or Pan-Turkism.

Of China's 30 provinces, three of the biggest (Tibet, Xinjiang and Inner Mongolia) are the homelands of non-Chinese people much closer culturally and linguistically to their other neighbours than to the Chinese. This, and inconsiderate behaviour from Peking, cause instability. China is spoken of as 'the only major power that expects to acquire substantial additional territories'.[1] These include Taiwan, a large number of islands in the South China Sea, plus parts of Kazakhstan. When this situation is combined with a very new one – the competition for resources to feed China's rapid economic development – it should not be surprising that Chinese leaders are concerned about security, particularly since for the first 30 years of the PRC their predecessors managed to disgust, or at least alienate, most of the world.

To keep up the momentum of development, China needs to import not only oil in great measure but a huge range of raw materials and food. For oil it is competing in particular with the world's biggest consumer, the USA, which has been taking steps to establish its supplies in the Caucasus and Central Asia as well as the Middle East. For the supply of raw materials, China is dependent upon sea lanes to and from Africa and the Middle East, which could be disrupted from South East Asian ports or by the Indian or US fleets. The great fear must be of coalitions, say of the USA, Japan and India, or Australia with Vietnam and South Korea. A US/Russian carve-up of Central Asia and Siberia is something China is keen to prevent.

China's leaders have therefore been dealt a bad hand. They approach foreign affairs inspired by some core beliefs: that China has a unique and leading place in the world; that China has been denied this for two centuries by outsiders who have weakened and dismembered the country; that strategic aims need tactical alliances.

As we have seen, China was the world's outstanding cultural and economic power from 221 BC until scientific and technological advances gave Europeans supremacy in the 18th century. The relegation was made clear by the Opium War of 1841, when China was forced to accept a relationship with Britain that it did not want. This, and other failures, resulted in exploitation and humiliation until 1949, when China could begin work to rebuild the 'wealth and power' appropriate to its status.

This view is held with an intense bitterness against 'outsiders' that has been fanned by politicians for generations.[2] Thus the return of Hong Kong to China was one more step back to the way the world ought to be. The separation of Taiwan from China, a result of the Civil War of 1930–49 but blamed on foreigners, must end. China cannot at present challenge the USA, Taiwan's protector, so it tries to divide the political classes of Taiwan; it seeks to undermine Taiwan's standing abroad and to create compromising economic ties. Force against Taiwan will be avoided only if the independence movement goes no further.

Chinese politicians have a global perspective. China has not yet recovered sufficiently to be a world power, so it will lead local consortia when there are common East Asian or Asian interests. China has agreed to a free trade zone with ten Asian countries and has cut import restrictions, inviting comparison with the protectionist US. During political summits, China sponsors large investment conferences, and it has established the Asean Regional Forum with 22 other countries. China is now engaged in more than 40 regional and sub-regional Asian security and economic forums, and is becoming involved politically. For example, China helped mediate a dispute between Cambodia and Thailand. According to the New China News Agency's *Foreign Policy Review* for 2004: 'China broke its traditional pattern by actively reconciling two other nations.'[3]

The overriding objective is to develop economically. For this, China wants peace, foreign investment and that other countries expend themselves on keeping order. China wants the status quo in international affairs. Once it has obtained its objectives, the international system – UN, WTO – may need to adapt, but not now.

The only real impediment to China's future position is the USA's pre-eminence. For the moment, China cannot challenge that pre-eminence culturally, economically, politically or militarily. However, it can seek to isolate it or confuse it by forming alliances with others, by undermining US relationships, by doing what it can to promote a 'multipolar' world. So President Hu Jintao addresses the Australian parliament, PM Wen Jiabao tours Europe to win support for lifting the arms embargo, and every opportunity is taken to flatter the pretensions of Europeans, Latin Americans and Russians. China has cultivated the Central Asian states, creating the Shanghai Cooperation Organisation, which has conducted military manoeuvres in Xinjiang and set up an anti-terrorism operation, and which is intended to check US influence in the region.

The nature of China's involvement in Africa has disturbed Westerners because, whereas they claim to tie trade and aid to improvements in human rights and better governance, Chinese aid is particularly welcome in Africa because it does not. With its increasingly great, and complicated, demand for energy, China has succeeded in sourcing 30 per cent of its oil from the continent. In 2006, for example, it took a 45 per cent stake in a Nigerian oilfield, made investments in other African countries, increased spending on goodwill programmes (health, education, satellite technology), and published a White Paper on African policy, which looks beyond the China Africa Cooperation Forum to a free trade agreement with Africa.[4]

China's diplomatic offensive is made easier by the US focus on its 'War on Terror' and the occupation of Iraq, which can make China appear a relatively benign partner. China has established close ties with Thailand, Laos, Cambodia, Burma, Mongolia, India, South Korea and Russia. It provides aid to Burma, Samoa, Fiji, Indonesia, Thailand, Laos, Cambodia and Vietnam, and invests in important trading partners such as Brazil. Opinion polls are starting to show that, while the US is feared, China is seen as the more benign ally.[5]

This is a view not shared by all. Japan's Foreign Minister states that Japan sees China as a military threat.[6] India, too, is suspicious of China's refusal to acknowledge its responsibility for the 1962 war, and for such unfriendly moves as arming Nepal.[7] While the USA is keen to involve China in discussions over the North Korean nuclear danger, it knows that China's interests are different: if the North Korean regime is the main impediment to the USA increasing its influence in North East Asia, then it is useful to China.

China has benefited from a rapprochement with Russia, whose biggest customer it is for arms, and with whom it wants to work to diminish 'US hegemony' and create alternative centres of power. In 2005, the two countries finally came to an agreement on border delineation. But it is questionable whether this amity will continue for long. China's growing involvement in Central Asia – the PRC buys most of Kazakhstan's oil and is the best prop of the Uzbek and Turkmen regimes – erodes Russian influence. Recently, Russia showed its nervousness by aborting cooperation over an energy pipeline in favour of Japan. Russians are intensely aware that some Chinese strategists may have long-term interest in Siberia and the Russian Far East.[8]

China's geopolitical momentum may be compromised by domestic problems. If the Chinese model is seen to be incapable of coping with the tensions within, it will lose its lustre. The underlying view of foreigners as having been the cause of all China's woes may make it difficult to establish warm long-term ties, and could be the source of more dangerous phenomena than the bouts of anti-Japanese or anti-American xenophobia with which we are already familiar.

Given China's vulnerability and need for stability, any serious crisis in its international relations is, with the single though important exception of a war over Taiwan, more likely to result from foreign initiative.

CHAPTER 25

Internet

The internet is changing China, but China may also be changing the internet.

China has around 103 million people online, 53 million of them broad-band users, giving internet access to over 400 million. This figure is expected to grow by 25 per cent annually.[1] There are over 500,000 internet websites, and about 1,400 news outlets have gone online. Chinese servers host an estimated 600,000 bloggers.[2] In Chinese terms these are rather small numbers, and illustrate information inequality: the division between those dependent upon conventional media and those with internet access.

Western observers long predicted that the internet would become a vehicle for opposition, for democratic forces in Chinese society, but this has not happened to the degree expected. Partly this is because internet users are not the people alienated from the new order, but its supporters – the urban, affluent young. Partly it is because internet users seem to be more interested in consumption and personal development. Although there is political discussion on the web, notably via the *People's Daily* forum, Chinese portals such as Sohu, Sina and Netease host vastly more bulletin boards (BBS) on relationships, art, residential property, cars, family life, grooming or nightlife.

The government has recognised the economic value of the internet, seeing its widespread use as offering an opportunity for 'leapfrog modernisation', bypassing stages of development through which other countries have gone, to build high-tech industries. At the same time, the government wants to control its undesirable aspects, from pornography to political subversion.

It has failed to limit the influence of the internet upon journalism and thence on policy. Manipulation of the news has become more difficult. Over the bombing of the Chinese embassy in Belgrade in 1999 and over the collision of US and Chinese aircraft in 2001, the government successfully hid the other side's view, giving the Chinese population a partial picture, but if anything the media hyped the nationalism beyond what was useful to the government.[3] However, over the 2003 SARS scandal, when the PRC was caught out suppressing data, and in notorious cases such as the cover-up by local officials of their complicity in an explosion in a school,[4] the government has found itself defeated by determined journalists who have ensured that the true versions of stories get out to colleagues in Hong Kong or elsewhere. These can then be posted on the internet or texted by mobile phone and re-transmitted around China until the official version of events is so undermined as to make its continued defence quite vain. Online condemnations of deaths in custody pushed the government into changing its policy on city migrants.

In a country where the potential for environmental and health disasters is great unless these are identified early – there is a dis-graceful pre-1992 tradition of truly horrific disasters remaining unreported, so that no action was taken until the problems were virtually unmanageable – this matters. By making cover-ups more difficult, the internet and mobile telephone are therefore forces for improvement, obliging some degree of transparency.

At the government's News and Communications Research Institute of the China Academy of Social Sciences, experts recog-nise that on-line forums have given a voice to the general public, including disadvantaged communities and marginalised groups: 'The vitality and scale of on-line public opinion have reached an unprecedented extent, and have generated enormous pressure which no government department, organs or even public figures can afford to ignore.' 'The popularity, timeliness, openness, its shared nature and interactivity of internet-based media have decided that the internet is becoming an increasingly important ideo-logical battleground.'[5]

The government is determined to police the internet. It is illegal to log on through other than official Chinese portals, which connect through a gateway controlled by the government. According to one study, 'China operates the most extensive, technologically sophisticated, and broad-reaching system of internet filtering in the world.'[6] In order to limit access to established websites, and to control what content can be posted domestically, the systems search for sensitive keywords. Packets of data can be filtered at 'choke points' designed into the network, with filtering undertaken by both machine and human censors. There are believed to be around 50,000 full-time personnel involved in censorship, and many volunteers.[7]

The requisite technology is supplied by Cisco, Nortel, Sun, 3COM and Microsoft.[8] Other foreign firms come to terms too. According to Reporters sans Frontières (RSF), Yahoo! has censored its China search engine for many years. This can be demonstrated by searches for such word units as 'Radio Free Asia', 'democracy', 'Taiwan Independence', 'June Fourth', 'Wei Jingsheng', 'Tibetan Independence' or 'BBC'. RSF believes that Yahoo! China's 'merger with Chinese-owned Alibaba will effectively sidestep any need for Yahoo!, as international partner and 40 per cent stakeholder, directly to negotiate censorship issues with Peking, devolving all such decisions to the local management team'. Google's Chinese partner Baidu filters.[9] In the week beginning 23 January 2006, two news stories appeared about Google: the first that it was refusing to cooperate with the US government in providing information that would enable it to track paedophiles; the second that it was helping the Chinese government identify dissidents. In February 2006, Yahoo! was accused of giving the PRC 'evidence to help jail [a] dissident'.[10]

Censorship is not the only means by which the PRC seeks to control netizens. It has introduced 'compulsory real name registration', with verification procedures, which has upset many, especially students running bulletin boards and instant message groups; held site administrators responsible for content; and imprisoned a number of bloggers for subversion.

In 2005, it was reported in *Southern Weekend*, the newspaper most famous for investigative work, that the CCP Propaganda Department of Suqian had recruited a detachment of 'undercover online commentators' or 'cyber agents', the prototype of many now being mobilised elsewhere.[11] Selected for their political stance and knowledge, 'They pose as ordinary internet users in on-line forums and chat rooms and defend the government against negative comments' in order to direct public opinion. The agents are undertaking training courses, are coordinated through regular meetings and are appraised for performance.

One agent, cited in the report, noticed that some netizens were complaining of police arrogance, in often driving with their sirens on. Many netizens posted follow-up comments, and the discussion gradually evolved into criticisms of the police force. The young agent immediately joined the discussion, suggesting that those policemen must have had urgent missions, were under threat of violence and should not be criticised.

China is regional internet access provider to other Asian states, notably the Central Asian ones, Korea and Vietnam. It seems likely that it will export its skills in internet control. Libertarians hope that technological progress will outstrip the CCP's capabilities. Networked communication is becoming ever more sophisticated, with RSS feeds (Really Simple Syndication, ultra-smart web pages read by computers rather than people), social bookmarking systems[12] like del.icio.us and Furl, and fledgling Voice over Internet Protocol (VoIP, or telephony over the internet) packages such as Skype.[13] The ingenuity and resources of the CCP may, though, outstrip theirs.

CHAPTER 26

Globalisation

Neither the hopes of the total modernisers nor the fears of conservatives are likely to be realised.

Not long ago, the sister of a Chinese friend brought her teenage daughter to meet me. Alice had been six years in the US before moving to Shanghai with her parents, father English-American. An avid reader of Harry Potter, she had demanded the right to go to an English boarding school and I was being asked to be her legal guardian. She went to an 'international' (read: American) school and claimed to speak no Chinese, not to like Chinese food and to have no Chinese friends.

Some might suggest that this is the logical end of China's passion for destroying its past: young people who are able to live in a location without having anything to do with it – truly globalised people. They would say that Alice is just advanced, and how she lives presages the standardised future coming to us all. Advocates of it foresee a homogenised world culture, where the traditions that hold us back and the differences which divide us have gone. To the suspicious, though, transnational companies and international agencies are really vehicles for US power, deliberately destroying those institutions and identities which give us the strength to resist conquest – cultural, economic or political.

In some ways China is well on the way. The elite has managed to get people to internalise a simplistic view of what constitutes progress and modernisation, so that they often express shame at Chinese characteristics, worshipping and blindly believing in things foreign, or *Chingyangmeiwai*. A study has shown that parents in the capital have lost faith in traditional approaches to children, buying anything as long as it is foreign.[1] With hindsight, a main achievement of

Mao Zedong may prove to have been so to wreck Chinese cultural traditions, habits and attitudes as to weaken resistance to commercialisation. Socialism, the necessary precondition for capitalism?

A particular **culture of food** is one of the main attributes of Chineseness. Among some groups this may be breaking down, as European cuisine is introduced in cosmopolitan centres such as Shanghai, and as fast food has been taken up by a few. Whereas in the West, fast food eateries are probably seen as the lowest order of eating – places which sophisticates would never dream of entering on grounds both of health and civility, and an expression of American society's failure to preserve a healthy eating culture – they are seen quite differently in China, according to anthropologists, as an indication of modernity 'synonymous with radical, progressive change'.[2] Considering that traditional Chinese food is nutritionally balanced and mostly fresh and healthy, even the limited success of McDonald's in China is difficult to explain. Does it appeal just because it is not 'what's good for you'? Because anything new or foreign 'must be good'? It may be that fast food is not really seen as food, but as a kind of exotic experience and a place where you can hang out (in Chinese restaurants you usually leave the instant the meal is over) with modern lavatories and little hassle.[3] One Chinese described McDonald's as being an advantageous meeting place. 'And the food?' 'Why spoil a visit to McDonald's by eating the food?' he replied.[4]

Globalisation works in different ways in different social classes. Wedding parlours have long been a feature of Chinese life: couples go there to plan their nuptials and, in particular, the all-important photographs of the wedding. It's rather fun watching through the windows dozens of earnest couples poring over catalogues, while models parade their gear and hairdressers work on their customers, all in one teeming mass of elegance and prettiness. Today, brides mostly seek a formal photo of themselves in white; it is rather as if an Italian woman were to dress in black for a christening. Curiously, although the photograph may be taken wearing 'Western'

145

wedding clothes, the ceremony itself will often be performed with the bride wearing the traditional scarlet.

Transnational corporations claim that they are 'glocal' rather than local, that they respond to, and fit in with, local cultures. Nevertheless, to observers they are engaged in attempting a cultural transformation of China, deploying 'a worldwide system of image-saturated information technologies to attract customers, including children'.[5] Among the results is the prevalence of commercially marketed celebrations. Christmas, Mothers' Day, Fathers' Day, Halloween, birthday parties with cakes, candles etc., Valentine's Day … all provide opportunities for spending and diminish the specialness of traditional Chinese festivals. Whereas in rural Cantonese society, celebrations of longevity were important features of family life, they are now being superseded by celebrations of youth.[6] All these involve children's food and child-focused entertainment. Apparently, they also involve hot dogs and hamburgers (no traditional parent would have bought 'composition foods' without knowing precisely what was in them!) and ice creams which have little connection with cows.

Toys and pets have appeared in great profusion, pocket money has been introduced, and, necessitated by high-rise living and the relative lack of siblings and nearby young cousins, as well as thanks to the models offered by books and TV, children's play has been 'commodified',[7] i.e. children are taken to commercial entertainment centres. What's more, seeing sitcoms from other countries may even make them behave differently. Interviewed soon after the first such American TV programmes were screened, parents complained that their children had started to try to kiss them when they got back from school! Truly, if, as Keynes said, 'all practical men are the slaves of some defunct economist', then all social innovators are the dupes of an advertiser's copywriter. Yet, because we use the same household appliances, live in the same kinds of homes, do we begin to think the same? Is the content of a Chinese text message made homogenous by the medium?

Meet Chinese academics today and you will find that many of them are working on projects of, or seeking funding from, wealthy foreign foundations and government institutions, naturally fitting in with the agendas of their paymasters. Some are so similar to their counterparts elsewhere as to seem part of a kind of transnational elite, rather as Peter Berger has suggested that the financial, media, NGO and diplomatic elites of the world have become, with their 'Davos culture' of common beliefs and behaviours which give them more in common with other transnationals than with their own fellow-countrymen.[8] The habits of foreign travel, with the standard Western-originated hotel experience, entertainment habits fashioned by the US culture industries, clothing designed for the world, and food which is a mixture of styles, made to offend few, are theirs. Even the anti-globalisers too may be globalised. When the environment activist leaves Hong Kong for a demonstration in Seattle, is she being Chinese, American or global?

Some have argued that globalisation will be constrained by cultural barriers.[9] Others note that in some ways traditional ideas have become more influential. Just as Islam and evangelical Christianity are spreading far and wide thanks to digital technologies, so Chinese outside China can strengthen their identities and maintain their ties by watching Chinese TV, congregating only with people similar to themselves, and using the internet in such a way as to become oblivious to the Indonesian, Venezuelan or Australian society around them.

I suspect that the tug of Chinese culture is too powerful for most Chinese fully to transform themselves into Anglophone individualists at home equally in any society as long as its demands are not too great, if that is what is meant by globalisation. Social psychology[10] has interesting things to say about Chinese traits and how distinct they are from Anglophone traits in particular, but it is enough to see how emotionally attached many Chinese are to homeland, the culture of food, a style of child-rearing[11] and a particular way of friendship and cooperation, to realise that this particular quarter of humankind is not likely to go globalised. Except at the edges.

CHAPTER 27

Population

Whether a large population is a benefit or a handicap is a moot point, but policies towards that population are having consequences that may damage China for many years to come.

Much disgust has been expressed around the world at the coercion used in the One Child Policy. What is perhaps more useful than condemnation of its cruelties is consideration of its objectives, whether they were laudable and whether they could have been attained any other way.

In 1949, China's population was 500 million. Although the 1950s were violent years for many, they also brought relative stability after decades of civil war, the Japanese invasion, hunger and widespread banditry. The new government introduced public health programmes and distributed land to the destitute through land reform; later it would guarantee a basic existence to most people through collectivisation. Although it is easy to see the years before Deng Xiaoping's ascent as all wasted, there were benefits of CCP rule, at least in its early years. Mortality and life expectancy both improved.[1] As a result, the population began to increase and the leadership, by the 1970s, feared that it would impede economic growth. The One Child Policy was introduced in 1979.

Fertility had already declined markedly before then, from six children per woman to two (with more like one per woman in the cities). Although this is partly explained by population control policies introduced in the 1970s, fertility had declined before then because couples had begun to want fewer children. This had come about also because the public health programmes of the 1950s had emphasised that less child-bearing benefited both mother and child. In the early 1960s, the government campaigned for smaller families, later marriage, and longer periods between births. A systematic campaign, *WanXiShao* or Later-Slower-Fewer, was introduced in 1971, and contraceptive and abortion services were extended to virtually the whole country. However, by 1979, the government had noted that, because of the large numbers born in the 1960s, there would soon be a baby boom. They had come to believe that more drastic measures were needed, lest economic development fail. This idea is a reversal of the way most development specialists think – that economic improvement is a precondition of population reduction. How China's leaders came to believe the opposite provides interesting insights into the mentality of Party leaders and policy development, and has been examined with great care by Susan Greenhalgh.[2]

In the 1960s, there was a panic in the USA about population in the Third World, with influential people concerned that the poor and culturally different were breeding so as to swamp the 'advanced' countries and generally bring calamity upon a world of finite resources. Population gurus, such as Paul Erhlich,[3] in essence adopted a view derived from Thomas Malthus (1766–1834), who argued that population grew exponentially unless slaughter and famine were at hand to save us. The underlying premise is that people – other people – are a threat. The UN and international aid agencies were urged to push population control programmes, not in the most densely populated countries such as the Netherlands, but in Asia and Africa and Latin America. Sceptics pointed out that population did not grow in a Malthusian manner, since as people became wealthier and healthier they chose to have smaller families, and that the best way of reducing population growth was to improve the conditions of life.

Unfortunately, by 1979, the conditions of Chinese life were bad. The early improvements had been followed by starvation and insecurity, such that the conditions for a reduction in population had not been met. Meanwhile a Chinese missile scientist, Song Jian, had been influenced by the apocalyptic vision of the Club of Rome, self-appointed prophets who argued for drastic control of population.[4]

He began to apply his particular skills in cybernetics and control theory to the problem of population, and produced impressive projections suggesting that China's population growth was a colossal threat not only to China's chances of economic development but also to the survival of the planet. The fact that he and the supporters he gathered around himself from the scientific and policy communities not only were basing their mathematics upon inaccurate empirical data but also ignoring the social sciences, and therefore all those factors other than the biological which influence population change, eluded the decision-makers. 'China's population would top 4 billion in 2080 and keep on growing … By eroding lakes, forests and other natural resources, and by polluting the environment, the rapid growth of human numbers, they suggested, would threaten the resources needed to maintain economic progress.'[5] Worse, the population explosion was a threat to national security, a 'strategic issue'. Song was, after all, a defence expert. There was nothing for it but rapid one-childisation (*yitaihua*).

The potential downside was recognised by some officials, but they were not heeded when they warned of the social costs, from the coercion of women to future labour shortages, disruption of families and rapid ageing. These were just human matters: the decision-makers were in thrall to **science**, or rather a scientistic view of humanity as merely one factor in a nature requiring exploitation if not subjugation.

Thus the national One Child Policy was declared, with targets that local officials were obliged to fulfil, their main weapons being benefit regulation and fines. Couples with only one child got access to health services, housing and job opportunities and schooling, denied to families which contravened. Couples were fined if they had more than one child, and were pressurised into sterilisation. By 1983, it was considered that too little had been achieved, and a big push started, forcing sterilisation of one member of each of the 21 million couples with two or more children, and 14 million abortions of unauthorised pregnancies, causing terrible suffering. The programme was toned down a year later, and by 1988, rural couples with a girl were permitted two children; subsequently the authorities are believed to have eschewed coercive methods and assured compliance through benefit regulation.

The consequences of the rapid reduction in fertility that has resulted from the One Child Policy extend beyond the physical and emotional suffering of women. There is the 'little emperor' phenomenon, by which the hopes of four grandparents and two parents are all fixed upon one child; a dwindling proportion of the population in the active workforce; and the spectre ahead of too few workers to support the rapidly ageing population (it is expected that 27 per cent of the population will be over 60 in 2050). There is the problem of the missing girls: in 1989, there were 105 boys to every 100 girls; in 2000, there were 120 boys to 100 girls, though in two provinces the boys numbered 135 and 138.[6] The reasons for this are debated, but include under-reporting, the adoption of girls, sex-selective abortion and, possibly, a small incidence of infanticide. Finally, there is the problem of the 'hidden population'. Chinese data are notoriously unreliable, but where such a draconian policy is being daily evaded, they must be even more so than usual. A substantial number of people now have no legal existence, surviving on the edge, without rights or benefits.[7]

Was the government duped by flawed but plausible science that it did not understand? Is it possible that, had the projections taken account of social and economic factors, they would have indicated that there was no crisis requiring such a drastic policy? Could the government have achieved the same reduction in fertility by other means, or did the earlier failure to develop materially make the One Child Policy necessary?

We do not know. But the unanticipated consequences of an inhumane policy have wrecked the lives of many and will dog policy-makers for years to come. Should we blame the Club of Rome or should we see the One Child Policy as merely a corollary of earlier policies – 'scientific socialism' – inspired by Lenin and Stalin? You choose.

CHAPTER 28

Agriculture

Can China feed itself, and does this matter?

China's agricultural problem can be summed up simply: less than 10 per cent of the world's cultivable land has to suffice for 25 per cent of the world's population. It has only 25 per cent of the average per person water resource.[1]

There are 200–300 million farms of approximately 0.6 hectares each (about 1.5 acres). And the lack of land is not the only concern; the fresh water, timber and energy available is so little as to make China one of the poorest countries in terms of natural resources relative to population. Over 80 per cent of water resources are concentrated in an area with only a third of the useable land, hence the attempt to transfer water north-west in the **Three Gorges** project. The need for land has forced people intensively to exploit every last crack of available soil, as any train journey through China will show you. The tiniest plots on steep hillsides are cultivated, demanding exhausting labour and the carrying of water, usually on the back, for long distances up high slopes.

After taking power in 1949, the CCP distributed land to the landless by expropriating categories of people – dubbed 'landlords' or 'rich peasants', though often in reality not greatly different from their neighbours – who were persecuted or murdered. It thus both reduced the number of those dependent upon temporary employment and without their own sustenance, who now had land, and terrified potential opposition.

Mainly for ideological reasons – private was bad, collective good – once peasants were too cowed to resist, land was collectivised into big public farms. Land holdings became of a much more sensible size for farming purposes, and the State assured security, but nobody felt responsible. Productivity plummeted, and there were manifold problems from which Deng Xiaoping sought to extricate the economy by introducing the Household Production Responsibility System (HPRS) in 1978.[2] Under the HPRS, land remained the property of the local authority but was leased to all local peasants, with an average farm size of 0.6 hectares for each of the approximately 300 million farming families. The reform brought about an immediate rise in productivity and most households became self-sufficient in foodstuffs, as well as exporting.

But the ideological climate had made other problems worse too. Over the last few hundred years, the forests in much of China had been reduced to almost nothing, and over-grazing and intensive land exploitation in areas with little water had created deserts of swathes of the North and West. Although the world average forestry coverage is 26 per cent, China's is barely 13.9 per cent.[3] Before the 1980s, virtually nothing was done to reverse the destruction of the forests or to reclaim land being gobbled up by deserts at an alarming rate, causing sandstorms. Ecology was out of balance because, for political reasons, the government required the peasants to produce staples and had penalised other kinds of production and conservation. Today, government policy to deal with these issues has four prongs: Marketisation, Reclamation, Urbanisation, and Internationalisation. The core premise is that people must be taken out of farming.

Marketisation allows people in the agricultural sector to use their initiative to develop their own sources of income. The first step was the return of land to private use in 1978. Real rural income rose three-fold between 1980 and 2000.[4] Marketisation reduces government interference in many ways: traditional markets have re-emerged, prices have been largely deregulated, and peasants will not in future be required to produce crops as stipulated by the government in its attempt at food self-sufficiency. Most of China's peasants had been producing crops which are much more successfully produced in land-rich countries, such as the UK and USA, with their large farms and few farmers. Where China has the advantage over them is in the production of people-intensive crops such as fruit and vegetables, flowers and plants. So one aim of marketisation is to absorb more rural labour by encouraging the latter; the corollary of this is that China now imports huge quantities of grains, particularly from the USA, which it must pay for in the export of people-intensive products, particularly to South East Asia. While these policies are showing signs of working, the gap between the urban and rural areas has continued to widen (in 2003, average urban income was over three times rural),[5] causing dissatisfaction, and the behaviour of officials and developers has resulted in ever more resentment.

Acknowledging this, the government has continued its gradual withdrawal from agriculture. The State involvement in, formerly monopoly of, the marketing and distribution of goods has virtually ceased. In the late 1990s, because the return of land to the farmers increased production, yet government controls still dictated what they should produce, there was a glut, such that farm incomes fell. In 2005, the national agricultural tax was abolished.[6] The abolition does not mean that the problems are solved, since that tax was only one of the many tribulations from which farmers suffer, but it is a gesture of symbolic importance because it demonstrates the government's concern for the plight of the rural areas. At the same time, travelling away from home to find work is being made less difficult.

Faced with a desperate peasantry, kept down only by coercion, the government's first priorities after 1978 were to return to free enterprise in the rural areas. Not only was agricultural production and quality improved beyond measure, but country people were encouraged to make their own alternative sources of employment, which they did spectacularly through the Township and Village Enterprises (TVEs) that sprang up everywhere. These not only provided new income in the countryside and reduced poverty; they also saved the urban areas from even greater pressure from migration. On one short train journey of 24 hours, I met young men from faraway provinces in cheap suits representing (1) a factory in the sticks which wants to put its plastic flowers on Shanghai tables, (2) a maker of plumbing bonds, (3) another of bicycle parts and (4) a noodle factory. There were, too, a well-dressed lady, accompanied by two young assistants, who ran a night club in a provincial town, and the owner of two clothing shops. The rural reforms and the creation of the TVEs have enabled some 400 million to rise above the poverty line in 1979–2007.[7]

The downsides have been, first, that the area of cultivable land has continued to decrease as it is taken for other purposes such as new private homes and factories, and second, that industrial pollution, hitherto the preserve of the urban areas, has become a rural problem as well, even as use of fertilisers and pesticides becomes more intense. The government is now attempting to regulate chemical discharge, as well as to enforce reforestation and introduce large-scale reclamation projects in desert areas. In doing this, international expertise and cooperation has proved invaluable.

Internationalisation means exposure, through accepting the rules of the **World Trade Organization**, to competition. For 40 years, the elite believed in autarky, as a result of which China is the world's largest producer of wheat, rice and soybean, all of which – along with other major products – can be farmed more efficiently and sold more cheaply by other countries. Entry to the WTO allows these competitors to import into China, removes Chinese government subsidy and potentially undermines the livelihood of vast numbers of farmers. Indeed, the main opposition to the WTO has come from those who feared the ruin of agricultural production, the instability which would be caused during a long period of transition, and the risk to food security should China become dependent for its staples upon foreign suppliers. Supporters of entry have argued that, with 20–25 per cent of the world's population, China has enormous power in the grain markets, which will stymie any thoughts of exploiting its 'dependence'. They have emphasised the benefit to the government of ending subsidies, which will also lessen the likelihood of the gluts that are a feature of the subsidy system[8] and which make farm income erratic, as well as the possibility of enrichment of the farmers through further specialisation in people-intensive production. China is already the largest producer of fruit, vegetables and meat in the world.[9] Further development of people-intensive production will mean that fewer young people are forced to leave home for work and, as the quality of product, promotion and presentation improve, it will also mean higher incomes. As a transitional arrangement, China still retains a National Grain Reserve, whereby it buys grain not absorbed by the market for the purpose of disaster relief; it may also continue to subsidise city dwellers from intolerable price rises during the course of market adjustment to State withdrawal.

The book *Who Will Feed China?* caused controversy in Chinese policy circles when published in 1995. Lester Brown, its author, predicts that China will have a population of 1.6 billion by 2030 and will probably need to import 1.5 times the present total world trade in grains. He touched a raw nerve, because the government is aware that it has been unable to increase production in recent years and that surplus rural labour and environmental blight impede solution. With its reforms, it is taking the risk of disruption now in order to provide for the future. But today there are desperate peasants on the march for survival and to right their grievances; unrest in many rural areas threatens stability, unrest which currently results more from issues of governance than immediate shortages. The measures taken by the government so far have achieved much. It is by changing the **rural China/urban China** balance that it hopes to find the long-term solution.

CHAPTER 29

Environment

China is the site on which the struggle to save our planet may be waged. More sharply than anywhere else, conservation confronts the dark lords of exploitation.

From Northern Tibet the Angry River twists and turns through the deep gorges of Yunnan until it enters Burma. In 2003, at China's behest, UNESCO declared those areas a World Heritage Site for their animal, bird and plant life. Within days, it was announced on Yunnan Televison that developers would uproot the entire area by building thirteen massive dams.[1]

The struggle to save the Angry River is unusual – in a country where numbers of building projects are created more to provide profits for builders than out of any proven need[2] – for the strength of opposition it has incited and the way it has helped the promotion of the green NGOs in China. Cambodia, Vietnam and Thailand all claim that the business plan to make Yunnan the main seller of power in the region has already reduced water flows, threatening the livelihoods of many millions and the feeding of millions more.[3] The three affected countries contacted China's environmental groups, Green Volunteers and Friends of Nature. Publicity in the Chinese and other media resulted, a website was created (www. nujiang.ngo.cn), and in April 2004, the Prime Minister ordered the project be suspended for examination.

If, braving the smog and wiping the sandstorm dust from your eyes, you visit the Temple of Heaven in south-east Peking, you will see a symbol of traditional attitudes to the environment, for it was here that the Emperor, until 1912, assured the almighty of his reverence. Before 1949, the conventional Chinese view saw heaven and earth in symbiotic relationship, with earthlings needing to respect nature, lest heaven take its revenge by drought or flood.

China is a country of climatic extremes: there has always been a need to manage water, and for several centuries huge dust storms have driven forward the great deserts of North and West. There are frequent earthquakes and, because of the long, low coastline, sensitivity to temperature change. So, for at least 4,000 years, the exploitation of flora and fauna was regulated and the culture extolled nature.

Then came the Enlightenment of the 1920s, greatly influenced by socialist Russia, and with it the belief that progress consisted in industrialisation and collectivisation regardless of cost, that the land and its product, like the human beings who got in the way of progress, should be conquered or simply destroyed. The results for China of the socialist vision have been well documented by Judith Shapiro.[4] Forests have been eliminated, nuclear waste dumped, rivers dangerously diverted, fishing stocks depleted, rare species extinguished, mining allowed to destroy huge areas, and pollution of earth, water and air has become among the worst on the planet. In a very short period of time, whole areas, such as the Tibetan Plateau, have been turned into desert.[5]

Now, State arrogance has been replaced by private ambition. Since the Southern Progress, mass production, mass consumption, mass dietary improvements, mass transport and the mass waste of a massive and growing population urgent to better themselves have negated whatever constraints remained.[6] Today the main problems, according to the State Environmental Protection Administration of China (SEPA),[7] are:

- lack of, and contamination of, water
- industrial discharges
- air pollution from vehicles and coal fires
- China's six largest cities are the most polluted in the world, such that respiratory diseases are the leading cause of death in urban areas and some rural areas

- soil erosion
- disturbance of the water ecosystem
- biodiversity destruction
- deforestation
- acid rain and greenhouse gases.

Policy-makers are now well aware of the scale of the problems.[8] TV transmits many news reports and documentaries on environmental questions, and you can read the level of alarm among the policy community from newspaper articles and slogans on the streets. And it is on the streets, rarely suffered by the leaders, who travel by networks of underground tunnels in the capital, that the problems present themselves most obviously to city-dwellers. In 1990, there were 1 million cars and in 2005 nearly 15 million.[9] If China apes the USA, it will have 600 million cars, more than the current total for the planet. Far from learning from our mistakes, China is building ever more and bigger roads to welcome more cars, banning bicycles when London and New York are encouraging them back, and confirming China's dependence upon imported oil.

Forthcoming international events such as the Olympic Games of 2008, Expo2010 and the Asian Games of 2010 have focused attention on the pollution of air and water in China's cities. In March 2005,[10] President Hu Jintao and the Premier Wen Jiabao both spoke of the need to adopt a 'new development mode' or 'new economic growth mode' within the overriding objective of achieving an all-round harmonious society or *xiaokang*.[11] This is a euphemism for growth that is 'green', assessed according to 'green GDP' criteria. The idea is to find a way of factoring in the hidden costs of change, and 'giving priority to human welfare and well-being rather than mere productivity'. There has been much discussion as to how the price mechanism can be devised to prevent wastage and pollution of water. Selected provinces or municipalities will carry out pilot programmes to calculate their green GDP from 2004 to 2006, and their experiences will be references for other regions.

In 2005, Xie Zhenhua, the SEPA Minister, confirmed that deaths from pollution-related illnesses are very high and that drinking water, acid rain and nuclear radiation are damaging.[12] He reiterated the need for development evaluation which takes resource consumption and environmental loss into consideration; and called for the government to consider environmental issues in the evaluation of local officials' work.[13] Some areas are reverting to traditional agricultural methods, establishing nature reserves, punishing the killing of protected animals, limiting logging and introducing reforestation programmes in attempts to hold back, if not yet reclaim, the advancing deserts. Energy conservation is being widely promoted and China is held up as a model in some of its policies. For example, efficiency standards for home appliances and cars may be better than those of the US. In 2004, China committed itself to generating 10 per cent of its power from renewable energy by 2010, and announced preparation of an energy law which will promote widespread use of renewable sources. In Xian, as in many other cities now, from the 14th-century city walls you can see thousands of solar collectors on the roofs of buildings, illustration of the remarkable fact that China had 75 per cent of the world market for them in 2003; China is now regarded as world leader in both small hydropower and solar water heating.[14]

The potential of China's problems to damage the rest of us is at least as alarming to observers as the crisis within. Fifty per cent of the world's population needs water that originates in Tibet, and could suffer terribly from mistakes made by the PRC; China's carbon dioxide emissions are seen as a major cause of global warming; the contaminated Yangtze River may be killing off fish stocks in the ocean; smog from China is acid rain in Japan. But the environment is bringing people together too. International green NGOs have joined forces with China's own nascent environment movement to influence policy-makers, and the government is involving international specialists in its policy consultations. In environmental matters, traditional beliefs, the plans of the leadership, criticisms by activists and the concerns of the majority for once coincide.

CHAPTER 30

Three Gorges

Mankind's largest-ever water control project is symbolic both of the enormity of the tasks facing China's rulers and of the dangers the country runs as it attempts to bring one quarter of humanity into the developed world.

The World Bank refused to fund it, as did the US Export-Import Bank. But the world's largest-ever water project is going ahead anyway. Suspicions that it is driven less by calm reasoning about its necessity than by vanity are not reduced when the Chinese government proudly reminds us that it is accomplishing what no ruler in 5,000 years of dam-building has been able to do, and what the first President of the Chinese Republic planned to do nearly 100 years ago: tame the Yangtze River.

Chinese engineers are world leaders in dam-building. China contains half the world's large dams, and its 5,000-year history of hydraulic management has led some historians to argue that the Chinese State originated in the control and management of water resources. China's oldest working dam is 2,200 years old today.

The Yangtze is the third-largest river in the world and dominates life in South China. It has 18,000 miles of dykes manned 24 hours a day, and 1,200 monitoring stations, needed for a river that can rise many feet in one hour. In Hubei Province, there are 300,000 soldiers permanently guarding the dykes and ready to create diversionary flooding to save cities such as Wuhan.

There are four principal reasons why the Three Gorges Dam has been advocated. Over the last 2,000 years, the Yangtze has had a major flood every decade, causing death to large numbers and the destruction of livelihood; so the first objective is flood control. Twenty million people will be directly affected, many more

161

indirectly. Second, it will make a mighty contribution to energy production, replacing the burning of 50 million tons of coal a year. The
Yangtze Dam will be the world's largest hydroelectricity plant. The
third objective is penetration: a direct route, much more navigable,
will be provided for shipping and travel from the Pacific to
Chongqing, opening up new markets. The fourth objective is to
provide fresh water needed for agriculture and industry as well as
human consumption; this will also benefit arid North China with the
help of an inter-basin transfer project which will irrigate 115,000
square miles. That similar outcomes have been achieved with
other dam precedents is widely acknowledged.[1]

Critics dispute whether the objectives of this particular project
can be achieved, and also argue that the benefits are outweighed
by the costs.[2] According to the World Commission on Dams, a
combined initiative of the World Bank and World Conservation
Union set up to examine why too many bank-funded dam projects
have failed to deliver benefits, the negative impacts are mainly
environmental, including the loss of forests and wildlife, greenhouse
gas emissions, loss of aquatic diversity and poorer water quality. It is
argued that the project is dangerous, since the dam is constructed
near an earthquake fault line. Others among the many critics note
that some of China's most productive farmland will be lost, reducing its grain supply by some 10 per cent; that the relocated inhabitants will be lost to subsistence farming and, given the record of
relocations on previous projects, may be lost altogether. Chinese
critics have regretted the fact that the Three Gorges, focus of art
and poetry for several thousand years, are to be so changed and
that some of China's greatest cultural sites are to be drowned,
along with thirteen cities, 140 towns and 4,000 villages. They have
asked why a number of smaller dams could not have achieved as
much as this mammoth project.[3]

This is a question that has exercised experts too.[4] The unanticipated consequences of large dam-building projects have in the
past included accidents due to faulty materials and corruption in

the building processes, both of which issues have already emerged on the Yangtze; much higher maintenance costs than budgeted; and failure to predict and then to relocate or compensate the millions affected. According to the World Bank, of the 10 million people displaced by earlier dam-related projects in China, about 46 per cent were still in 'extreme poverty' years later.[5] Only 31 per cent of the contracts issued for the project are to Chinese companies, so that cost overruns pose risks for the Chinese economy. The number of possible things that could go wrong, and the magnitude of the possible disasters, are in other words proportionate to the scale of the project.

The Yangtze Dam Project was initially conceived by Sun Yatsen, father of the Republic, in 1919, and was being seriously considered once the technological expertise was available in the 1980s. In 1986, a report by qualified scientists and engineers was submitted to the Central Committee, recommending that the project be put on hold. However, 'no widely circulated, non-specialist newspapers had objectively reported the findings of their study'.[6] A *Guangming Daily* correspondent and trained engineer, Dai Qing, the adopted daughter of Marshal Ye Jianying, a founder of the PRC – and thus well connected – covered the meeting of the Chinese People's Consultative Conference at which the report was being released, and found that the story she subsequently wrote was spiked. When she took this up with the editor, she was told that there was a 'spirit' abroad which permitted only positive reporting of the project. She tried various magazines to get publication but failed at every attempt; after trawling many potential publishers, she eventually found a provincial book publisher prepared to take the risk.

On 28 February 1989, Dai,[7] along with associated journalists and academic experts, held a press conference to release the book, now called *Yangtze! Yangtze!* It was a compilation of articles and reports that they had been unable to get published by their employers, and amounted to an indictment of the manner in which decision-making over the largest-ever Chinese construction project had proceeded, as well as a questioning of its development value and its potential effect on the environment.

In the months following the publication of the book, government agencies retracted their commitment to the project. There was a feeling in the policy-making community that the project was a major error, and should at least be shelved for further consideration. However, in June 1989, the Tiananmen massacre of protestors took place, and the left wing returned to power as the modernisers were blamed for the demonstrations and disorder that had taken place in many areas. The Three Gorges was particularly a dream of the left, and in October, Dai's book was banned and she was imprisoned for nearly a year. In April 1992, the National People's Congress (NPC) reinstated the project. What had happened in the meantime?

To impose this grandiose project, the processes of consensus-building, developed in the 1980s, were undermined. Those whose consent was looked for were kept ignorant or fed with partial information using techniques familiar to Western public relations practitioners; engineers were protected from exposure to questions;[8] and procedural rules of the NPC were used to prevent the distribution of information and to manipulate data in the manner to which citizens of many countries have become accustomed.[9] Notwithstanding all this, a third of NPC delegates either opposed or abstained on the issue, an unprecedented opposition, perhaps related to the fact that a dozen newspapers, including the *People's Daily* and the *Guangming Daily*, had managed to carry reports of the book's publication.

Nevertheless, by 1994, works had begun and, soon after, well over 1 million people had said farewell to their ancestors and paid their last visits to their parents' graves, their family homes, their land and their temples. The impression given was that, as so often when politics refuses to allow proper debate, where planning involves no participation by those affected, all considerations had become subsidiary to the economic and technical feasibility of the project.

CHAPTER 31

Regions and Languages

China is not the homogenous country it appears to outsiders, but the government seems to be succeeding both in permitting regional identity to flourish and in keeping the country united.

When my friend Xie first came to Paris twenty years ago, he was irritated to find that no one spoke the 'European language', English, that he had put such efforts into learning; he was non-plussed when he found that, to study science in Germany, he needed German. He had assumed English to be the language of the educated in Europe, and that other languages were merely dialects.

Just as some Chinese are unaware of the variety of cultures and languages in Europe, non-Chinese are sometimes surprised to find that differences between Chinese can be almost as great. Although the analogy with Europe should not be stretched too far, it is useful.

In the north, China touches the cold Gobi Desert, in the south it is humid and tropical; the east coast is fertile and overpopulated, the west is often barren and empty. The most populous and third-largest country in the world, after Russia and Canada, China is about 3,000 miles from east to west and 2,000 miles from north to south. Nine areas are normally identified as distinct. Most people live in the basins of the Yangtze, Yellow and Xi rivers, the three richest agricultural regions. The main area of growth has been the south-east coastal area to which, increasingly, people gravitate because of the extraordinary expansion of business. It is, like the fifth area, the Yunnan-Guizhou Plateau, in South East Asia, traditionally a rice-growing area, though less fertile than the basins. Manchuria, as with other northern areas a wheat and soybean economy, has the PRC's greatest concentration of heavy industry. Xinjiang and Mongolia consist largely of oasis-like pockets within arid deserts, and Tibet contains pasture lands at high altitudes. In the north and west of the PRC, rain is scarce and temperatures can be extreme. In the south and east you are more likely to encounter monsoon rains and tropical humidity. With such differences in geography, you can expect variations in culture, inviting the question of how such diversity can possibly be held together.

European religious ideas, manners and way of living and **culture of food** have common roots; so do the Chinese. The most obvious divergences are in language, for while the written language can be used by all Chinese, the spoken languages can vary as greatly as do European languages.[1] Over 70 per cent of the population, living north of the Yangtze and in certain north-western parts of southern provinces, speak a form of Mandarin (Putonghua), albeit with local dialects. By contrast, the languages of South China are mutually incomprehensible. They include the Wu languages around Shanghai, Xiang in central and southern Hunan, Gan in Jiangxi, Northern and Southern Min in Fujian, Yue (including Cantonese) in Canton Province and part of Guangxi, and Hakka, the language of a people scattered in various parts of China. Not long ago, I was in Hangzhou with a student (a native of Hangzhou) who took me out for the day into the nearby countryside, during which trip we encountered two distinct Wu dialects, of neither of which could she understand a word, being reduced with one person to writing in order to communicate.

Standard Putonghua, which used to be known as Guanhua, the officials' language, is always that of administration. Until recently, the government allowed no broadcasting in anything other than Putonghua, but increasingly radio and local TV are using the area speech.

The Chinese written language unites all Chinese; until recently, it was used in common with linguistically quite different Japanese, Koreans and Vietnamese too, since it is ideographic rather than alphabetic. What this means for practical purposes is that even when people cannot understand each other's speech, they can communicate in writing, writing which each will pronounce completely differently. In theory, any spoken language such as English might be written in Chinese, though, as with Japanese, it would need to acquire grammatical particles and the ideographs would be given an English sound.

In Chinese, each ideograph represents a syllable and, often, a complex of ideas and associations connected as much to the symbol as to the syllable. The very oldest are stylised pictures: a sun, a moon, a well. Others are ideas based on pictures: a woman under a roof (peace), a boy under a roof (study). Some have an element which is a guide to pronunciation. The early written language was monosyllabic, but in the modern language, ideographs are combined to make polysyllabic words. The word 'culture' consists of two ideographs, *wen* ('learning') and *hua* ('transformation'). 'Imperialism' consists of four ideographs, amounting to 'territorial aggrandisement' with two of them, and 'ideology' or 'ism' with the other two.

Before the 1920s, official writing was in virtually monosyllabic literary Chinese (*wenyan*) which bore little relation to the by now polysyllabic spoken language (*baihua*), but, after reform, writing increasingly reflected spoken Chinese. In Hong Kong, Cantonese will read Chinese not in Putonghua but in their own language, and for local literature and journalism there are ideographs particular to Cantonese. In Zhejiang (south of Shanghai), a scholar once lamented to me that, because in his area all were obliged to read in Putonghua, they found it difficult to express themselves in writing; it was like speaking English but reading and writing only Latin.

Since 1949, the government has been at pains to get people to forget their regional identities and to think of themselves as 'Han', embracing one identity and one language. Identities such as Tang, southerner, or Wu, Shanghaier, have been frowned upon and the expression 'Chinese' (Zhonguoren) has been used to embrace everybody in China, including those of different cultural identity. For aside from the differences between Chinese, in language as in custom and food, there are 56 'minorities', most of whom have languages quite distinct from Chinese, and these have been permitted to use their own, although it is said that there is great pressure to insist on Chinese from secondary school – and that no officials ever learn any language but Chinese.

In Xinjiang Turkish is spoken, with an Uzbek accent, as is Kazakh, a Turkic dialect which is linguistically related to Mongolian. Tibetan is used in both Tibet proper and Greater Tibet, now incorporated into the Chinese provinces of Qinghai and Sichuan; various Thai Group languages are spoken in Guangxi and Yunnan. Since those designated minorities comprise less than 10 per cent of the population of the PRC, none of this would matter very much but for the fact that several have geopolitical significance beyond their numbers, and secondly that the numbers of those wishing to be designated 'ethnic minority' is growing. This is partly because the government has deliberately courted ethnic minorities, allowing them less restrictive birth control policies, for example, and sometimes subsidies, on account of political sensitivity and the consciousness that ethnic minorities are disproportionately poor. According to the World Bank, 40 per cent of China's poor are from the 9 per cent making up the ethnic minorities.[2]

As the homogenising urges of the CCP have lessened, and perhaps too because migration is affecting so many families and change coming to so many places, there has been a general interest in identifying yourself by your origins and claiming identity as a 'Hakka' or a 'Hainanese' or a 'Miao'. There are outside influences at work as well. Not only do the Mongolians have kinsmen across the border – to whom hundreds of thousands have fled during periods of turbulence – so do the Miao and Zhuang in Burma, Laos, Thailand and Vietnam. There are Chinese Muslim and Chinese-Turkish Muslim communities in the Middle East and, very important for investment and the repatriation of management skills, there are wealthy Fukienese communities in South East Asia, Cantonese (and, increasingly, Zhejiang) in Europe and Shanghainese in the Americas. These communities help to keep alive their particular identities.

At home they are held together by four powers: the prestige and pull of the Chinese cultural world; the appointment and rotation of officials by the **central government**; the tradition of a national, professional and dedicated hierarchy of State officers; and the centralising impulse of the **Party** system.

PART FIVE

Society

CHAPTER 32

Health

One achievement of the closed, controlled society of 25 years ago was that it had extirpated, or could manage, the dire illnesses that are endemic in pre-modern societies, and could maintain basic health through a rudimentary health service. The market society has ended that, and the Open Door policy has allowed in some destructive pests. The government has just discovered that it cannot cope without international help and that it needs to stimulate the market into providing a modern healthcare system.

Children throw rocks or run away when they see their former playmate. Their parents pushed the school into expelling Li Ning. Neighbours are moving house. And all because, one day, the ten-year-old boy fell off a roof, was taken to the local hospital, needed a blood transfusion and got it. But he also got HIV.[1]

It is believed that very large numbers, certainly in the 100,000s, have been infected with HIV on account of the activities of commercial blood collection companies targeting the poorest villagers of China and buying from them frequently.[2] The 'mass production' technique used has multiplied the dangers. When collected, the blood is mixed up and then the pooled plasma is separated from the red blood cells, which are re-transfused back into donors. This reduces anaemia and enables the sellers to provide plasma regularly. But because of the re-transfusion, there is the risk of mass infection. In one seizure of over 6,000 bags of blood from a blood farmer, over 98 per cent of the random sample screened contained HIV-positive blood.[3]

In this saga are illustrated all the components of the public health crisis that affects China. The reforms which liberated people to use their initiative and enterprise have been accompanied by a collapse of the near-universal basic access to health which was the principal achievement of the government since 1949. In the 1950s, energetic campaigns had virtually eliminated TB, smallpox and STDs, as well as successfully reducing the incidence of many other illnesses. By 1990, virtually all infants were being immunised against polio and measles, and medical auxiliaries carried preventative measures and basic healthcare to even the most remote areas.

Today there are few medical personnel outside the cities, with most villages and townships lacking both facilities for diagnosis and treatment and physicians and nurses. Most practitioners have a middle school education only, if that. Access to healthcare and immunisation is much less, TB is common[4] and the ability of the authorities to deal with major health risks such as SARS, HIV/AIDS or bird flu is in question. What has caused this change?

First, healthcare was originally provided via State work units, which no longer exist for any but a declining minority of the working population. Second, central subsidies have been reduced and the provincial and local authorities have chosen to invest in other ways. Sixty per cent of total public spending on healthcare is consumed by 15 per cent of the population, mainly the east coast cities.[5] Third, private health services are too expensive for most of the population. They are expensive because the government has not only obliged hospitals and medical personnel to earn their own income, but has also continued to enforce public sector staffing levels and to control prices for consultation, basic services and hospital beds, for which unrealistically low fees are charged, often well below the costs of provision. In order to raise enough income, health personnel therefore rely on sales of medicines and on operations, which are not only very expensive but also often prescribed unnecessarily.

The high price of medicines, the decline of standards enforcement and the lack of qualified personnel outside the cities has led to the production and sale of sub-standard or even counterfeit medicines. Hospitals are believed to countenance dubious practices in order to make money,[6] one of which is the subcontracting of STD clinics, notorious for overtreating, as money-making ventures.

The SARS epidemic in spring 2003 and the anger expressed around the world at China's dilatory admission of it, obliged the government to focus on the public health crisis and cooperate with the World Health Organization, United Nations and US agencies. The extent of the crisis was made apparent to the world only because of the courage and public-spiritedness of one physician, Jiang Yanyong, who knew from his day-to-day dealings with other hospital medics around the capital that the Minister of Health was lying when he went on television to deny that there were more than a few unrelated and imported cases of SARS. Dr Jiang promptly wrote a refutation of the Minister's statement, which was published by *Time*, causing the World Health Organization to raise with the Chinese government the discrepancies between the specialists' account and that of the Minister. Emboldened, other medics came forward to testify and to show how the real situation had deliberately been hidden from WHO inspectors. As soon as the PRC government was apprised, it sacked the Minister and set up an efficient system of monitoring and prevention.

Once the problem of SARS had been acknowledged, it was dealt with rapidly and efficiently. The government carried out an examination of its procedures in dealing with infectious diseases, promised no more media cover-ups and began to deal seriously with the problem of HIV/AIDS.

An authoritative report has described the HIV/AIDS situation as follows: 'China is on the verge of a catastrophe that could result in unimaginable human suffering, economic loss and social devastation. Indeed, we are now witnessing the unfolding of an HIV/AIDS epidemic of proportions beyond belief ...'[7] Since then, China has participated with the global fund to fight AIDS, TB and malaria, and established several organisations, including CHINACARES, to respond with treatment, education and services to dependents.

International NGOs have been welcomed, and the government has encouraged the formation of domestic equivalents such as the China Association of STD/AIDS Prevention and Control, implicit recognition of the need for **civil society** institutions in tackling the epidemic. Aware that its reporting systems are inadequate, it is attempting to improve data collection and remove the stigma that obliges people to hide the problem, and has set up parallel services in order to avoid the corrupted public health system. One indication that public acknowledgment and understanding of the problem is growing, such that cases of persecution like that of ten-year-old Li Ning should become fewer, is that the number of lawsuits taken out for healthcare malpractice by hospitals supplying contaminated blood has rocketed.[8]

The majority of the population is likely to be without health insurance, and because of its cost simply leave their illnesses untreated. Credibly, an American journalist noted that: 'Among those who did go to a hospital, nearly half discharged themselves against a doctor's advice because they could not afford continuing care.'[9] This is the case at a time when Chinese are beginning to suffer from the ailments that afflict rich Western countries, such as lack of exercise, air pollution and higher cholesterol intake. Heart disease is rapidly becoming a major cause of death. These changes and the ageing of the population make it clear that there is a growing market for healthcare and medical technology, but so far, few suppliers have set up since the population is not well off enough to afford them. This will change. Aware that it cannot afford a universal public health system, the government's policy is to try to ensure that people can afford to insure themselves, and to maximise the number of, and competition among, suppliers, so that quality is improved.

CHAPTER 33

Law

Arbitrary power always trumps law, but domestic and foreign pressures are helping those in China who are trying to change this.

A Chinese student of journalism in the UK not long ago made a TV feature about a curious Shanghai redevelopment project. A two-year-old block of flats had been scheduled for demolition on the grounds that its land was required for a public park. The proud owners of the very splendid modern apartments demonstrated, petitioned and used every connection they had, but to no avail. When the bulldozers were ready, the police simply manhandled out the last residents, who then watched the destruction of their homes and investments; among them were several judges. The developers were not interviewed in the feature. Why? 'I want to live', was the student's answer.

In a country where 'democratic centralism' has long been a euphemism for gangs of powerful people using their political muscle to seize what they want, such instances are common. However, there are systems which may in time control such behaviour, and some believe that they are beginning to do so; courageous lawyers are trying to make them work. In 1949, both traditional limitations on arbitrary power and the modern legal procedures introduced under the late empire and Republic were abolished, as China travelled the same road as the Bolsheviks and the Nazis. The Republic had legislated against torture and corporal punishment, but now China was kept under control with violence and caprice. Only in the 1980s did China start to rebuild its legal institutions, and there has been dramatic progress in institutional change as well as in popular understanding.

The organisation of the legal system mirrors the administrative.

At the highest level is the Supreme Court, at provincial level are the High Courts. Below these are Intermediate Courts and below them a variety of county, city and district courts. At the lowest level, labour camps have their own separate courts. There also exist autonomous national jurisdictions such as the Military Court System, Maritime Court System and Railway Transport Court System. In all such courts, the judges act in college; there are no juries.

Below the lowest rank of court are People's Tribunals, which handle minor civil disputes and criminal offences; where these involve trial, they go to the lowest level of court. Intermediate Courts are required to handle offences against national security, crimes that may incur life imprisonment or death, and crimes involving foreigners; they also deal with appeals against, and supervise, lower courts. High Courts handle complex cases, appeals and reviewing of death sentences in certain cases.

The Supreme Court consists of the three highest ranks of judges and has a president nominated by the Presidium of the National People's Congress (NPC) and elected by the NPC.

The Procurate is organised in a similar hierarchy. It not only receives cases referred by the public security offices but also initiates investigations, particularly in matters of public administration, and in effect also acts as inspector and supervisor of State functionaries in the area under its jurisdiction.

The description above is misleading if it is assumed that judicial power is separate from executive, legislative and Party power;[1] the judicial bodies are tangled up with the Public Security and State Security systems. For example, a prisoner can be sentenced for up to three years (extendable to ten years) simply by administrative order.[2] Because of this kind of procedure, Western observers sometimes assume that there really is no concept of the rule of law (as opposed to rule *by* law). But there have been many changes over the past twenty years, such that the legal system offers more hope for redress, both to Chinese and to foreigners engaged in business with China, and there are pressures on the Chinese establishment which are helping to push forward further improve-ment.[3] The government aims to ensure the primacy of law over administration, but this is not simple in a country with a long history of government in which Western concepts of the separation of administrative, legal and moral authority have had no place.

Foreign businesses in dispute with locals cannot be assured of a fair hearing, and dissidents or merely inquisitive journalists may be harassed, beaten, imprisoned or murdered. These are symp-toms of underlying failures, by international standards. The courts' powers to deal with official malfeasance are limited, as is their abil-ity to get judgements enforced, for they receive little or no help from **central government** in obliging local authorities to obey; both Party and State officials interfere with court deliberations. Criminal law is often overridden by political exigencies, as in anti-crime campaigns, when serious violations of rights may occur. It is often unclear as to what is or is not legal; when it is clear, the law is by no means supreme. Equality before the law is a chimera, and State and Party officials behave pretty much as they want. Foreigners note that there are many breaches of **intellectual property** rights, that both rules and policies are followed that are contrary to the obligations undertaken following international treaties, and that the courts can be unwilling to uphold the rights of foreigners.

Nevertheless, policy-makers appear to be in agreement on the changes that must be made, and officials and the media constantly emphasise the importance of a modern legal system for China's development. Accession to the WTO has given further impetus to the development of law in such areas as property rights (including intellectual property), equity, insolvency, company regulation and so forth, and the volume of litigation has increased as people have taken advantage of the possibility. A legal profession has emerged, is developing status and attracts young people both ambitious and idealistic, just at a time when a new consciousness of rights and expectations of government appears to be developing among the citizenry at large, promoted by the media and by newly-created

Legal Aid Centres. The national Constitution has been revised to strengthen private property rights and reassert the idea of equality before the law. Reforms in court procedures have improved the situation of the accused, and experiments are taking place, with single judges sometimes replacing the collegiate system (considered more open to Party caucus manipulation) and written judgements being instituted.

While corporate lawyers are optimistic, the experiences of some of China's new breed of rights lawyers are depressing. Gao Shisheng runs one of the best-known law firms, yet it was ordered to close on a technicality. In December 2005, his personal licence to practise was suspended. The real reason may have been that he was representing members of a Christian sect who sought to sue the police. But, as Gao says, 'you cannot become a rights lawyer in this country without becoming a rights case yourself',[4] and there are now many instances of lawyers having been harassed or imprisoned for taking on cases which encourage the idea that anyone, no matter how well connected, can be held accountable.

So, are the changes cosmetic or do they really mean that international legal norms are becoming accepted? On the one hand, both internal pressures – the views and interests of the developing middle class – and external pressures – the requirements of international treaties and global commerce – are pushing China towards adopting international standards. On the other hand, it is difficult to see how, as long as the Party claims the right to override all other interests, the expectations of China's litigants and lawyers can be realised.

CHAPTER 34

Human Rights

People are still subject to an approach to human beings learned from the Soviet Union in the 1930s by a Party which, in its pursuit of total power, abandoned all civilised values.

The police held back the crowd of roughs from *The Guardian*'s car while they checked the reporter's identity and that of his companion, peasant rights activist and provincial Deputy, Lu Banglie. They were in Taishi, Canton Province, not far from Hong Kong, on their way to discuss local elections. After the police evaporated, the Englishman, Benjamin Joffe-Walt, feared for their lives as Lu was dragged out of their car and savagely beaten. Walt lived to file.[1]

China is regularly portrayed in the Western media as a country in which rights expected elsewhere are given short shrift. The Chinese government resents this and claims it is exaggerated; or it characterises criticism as interference or as attempts to diminish or undermine China's political and economic advances. It has sometimes been argued that critics wish to impose foreign values, which are contrasted with Asian values.

The PRC is a one-party State in which executive, judiciary and trades unions are subject to Party dictates, and in which censorship is pervasive. In 2005, controls on journalists and on religion were revivified and people were imprisoned, often in degrading conditions, for offences which include accessing foreign websites, informing people abroad about regulations, advocating ethnic rights, being involved in worker protests or overstepping the line as a journalist.[2]

There have been improvements. In 2004, the Constitution was amended to recognise the expression 'human rights'; in 2005, regulations were promulgated to punish officials who take revenge on whistle-blowers or who fail to deal reasonably with petitioners.

From the 1980s, there have been many initiatives aimed at reforming the administration of public order, making it less arbitrary. But this is a society in which, for generations, cruelty and contempt for human life were deliberately fostered. As many reminiscences have eloquently reminded us, under Soviet instructions in the 1920s, the communists deliberately set out to be savage, to turn people against each other, to abolish all rules and inhibitions, and to harden their hearts against pity so that they would not blink as they saw their neighbours tortured to death before their eyes.[3] After the victory over the Nationalists in 1949, the wanton brutality got worse, with the slaughter of hundreds of thousands in campaigns against this or that category of people, the purposes of which were to terrify the remainder, to give employment to thugs and to create complicity in those who were incited to seize the property of the persecuted, or forced to witness their destruction. The most decent of instincts – empathy, altruism and charity – were made shameful, or dangerous.

It is not therefore very surprising, now that the Party is trying to re-establish the civilisation – attitudes and institutions – it destroyed in the period 1927–76, that it finds this difficult, not only because power, unchallenged and unaccountable, is still largely in the hands of a small ruling class, but particularly since many of its own personnel have been reared in a mind-set completely at odds with either traditional civilised virtues or modern sensibilities. How can such people have any care for the kind of human rights that brave farmer representatives deserve or idealists expect? What does it matter to them if the cities and villages that have survived communism's onslaught and still provide the ecology of decency, are available to be smashed to become mere real estate opportunities?[4] The **law** can protect only if there are people prepared to abide by it.

Public order is the responsibility of two ministries, the Ministry of State Security (MSS), which is the intelligence agency of the PRC, and the Ministry of Public Security (MPS). The latter is more akin to a Western ministry of internal affairs, dealing with day-to-day police work, while the MSS's main responsibilities are counter-espionage at home and intelligence-gathering abroad. One very particular function of the MPS is its responsibility for the Household Registration or *hukou* system, which determines where you are allowed to live.

What is often referred to as the Chinese concentration camp system, or *laogai*, in fact covers two types of incarceration, *laogai* and *laojiao*. *Laogai*, or 'remoulding through labour', is the harsher, and in principle reserved for enemies of the State and criminals, whereas *laojiao* (*laodong jiaoyang*) aims to provide 're-education through labour' for troublemakers.

Although in the 1980s *laojiao* sentences were restricted to three years (having previously been open-ended), sentencing remains arbitrary, the decision of a local police officer. Prisoners of both categories are often obliged, upon 'release', to settle in the vicinity of their camps, into a regime which may differ little from that within; however, the number and conditions of those in this situation (*jiuye*) have improved greatly since 1988.[5] The word *laogai* is no longer official, having been replaced by *jianyu* (prison) in 1994.

It is believed that there were about 2 million prisoners in the late 1990s, with only 10 per cent being politicals, compared with 4–6 million in the early 1950s, of whom 90 per cent were politicals.[6] It is possible that since the repression of the Falungong (see **Religion**), these numbers may need to be revised.

A historian of the *laogai* system[7] has wryly suggested that the CCP put fewer people in camps than Soviet Russia only because its oppression of the population at large was more extensive and brutal. In 1949, the CCP, which had controlled only limited areas of China before, extended methods of oppression learned from Russian advisers to the whole country.[8] Socialism provided the pretext for throwing out all laws and restraints as 'bourgeois'. Once the CCP got power in an area, it behaved exactly as its counterparts did in other socialist countries such as Poland, Albania,

Bulgaria or Hungary – and eliminated anyone who might form the bases of opposition. The CCP categorised people according to arbitrarily awarded class origins – excepting its own leadership, most of whom were from affluent families – and in that category you and your descendants would stay in perpetuity. During all subsequent campaigns, anybody left from the undesirable categories would be brought out for public vilification, torture and assault, including the very old and the children. The idea of equality before the law was anathematised.[9] The same 'crime' might be punished with execution for the offspring of a farmer hiring labour, but with 'merely' hard labour for the hired hand.[10]

Today the terror campaigns and the categories have gone, but the *laogai* system remains. Its distinguishing characteristics have been: (1) the ease with which you can be admitted and your term extended indefinitely, by mere administrative order or judicial process that is in fact controlled by the Party; (2) thought-reform techniques intended to abolish the personality of the prisoner; (3) the mixing together of criminals with, say, religious or bourgeois or dissident inmates; (4) unrewarded forced labour; (5) starvation; (6) torture; (7) the isolation of the camps from society as a whole, made possible by geography.

Once Deng Xiaoping came to power, hundreds of thousands of innocents were freed, and conditions in the camps are believed to have improved. Yet many people who would not be considered criminals elsewhere have continued to be imprisoned.

In its international dealings, the PRC has regularly sought to impede the investigation of human rights in other countries, for example Sudan, Burma, Korea and Uzbekistan, and is working to suppress the issue generally. One fruit of recent cooperation with Russia has been that Russia helped China ensure that 'discussion of human rights policies was not placed on the agenda of the human rights conference held in Geneva in the middle of [2005]'.[11] Nevertheless, and despite obstruction, human rights projects are growing in number in China, and the objectives of activists are understood widely. Heroic individuals in China, and campaigners in Hong Kong, Taiwan and abroad, prove that it is not merely foreigners who regard these questions as important.[12] By contrast with communism, Confucianism regards people as precious, and those mistaken are to be remonstrated with rather than treated as misshapen objects. Moral suasion rather than cruel repression is the Chinese traditional ideal.

CHAPTER 35

Civil Society

Enterprise is not restricted to making money: modern Chinese are well into the business of remaking society. An indication of that is the growth in the number of non-official organisations bringing together people of common interests and intentions. China is fast becoming a more plural society, though it is not necessarily sensible to draw conclusions about the political implications of this.

In recent years there has been debate in England as to the extent to which ordinary people's part in running society has been weakened, first by the State taking over more and more areas of life, propelled by politicians' promises to electors and their urge to control, and second by the advance of 'professionalism' or the claims by certain interests that they alone are qualified for jurisdiction.[1] China's situation is different in that, by 1978, the country had been cleansed of any organisation not directly part of the State.

Many of the institutions and practices taken for granted in Anglosphere societies – schools, hospitals, insurance and savings arrangements, concert and meeting halls, to name just a few – were originally local not-for-profit initiatives, only lately taken over by the State or commercialised. Some of these initiatives, and accumulations of them, have long been strong enough to challenge and mitigate State power. In fact, modern capitalism probably first developed in England, at least in part, on account of a cultural disposition of the English to be enterprising, and not just in making money. The equivalent institutions in continental Europe originated later, and top-down.

In China before 1949, there was a very large number of quasi-autonomous bodies carrying out the same kind of functions, though rarely influential beyond their immediate localities; in fact,

Chinese were as famous as the English for their 'voluntarism'. As in communist Eastern Europe, they were destroyed or else mopped up by 'mass organisations' such as the All China Federation of Trades Unions, the All China Women's Federation or the Youth League. Today, the Europeans are consciously trying to rebuild the civil society of intermediate bodies, thinking of them as essential to the distribution of power – businesses as well as voluntary organisations which stand between individual and State – but in China the reasoning is slightly different. The government is permitting the development of associations attempting to perform functions similar to their counterparts elsewhere, on the grounds that – as society has become more complex and as the interests and needs of a greater diversity of people need to be considered – government just cannot, on its own, monitor compliance with regulations. It needs allies if it wants policy implemented and if it wants some independent evaluation of it.

According to the Ministry of Civil Affairs,[2] clan associations, temple committees, benefit and charitable operations are being set up and may now number over a million; there are 133,000 registered bodies collectively referred to as 'social organisations', 'non-profit organisations' or 'the third sector', and 1,268 foundations.

In the Anglosphere, out of the voluntary sector came non-governmental organisations (NGOs), in effect lobbying, campaigning and sometimes executive bodies which oversee government and powerful corporations and try to hold them to account or provide what they cannot or will not provide, in areas as diverse as juvenile justice, conservation, cancer research and the rights of small business. Hindering an exact replica of this in China are the facts that so many Chinese voluntary bodies were by tradition based in lineage and locality rather than in wider concerns; the lack of a political opposition to champion contrary interpretations of events and activities; and the unwillingness of some powerful people to accept that they may be accountable. Nevertheless, associations now exist which represent constituencies as varied as artists, *qigong* practitioners, musical societies, lawyers and anti-tax groups.[3]

Legally, all such bodies are required to register with their local Civil Affairs Office and to have a sponsoring body ('mother-in-law') to supervise them. In practice, activists note that the laws are not enforced, and they classify organisations as either Government Organised (GONGOs), or properly registered bodies, and a much larger number of NGOs, which are citizen-launched and unregistered.[4] They are concerned with the environment, health issues, education, scientific research, cultural services, poverty relief, legal aid, social welfare and the provision of services to the disadvantaged. One notable omission is workers' rights; a small number of groups have got together to demand better working conditions and for the redress of specific grievances, but when they appear to be nascent trades unions, such initiatives are immediately dealt with.[5] World Bank funding has enabled the Ministry of Civil Affairs to study NGOs in other countries, the laws and fiduciary regulations related to them, and to create a best-practice handbook. World Bank small grants and international companies such as Hewlett Packard have given NGOs the wherewithal to provide access to support and data, set up forums, publish newsletters, hold workshops and provide training in areas such as disability, drug control, HIV/AIDS, water usage, unemployment counselling, and services to disadvantaged groups. Project Hope and Spring Buds are indigenous initiatives to help poor children go to school; World Vision, an international charity, is active in China with similar aims.

In the matter of HIV/AIDS, the government has been keen to set up GONGOs to be active in ways that could not be countenanced by government departments themselves. These include the Chinese Association of STD/AIDS Prevention and Control, the China Preventive Medicine Association, the China AIDS Network and the Institute for Gender Research. International NGOs have been permitted to get involved in HIV/AIDS-related activities, for example the Ford Foundation, Save the Children UK, the Australian Red Cross, Marie Stopes International, Médecins Sans Frontières, the Salvation Army, Oxfam-HK, and others.[6]

The biggest single interest represented by NGOs is the **environment**, reflecting concern at the surrounding degradation, the government's commitment to raising awareness of the environmental limitations to improved development, and health and overseas interest. The capital is home to, among others, Global Village of Beijing (GVB), China Environmental Culture Promotion Association, World Wide Fund for Nature (China), China Association for NGO Cooperation (CANGO), Friends of Nature, the Institute of Environment and Development, Green Earth Volunteers, Friends of the Earth (HK) and Conservation International. Local operations specific to local problems of pollution, wildlife management, energy-saving and water conditions have been set up, and some, like conservation activists attempting to save architecture from the developers, have fought campaigns in the courts and media.

Others have carried out surveys of conditions, questioned the value of (e.g. dam-) building projects, formed residents' environment committees to raise awareness, and set about encouraging communities to recover discarded traditional knowledge and beliefs about conservation and energy-saving. Major propaganda achievements have included a ruling on the conservation of the Round Bright Garden Lake, near the capital, where financial interests were pitted against cultural and ecological ones, persuading the Standing Committee of the NPC to introduce energy-saving measures into the management of the Great Hall of the People (Parliament), influencing Shanghai municipality to project a Green City for the forthcoming development of a Shanghai borough, and stopping work on the Angry River Dam Project. These and other activities have increased public awareness and public participation.

The 'third sector', as it is sometimes called, may still be weak and, to extend its influence and reach, needs the protection of **law** and of those in authority who will implement the law. Yet the very

189

gusto with which the third sector is establishing itself is a tribute as much to the foresight of the often maligned leadership as to the altruism and energy of the social entrepreneurs.

CHAPTER 36

Welfare

The lack of a social security system threatens stability yet, with such an enormous population, widespread poverty, an expensive public sector pension scheme, an uncooperative private sector and a growing proportion of non-earners in the workforce, China has a problem to solve that dwarfs the pension crises of other countries. And its population may become dependent before the country becomes rich, threatening everything for which it is now striving.

Recently there was a programme on Chinese TV about people who used to manage State enterprises. A former factory manager was assembling plastic Christmas lights. Her husband, the former General Manager, was running a food-stall. They had never received the stipulated compensation for the loss of jobs, homes, health services, schooling and peace of mind. Not long ago, I took a pedicab whose driver told me that a flood had submerged his home and land; he had tried to make a living nearby from breeding eels but that had failed, so he had moved to the town where a cousin had set him up with a bicycle, which he adapted into a taxi. He had had government handouts for two months after the flood, but was now on his own. He remits most of his earnings back to his wife and two children.

Social security under socialism was provided by the work unit. When first I stayed on a Chinese campus, I was surprised to see many elderly people, until I realised that they were retired lecturers, doorkeepers, cleaners or whatever, who had lived there ever since taking up their first post, and would certainly end their days there. So it was with factories and ministries and rural communes every-where. As long as you had an official job, you shared in the com-monwealth of poverty and security.

But then came reform. Hundreds of State enterprises have been privatised or broken up or allowed to go bankrupt. In some cases the local authority has negotiated a saviour, as in the famous case of Wahaha, a drinks company which had already proved its patriotism first by launching a range of healthy drinks to compete with the transnational companies' carbonated and sugar-loaded cans, then by agreeing to establish factories which would absorb some of those rendered unemployed by the **Three Gorges** project. Its final big act of social responsibility was to agree, reluctantly, to take over a huge and thoroughly overmanned manufacturing complex in Hangzhou, which it proceeded to incorporate into the Wahaha empire and to ensure it made profits without shedding staff.[1] It was therefore able to continue providing benefits.

But Wahaha is probably unusual. In effect, China has needed to design a social security and pension system from scratch, and to try to ensure that it can both afford it and operate it. The difficulties are compounded by the poverty of the workforce, with no surplus to invest in insurance schemes, by its mobility, and by the fact that small and ephemeral companies provide so many of the jobs. From a 'unit person' the Chinese worker is being transformed into an 'individual'.[2]

In 2004, the government issued a Social Security White Paper, which both summarised progress to date and set out new aims in developing insurance programmes for old age, unemployment, medical care, workers' compensation, maternity care, social welfare, special relief, housing security and social security in rural areas. The biggest issue is pensions because, thanks to the dramatic fertility decline, the population is ageing so fast. The proportion 60 or over increased from 7 per cent in 1953 to 10 per cent in 2000, and will be 27 per cent in 2050.[3] To put it another way, today there are six workers to every retired person; by 2030 there will be two.[4] The main sources of the policy-makers' troubles, apart from the fertility decline, are improved life expectancy, the One Child Policy and the socialist welfare system, which has collapsed for most, but which featherbeds some.

There are about 11 million retirees from public institutions draw-ing generous socialist-era pensions of about 80 per cent of final salary, plus benefits. The government hopes to reform this, as its implicit pension debt – the amounts it may be expected to pay out if it does not reform the public sector schemes – is unsupportable. It wants to replace these with a new scheme that it has first promoted for the employees of urban enterprises.

The 'social-pool-plus-personal-accounts scheme' was introduced in 1997. The old-age pension consists of a base pension (about 20 per cent of average monthly wage, adjusted for cost of living) and a pension from a personal account, which has been accumulated through monthly contributions. In 2003, there were 155 million par-ticipants, of whom about 40 million were self-employed. There is a number of pilot projects being undertaken in several localities – the pensions are administered locally and vary according to local con-ditions – to try to improve the operations of personal accounts, which at present involve such substantial contributions from employers as to put off many of them. In order to try to keep down the level of contribution required, the government is earmarking subsidies and establishing a National Social Security Fund, oper-ated on market principles as a financial reserve for social security programmes.

In the past, enterprise administered and delivered pensions, but the government is trying to ensure that these tasks are performed by professional social service institutions with computer-based net-working of social security information, so as to serve ever-more mobile workers.

Rather similar systems are being set up to cover other security needs. By the end of 2003, there were 104 million participants in the unemployment insurance scheme, which is now compulsory for urban employers and employees and appears so far mainly to be for ex-employees of State Owned Enterprises (SOEs). Shortfalls are made up by local government. This is part of the 'Three Guarantees System' that provides a basic livelihood guarantee to laid-off persons from SOEs, an unemployment insurance guarantee and a minimum living standard guarantee for urban residents.

A re-employment service has been set up both to help registered people find and equip themselves for new jobs, and to pay medical and other benefits. Insurance for work-related injuries and maternity insurance programmes have also been introduced.

With the public **health** service parlous, an attempt has been made from 1998 to establish a basic medical insurance system for urban employees. This encompassed some 109 million people by late 2003. Again, the funds come from premiums paid by both employers (about 6 per cent) and employees (2 per cent). The individual's premiums and 30 per cent of employer premiums go to the personal accounts, and the remaining 70 per cent of the employer premiums go to the social pool programme funds.

Welfare services for the elderly, orphans and the disabled are being set up.[5] To date, there are 38,000 social welfare organisations of various kinds for elderly people, with 1.1 million beds, or 8.4 beds for every 1,000 people over the age of 60. By 2004, there were 32,000 Starlight Homes for the elderly. There are nearly 800 welfare institutions accommodating 54,000 orphans and disabled children. There are also nearly 10,000 community services for orphans and disabled people, such as rehabilitation centres and training classes for mentally retarded children, and since 2004, a major programme, in addition to existing services for the 30 million disabled, has been undertaken. The 'Tomorrow Plan' is to provide operations and rehabilitation services for 10,000 disabled orphans over three years.

Other introductions have included systems of Natural Disaster Relief, Relief for Urban Vagrants and Beggars, the System of Publicly Accumulated Housing Funds to contribute to home-building for people whose work units would in the past have provided housing, and the Low-Rent Housing System for low-income families.

Seventy per cent of the elderly live in the countryside, so comparable schemes in **rural China** are being tried, since the government acknowledges that families cannot always carry all the burden, especially now that people are living so much longer. Fifty-four million people had signed up to the old-age insurance programme by late 2003, and nearly 2 million farmers were drawing pensions. One way of giving security would be to confirm land rights so that they could be sold or used as collateral, but this is not yet under consideration. In 2002, a New Rural Cooperative Medical Service System, by which local and central government and members contribute, was introduced experimentally. There is also a Minimal Subsistence and Medical Relief for the destitute.

This is a sketch of the welfare system as it is being developed. Foreign observers are concerned that there are few incentives for the private sector to participate, that there is much non-compliance already and that there are fundamental weaknesses that must be resolved. One is the lack of well-defined property rights to pensions; another is the absence of actuarial and other necessary skills to provide professional competence; and another is that investment decisions on pension funds are political. They see both community-based schemes and the very active private health and life insurance companies as offering more trustworthy solutions.[6] When the British Welfare State was introduced, it was in many ways simply an amplification, generalisation and systemisation of an existing array of voluntary institutions and networks of support that were well established, with their procedures, professionalism and public service ethos. What is being attempted in China is the creation of a social security system in a country with nearly 30 times the population of Britain, mostly much poorer than were the British then, and without any institutions upon which to build. This is awesome.

CHAPTER 37

Intellectuals

Intellectuals are now rarely persecuted; their interesting ideas are often co-opted, at least tolerated and may influence the governing class; any challenge to order comes no longer from them but from the poor.

From the international media you can get the impression that a few brave dissidents represent all that is left of China's conscience. In fact, there is a ferment of ideas in many of the thousands of newspapers and magazines. Journals such as *Law and Democracy* advocate transparency and rights, newspapers such as *Southern Weekend* publish investigations of abuse, and intellectual organs such as *Reading* and *Public Weal* call for liberalism and democracy. The intellectuals who are most active with these theses, issues and debates have a wide variety of perspectives, from New Left and Neo-Marxist to Liberal, Neo-Conservative or Traditional Conservative. The matters of interest include: globalisation and whether it is to be welcomed or not; the idea of American scholar Samuel Huntington that a clash of civilisations is inevitable, and the contrasting Fukuyama thesis that every nation will become like the USA; and whether China should modernise according to a Western model, buy in to universal values (even if they are really American), accept the international treaty and trading system and swallow the Anglophone doctrine of humanitarian intervention. The survival of traditional culture and the place of law and human rights in China's development are also much debated.[1]

For Chinese intellectuals take themselves seriously and are convinced of the value of their role in assisting China's rise; they are committed, whether they work in universities, the culture industries more generally, or the think-tanks and NGOs which have been springing up. There is a particularly Chinese aspect to this class, much despised under Mao, and that something has persisted despite the great changes since 1992.

The Imperial examination system tested applicants on their knowledge of, and ability to reproduce, classical literature. Those who ran China until recent times were experts in the humanities who considered themselves responsible for the maintenance of the State and the transmission of culture. Even before the collapse of the examination system, in the late 19th century when it had become clear that China needed to adapt if it were to resist the threat from abroad, young men from the kind of families that in the past had expected their sons to become officials, plus some from the newly successful trading families who had travelled abroad, were updating that sense of common purpose into a determination to use modern methods to save China. They were, in the much-to-be-used phrase of a 19th-century translator of Western philosophy, Yan Fu, 'in search of wealth and power'. For them, personal enrichment would not be an aim until the 1990s.

By 'intellectuals' here we mean those, usually with higher education, who make it their business to concern themselves with patriotic and public issues. In the first quarter of the 20th century they were very varied. One gave up a civil service career for journalism in order to mobilise opinion; another gave up medicine for literature, to hold up a mirror to his compatriots. Others translated Western books unendingly, set up lobbying organisations for reform of every institution from the courts to the written language, or sought examples of renovation in the then recent Italian movement for liberation and unification, and later in the inspiration of the Russian Revolution.

They were influential, partly because of their ability to mobilise public sympathy on account of their youth and patriotism, partly because of their class connections, partly because of their knowledge of the world and communication skills relative to the officials. They denounced, demanded, demonstrated. The most famous of all the great demonstrations has become iconic, symbolic of the urge by the intellectual to eradicate, or at least utterly transform, traditional Chinese society. On 4 May 1919, demonstrations forced the government not to sign the Versailles Peace Treaty, on the very true grounds that it did not take into account Chinese grievances or treat China as the ally it had been. May 4th radicalised the intellectuals, and many others. After it, language reform took off and in a few years the vernacular was the main medium of writing, rendering the literary language as current as Latin in Europe. For the opinion-formers, Confucianism was rejected in favour of 'science and democracy', themselves soon to be dethroned in favour of 'socialism' as the answer to China's ills.

A tendency to idealism was the intellectuals' undoing. In the turmoil of the 1920s, more and more were persuaded to sympathise with, if not actually join, the Communist Party. It promised a heavenly future of unity and equality in a country which the Nationalist heirs to the first revolutionaries were struggling to pull together with myriad messy compromises, a country pulled apart by factions, foreign interests and regional disparities. Those who made the journey into the Communist base of Yanan in the 1940s summarily came to realise that they were the slaves of the capricious leadership, and useful only in performing propaganda functions.[2] But most did not, and found out only in the 1950s.

The odd thing about Chinese intellectuals is how long it took them to realise that the kind of contract with their country that they had enjoyed before 1949 – by which they, as heirs of the ruling elite, continued to speak for and seek the good of Chinese civilisation – had been spurned by Mao. Either because Mao was not omnipotent, initially, or because he had not yet come to the conclusion that he could do without them, intellectuals fared well in the early years, as long as they declared loyalty. The Soviet system of ranks and safe jobs allowed many to lord it over the people in ways at least as hierarchical as in Imperial China. There were academies to staff, universities and the culture industries generally to reorganise for New China. Not until the failure of the Great Leap Forward had become clear did many of them start offering their advice with any courage, only to be chopped down in the infamous Hundred Flowers affair (see Glossary). The Cultural Revolution was directed in great measure at the educated, the erudite and the exceptional, and the intellectuals suffered terribly; they were cruelly re-educated where not murdered or dispossessed.

After the death of Mao, they re-emerged – as dissidents. In 1978 and again in the 1980s, intellectuals, frustrated at the slow pace of change, took up their pens and took to the streets. They were knocked down. In the 1990s, reforms in **science**, the **media** and the **economy** removed security of tenure from most of those not established in universities and academies, and forced many to compete in the market – as popular writers, producers or think-tank operatives, or simply hassling for whatever work was available to people with ideas and word-processors. They had to adapt. Literary novels were less likely to sell than popular handbooks or steamy and seamy stories; copywriting was more welcome than poetry. Where they were not dependent upon the market, they could still be patronised as consultants and policy advisers by Party and State bodies. Seeing these new types of intellectual develop, the university originals sought to distinguish themselves as scholars (*xuezhe*), as opposed to intellectuals more generally (*zhishi fenzi*). Yet in some senses they are all still part of the power elite. The gulf between their income and contacts, and those of the bulk of society, is huge; they tend to despise the poor, and are also scared of unleashing the kind of destructive passions witnessed in the Cultural Revolution. They cannot imagine that democracy will lead to more than violence. Often isolated from the concerns of their fellow countrymen, as they are from their conditions, they also have a missionary self-image both to 'save' the nation and to serve the State with advice and admonition.

The 1994 publication *Looking at China Through a Third Eye*, by Wang Shan, vilified the Tiananmen protestors as having been manipulated by the USA, but was remarkable because it went further than any previous book in questioning international, as opposed to merely domestic, policy in public. This has since become commonplace, with such works as *China's Road Under the Shadow of Globalisation* by Wang Xiaodong criticising 'unrelentingly' those who are perceived as selling out to the West,[3] and *The Pitfalls of Modernisation* by He Qinglian making sharp criticisms of policies.[4] *The Pitfalls* argues that China has failed to get to grips with reforms which are fundamental if the country is to compete in the modern world. To back this up, the book exposes the theft of State assets, manipulation of prices and graft, and it did get its author into trouble.

From time to time today, intellectuals cross the boundaries or irritate powerful politicians; they go to jail or lose their careers. But on the whole, the government lets them talk and argue, knowing that calls for full legalisation of private property, more distance between Party and business, greater market freedom and some democracy too, are far less dangerous to stability than the battles being waged by peasants, migrant workers and religious disciples. Thus, while a few intellectuals have been castigated as dissidents, more have either gone into commerce or morphed into 'policy wonks'.

CHAPTER 38

Universities

China's higher education system is so huge that, despite problems, it has the potential to dwarf the rest and to compete fiercely against those Western universities which now think they have the market sewn up.

In recent years, British universities, like their counterparts in many other countries, have congratulated themselves upon the large numbers of Chinese who have chosen to study in the UK.[1] They have been welcomed for subsidising the uneconomic fees paid by UK students, and have become necessary to the survival of some departments and courses. Chinese families are famously prepared to pay fabulous sums to prepare their children for glorious futures, and many Chinese institutions have paid for others.

The reasons why they choose the UK are various, but one important reason – the lack of appropriate courses at home – is fast becoming obsolete as Chinese higher education develops. The traditional elite universities have taken stock of international examples, welcomed new staff out of foreign postgraduate training, recruited foreign lecturers, started to reform teaching and curricula and developed new courses.

They started almost from zero. Because the cultural revolutionaries despised learning, all schools and universities were closed 1966–68. When they re-opened, only those from poor backgrounds and with the right political credentials could get in. Once Mao's heirs had been seen off, reform could start, but even then it took careful introducing, in phases. In the early 1980s, academics were rehabilitated, foreign staff brought in to introduce them to modernity, and tens of thousands of students sent abroad. In phase two, from 1985 to 2000, the government addressed other problems by decentralising, giving the regions and localities the responsibility for education, and by depoliticising education, telling the CCP committees to confine themselves to narrow tasks, and by giving academic bodies power over their own affairs. It also exhorted local educational authorities to partner industry and create vocational and technical skill courses at every level.

Pushing vocational training was partly an answer to a skills shortage, partly a policy to prevent over-academicisation, and partly because the government realised that it cannot supply enough places for all those who want to attend higher education. It has encouraged some 1,300 private universities to be established, usually with flexible, practical and very work-orientated courses and modules. Fees are high by Chinese standards, but the subjects of study, the teaching and learning techniques and the emphasis on contact with employers through work placements and in curriculum design all make them a good career investment.

Conventional State universities, numbering about 1,800, include both general ones covering most subjects and subject-specific ones, such as China University of Communications (formerly the Beijing Broadcasting Academy) or Beijing Sports University. 'Normal' (*shifan*) universities provide teacher training. Fees are now payable in the State universities, with a scholarship and loans programme for poorer students.[2]

In 1997, 'Project 211' was launched to ensure that key branches of learning were adequately resourced and that resources were not frittered on non-performers. A hundred elite institutions were identified, into which the government pours money for research; they include those that were seeking to emulate Harvard, Yale and Oxbridge until 1949. Today, these universities, such as Tsinghua, Peking and Fudan, are ambitious to be world leaders in scholarship and are also fired with enterprise: they are using their estate holdings as collateral in establishing money-making ventures such as science parks and business services, whose profits support further research and innovations. Examples include Tsinghua University's Ziguang Corporation, Xian Jiaotong University's Kaiyuan Corporation and Peking University's Founder Corporation. Moreover, like the science academies and other State institutions, the universities are often incubating enterprise, particularly in bio-engineering, information and digital technology applications.

Far from allowing the elite institutions to cut back on science and technology courses, as has happened in the UK, the government has insisted on their primacy. The number of science and engineering PhDs doubled between 1996 and 2001,[3] although higher degrees may be offered by only a small minority of institutions, lest too many become too theoretical.

Traditional pedagogy, with the emphasis on fact learning, dreary lectures and the passing of tests, still exists in the State institutions, but the private operations, 'unencumbered by tradition … mandated state curriculum plans or tenured dead wood', are thoroughly practical.[4] There is little quality control such as was introduced in the UK in the 1990s.

Higher education is essentially about the needs of the national economy and fitting people for jobs, rather than personal development, and the tiny proportion of the population who get into the State institutions will mostly take up posts in the professions and civil service; the emphasis on conformity, moral behaviour and relationships makes the experience distinctly Chinese. Students live in dormitories, sharing rooms, and undertake military-style drill at prescribed times, usually in attractive, spacious campuses with good restaurants. Particularly in the social sciences and humanities, academic work is strongly influenced by politics, and scholarship is not noted for objectivity or empiricism.[5] On the other hand, the increasing commercialisation of society generally has affected these institutions too, and there are many partnerships with industry, consultancy projects and academic moonlighting.

While the number of foreign students in China is still small, the biggest single group being Koreans, the fact that universities are both increasing the number and quality of preparatory Chinese-language programmes and introducing courses taught in English, means that this will change. Elite individuals and cadets of multi-nationals such as IBM and Volkswagen now attend business schools in China; formerly they would have chosen Harvard. Governments are following suit. The Singapore government, long an important customer of top UK universities, now funds as many students in China as in the UK.

Foreign corporate investors in higher education have been welcomed: the China Europe Business School is funded by, among others, Philips, Bayer, Alcatel, Colgate, AXA and LVMH. Some foreign institutions are establishing campuses in China, notably Nottingham University at Ningbo and Liverpool University at Suzhou.

China presents three challenges to higher education elsewhere. First, the challenge of upgrading. China will not for long be a source of overseas students if its own universities continue to improve in the range and organisation of, and facilities for, what they offer. Second, since Chinese higher education intends to offer its services in the world education market; existing market leaders may need thoroughly to rethink, to take account of what China can offer.

The third challenge is of product. In China, there are around 23 million[6] students in higher education. There are plans for 25 per cent of secondary school leavers to be in higher education by 2010, and 40 per cent by 2020. If even a small proportion of these have first-rate education and can use English, they will compete with Western graduates in virtually every field, unless, again, European and American institutions can provide something very special. In the USA, 38 per cent of the nation's scientists and engineers with doctorates were born outside the country. And of the PhDs in science and engineering awarded to foreign students in the USA from 1985 to 2000, more than half went to students from China, India, South Korea and Taiwan, and a third of high-tech start-ups are by people with Asian passports.[7] In other words, Western universities may suddenly find that they have transferred abroad the motor of their economies.[8]

CHAPTER 39

Schooling

If there is one enterprise in which China is most likely to outstrip the rest of the world once it has the resources, it will surely be education.

'In what land but China would it be possible to find examples of grandfather, son and grandson all competing in the same examination for the same degree, age and indomitable perseverance being rewarded at the age of eighty years by the long-coveted honour?' The incredulity of the 19th-century Englishman,[1] commenting on the Imperial examination system, refers to an attitude to learning that has remained constant, even while the system and content is unrecognisable. There are probably still boys who tie their books to the horns of the ox with which they are ploughing, and there may too be girls who study by the light of the glow-worm.

Not only has formal education existed in China longer than anywhere else, but so has the respect for scholarship, for education as means of advancement, and for examinations as criteria of merit. A fisherman described his three children to me: 'The clever one is a lecturer in philosophy; the daughter is a doctor; the numbskull became a businessman. Fortunately, the numbskull now owns a lot of factories, so he paid for the doctor's education and still supports the lecturer.'

So even today, when the routes to success are many and often do not require certificates, the status of scholarship is high. In the information economy this matters. Since the mid-1990s, Chinese **universities** and research centres have been developing very fast and will soon be challenging the best in the world, both in the quality of their research and in their attractions for foreign students. Such a challenge would be impossible without the basis of attitudes and behaviour evident in the school system.[2]

Schooling is compulsory for nine years: six years in Primary (ages 6–12) and three years in Junior Middle School (JMS, ages 13–15). Nearly 90 per cent receive primary schooling, 65 per cent middle schooling.[3] There are six channels, each of which will have both a State and private provision, and each of which has, or is developing, a distance-learning dimension. Comprehensive schooling is essentially academic, though these schools may, particularly in cities, have specialities. The subjects emphasised at Primary are arithmetic and Chinese with romanisation (i.e. children learn how to use the Western alphabet applied to their own language), and those at JMS are arithmetic, Chinese, English, Physics and Chemistry. At the end of JMS there is an examination called *Zhongkao*, which decides whether you can move on to Senior Middle School (SMS) or whether your formal school education ends. Those who fail to move on will either choose a vocational school or start work with the possibility of participating in adult education later.

Graduation from SMS may mean, for the most competent at academic examinations, university, depending upon performance in the national exam, *Gaokao*. It may also mean transferring across to one of the other channels for further or higher study. The system is flexible in that it is quite possible to transfer between the comprehensive and the other channels: Vocational, Technical, Rural Vocational, Adult (usually older people) and Normal (teacher training).

The non-compulsory elements, kindergarten before or SMS after, must now be paid for, with varying levels of contribution. In principle, the compulsory nine years' schooling is free; however, some poor families cannot send their children to school because they cannot afford books or clothes, or because the children are essential breadwinners. Although it is illegal to charge, it is increasingly common for schools to devise ways of demanding contributions, and the desperate parents pay them if they can. To help those who cannot, various charitable foundations have been set up, energetically promoted both by the government and by foreign foundations. Free schooling may be coming to an end.

Chinese schools are thought of abroad as practising only rote learning.[4] True, until recently they were geared mainly towards getting students up the ladder, providing an 'exam-oriented' education. Since 2000, the Ministry of Education has been changing the curricula away from mere subject study to education to promote thinking ability, creativity, initiative and problem-solving. This is particularly so for 'Key Schools'. Extra-curricular activities after school or at weekends are increasingly many and varied, perhaps including music, martial arts, painting, modelling, dance, writing, sports, IT and so forth. City schools can be very well equipped with IT and science equipment, while rural ones have nothing. School facilities vary greatly, as do conditions for teachers.

At both Primary and Middle levels, about 15 per cent of schools are designated as 'Key Schools' because of their academic emphases and their facilities. Entrance is competitive at ages 6 and 15. At Key JMSs, pupils are grouped either in humanities or in science pathways, with curricula determined by the university entrance examination which emphasises Chinese, English, Mathematics and an optional subject. Key Middle Schools may also contain fast streams for those sufficiently academic to be able to foreshorten their schooling by two years. Once in a Key School, it is rare that pupils do not continue along the Key track and get into university.

In general, the Chinese provide schooling that, though now allowing more initiative and self-development than before, is more disciplined and focused than Anglophone schooling. The State school systems of the USA and the UK have similar problems of low expectations among the majority, as compared to those for a small elite. So alarmed are US educators at the superiority of Chinese schooling – in science and mathematics certainly, and to an extent in all other subjects – that some have begun to adopt Chinese course books and teaching methods. Over 200 US secondary schools are reported to have now replaced their own curricula with Chinese ones.[5]

In the early 1980s, it was realised that there was a shortage of primary technicians, supervisory personnel and skilled workers in both urban and rural areas, and that far too many secondary school graduates aimed for universities. There was a risk of having an excess of graduates with insufficient jobs, and qualifications inappropriate to industry and commerce. By 1998, this situation had been rectified. Vocational training is now rated highly, to the extent that 55 per cent of secondary school pupils are in *vocational* secondary schools. All education is shifting its objectives from meal-ticket provision to lifelong skill-learning, and so the status of vocational, or professional, schooling has risen. It is the experience of Germany and France that is seen as a useful exemplar for vocational training, rather than that of the Anglosphere.

For those in work, or who have missed out on education for some reason, there are both the extensive Adult Education system – at all levels – and many distance-learning bodies. There are now 29 radio and TV universities, with 600 branch colleges; Hunan University set up the first internet university in 1997, but by the following year, five other national institutions had established e-universities, several interactive. The government is investing in R&D aimed at upgrading, speeding up transmission, integrating with satellite and making other improvements, and has authorised over 30 institutions to comprise the Multiform Education System, of which around 14 million students now take advantage.

Pre-school provision varies. In the countryside, most children are looked after by parents and grandparents, whereas in the cities, with parents blissfully unaware of Western research – which points to the inadequacies of pre-school provision and shows the importance to young children's development of spending as much time as possible in the family – there has developed a tendency to put children into pre-schools ever younger and for ever longer. Some even board. Most kindergartens are now private enterprises.

Where new schools are to be established, the funding may come in a variety of forms; not being State-funded, they are termed *minban* or 'people-run'. Associations may receive government aid to set up schools, raise equity investment and charge newly-enrolled students substantial deposits. About 7 million pupils were enrolled in *minban* schools in 2000.

Registered teachers – *minban* teachers are not always regis-tered – are trained in State-controlled Normal Colleges. Although they have lost tenure and are now employed under contract, they can benefit from better training and incentive systems. Schools run business enterprises and undertake work-study programmes in order to make up for funding shortfalls.

A tradition of education which has survived the revolution, science parks for children, wide deployment of new technology, disciplined schooling with clear narrative, and parents who believe that education provides advancement through merit, all combine to create a climate in which learning is valued and those who transmit learning are respected.

CHAPTER 40

Rural China/Urban China

The government is determined to close the gap between the city and the country, mainly through urbanisation. Cities provide opportunities that the country areas cannot. But urbanisation has to be managed carefully if the risks are not to outweigh the rewards.

At every city railway station, you will see hundreds if not thousands of patient men and women, shabby and weather-beaten, waiting for the gangers to choose them. All around the city, their cousins squat on the pavements, selling a chick or a few persimmons, until the police shove them away. Outside many television stations and newspaper offices are similarly humble petitioners, prostrating, kneeling, begging the slick reporters and cool presenters to take up their cases. This is the China of the hungry millions, not one of whom knows what is an iPod.

Even after the colossal changes which have turned China into the world's workshop, over 60 per cent of its people still live in the countryside, a much higher proportion than in Japan at the same stage of development.[1] That is around 900 million people.[2] Although Deng Xiaoping's first reforms helped improve conditions in agriculture greatly, the limitations of the initial privatisation have become apparent. Local officials have begun to act like the wicked landlords of communist fiction, expropriating peasant land and leasing it or selling it to benefit themselves. At the same time, these 'landlords' exploit the peasantry with innumerable different local taxes, or demand unpaid labour in lieu of tax. Revolts have become common, such as took place in Shanwei in December 2005, when peasants refused to pay exorbitant fees for burial lots and several people were shot in the ensuing violence.[3]

Although media coverage of the crises in the rural areas is

restricted, much of this had been guessed at by foreign observers through the reports of demonstrations and riots that have seeped out over the last decade, but it was more precisely clarified by a book published briefly in China in 2004, and which is claimed to have sold over 7 million (mainly illegal) copies. *An Investigation into China's Peasantry*, by Wu Chuntao and Chen Guidi, is the result of detailed studies of peasant life in Anhui Province.[4] According to them, such improvements as peasants obtained through the 1980s reforms have disappeared, as taxes have increased to between four and five times their original level. Although a farmer's annual income is but one-sixth of a city dweller's, he pays three times more tax. Wu and Chen write of families living in mud huts on annual earnings of £20, who cannot afford to eat the produce they sell for pennies, and get through the winter by selling blood. Yet nearby are the smart cars and new houses of the officials, with their entertainment accounts and nightclubs and supplies of girls. They describe how officials seize what they want and use the local police as their personal thugs.

An Investigation details how officials hoodwink senior leaders and inspection teams from central government. In scenes which would be comic if not tragic, Wu and Chen describe mountains of grain being imported to make empty granaries look full for a Prime Ministerial visit. The grain workers were dismissed and officials, well briefed with false statistics, took their places to be ready for questioning by central officials or media. The Prime Minister was duly filmed for TV on top of the grain mountain!

The murder of a farmer called Ding, who demanded an audit after uncovering corruption, is investigated. The protests of Ding's fellow villagers eventually resulted in intervention by central government to punish the killers. Similar tales can be found in accounts by others; one of the most moving is that of the self-taught village lawyer, Ma Wenlin, written up by *Washington Post* journalist Ian Johnson.[5] Ma has struggled for years to prevent exploitation and expropriation of poor peasants by grasping officials, and has suffered brutality and indignity despite keeping carefully within the law as proclaimed, though rarely implemented.

The government's answers are the marketisation and inter-nationalisation of agriculture, plus more mobility, leading to urbanisation. In the past, the autarky policy required that China tie the bulk of its people to the land. This was legally enforced through the Household Registration system (*hukou*), by which most citizens were tied, like feudal serfs, to their place of birth, where their employment, housing, social services (if any) and family circumstances were determined for them by the same officials. More and more peasants have been leaving their families to seek work in the cities of the East, becoming clandestine immigrants, contravening the *hukou* rules and so becoming prey to exploitation and maltreatment. The government kept the system in place, both in order to restrict pressure on the eastern cities and to promote urban development in the central regions. Accepting the impossibility of totally controlling migration, the government has introduced reforms which have helped make labour mobility, under certain conditions, legal.

Documentation is provided by each administrative locality, and identifies the bearers first of all as rural or urban. Although they are usually 'circular migrants', i.e. intending to return, they need registration documents in order both to be safe from police harassment and to benefit from local services, particularly schooling. The reforms have made it possible for them to register, rarely in the big cities but in either the periphery of those cities or in the smaller urban centres, if they have stable jobs and fixed places of abode. Some administrations make registration further conditional, for example, upon qualifications, origin or capital.[6]

These reforms may stem the flow of migrants but they do not halt it. In 1978, there were 193 cities and 2,173 towns. There are now 660 cities and 20,000 towns, and the urban population has grown from 170 million to 456 million. Shanghai may have as many as 20 million, Peking is over 15 million, and Chongqing nearly 33 million. By 2010, 40 per cent of China's population is intended to live in cities. Why? The richest countries of the world are 78 per cent urban, middle-income countries are 58 per cent urban, and China is only about 35 per cent urban. The government therefore thinks it has plenty of scope.[7] The third arm of a modern economy, services, can develop fully only with urbanisation.

Yet the government is also worried about migration, afraid that it puts too much of a strain on cities' housing, health, schooling and public safety. They are conscious that local jobs can be undercut – it is supposed that at least 40 per cent of construction workers in the capital are peasant immigrants. So, probably, are the restaurant workers; anyway, the waiters I talk to never seem to come from the city, nor do those who call out to me to offer goods and services along the streets. In January 2006, they seemed mostly to be from the West and South West.

Precedents from elsewhere for controlling migration are not encouraging. Mexico has tried to funnel migration away from Mexico City (population 30 million) to regional centres, Indonesia invested heavily in trying to divert people from overpopulated Java; both have failed. Despite heavy subsidisation of rural areas in the EU, population decline has not been arrested. What China would have to have, if it were to balance its urbanisation, according to experts, would be 'an urban development plan that will project and build the necessary infrastructure (housing, public transport; and sewage, water supply, and waste disposal systems) before the wave of rural-urban migrants suffocate the existing urban agglomerations in the coastal provinces of eastern and southern China'.[8] Meanwhile, urbanisation in China is affecting global warming at a rate greater than that found elsewhere. Land use changes on account of urbanisation create an urban heat island due to the coverage of the land by buildings, roads and paved surfaces, as well as because of emissions.[9]

Urbanisation as a solution to the problems of rural China raises as many questions as it answers; for the moment, it does not allow the government to avoid the challenge of creating institutions to defend the peasantry and forcing its agents to curb their behaviour.

Notes

Introduction

1 The official population is 1.3 billion, but this is widely thought to be an under-estimate.

2 Ted C. Fishman, *China Inc.*, New York: Scribner, 2005.

3 Martin Wolf, 'The World Begins to Feel the Dragon's Breath on its Back', *Financial Times*, 14 December 2005.

4 Lester R. Brown, *Who Will Feed China?*, New York: Norton, 1995, p. 133.

5 Ibid., p. 140.

6 *Rising Above the Gathering Storm: Energizing and Employing America for a Brighter Economic Future*, Washington, DC: National Academy of Sciences, 2005.

7 Nancy Bernkopf Tucker, 'Dangerous Liaisons: China, Taiwan, Hong Kong and the United States at the Turn of the Century', in Tyrene White (ed.), *China Briefing*, Armonk, NY: M.E. Sharpe, 2000, pp. 264–6.

8 A 2005 survey found that attitudes in fourteen countries were positive towards China's burgeoning economic resurgence but suspicious of her military potential: 'China is Seen More Favourably than US or Russia', BBC press release, 2005, at: http://www.bbc.co.uk/pressoffice/pressreleases/stories/2005/03_march/07/china_poll.shtml

9 Peter Nolan, 'A Third Way: China at the Crossroads', in Hugo de Burgh (ed.), *China and Britain: the Potential Impact of China's Development*, London: The Smith Institute, 2005a.

10 Russia is weak, Japan is feared, India is a rival and the EU generally goes along with the US.

11 http://www.china-embassy.org/eng/xw/t230375.htm, although some say third; see: http://www.miamitodaynews.com/news/050324/story4.shtml

12 Phillip C. Saunders, 'Supping with a Long Spoon: Dependence and Inter-dependence in Sino-American Relations', *China Journal*, number 43, 1999.

13 Ibid.

14 Sir John Pratt, *China and Britain*, London: Collins, 1940?, pp. 24–37.

15 Wang Gongwu, *Anglo-Chinese Encounters Since 1800*, Cambridge: Cambridge University Press, 2003, p. 5.

16 Ibid., p. 142.

1 The Party

1 Carol Lee Hamrin, *China's Tenth National People's Congress: Promising Shared Prosperity and Good Governance Under Party Rule*, Institute for Global Engagement, 4 April 2003, at: http://www.globalengagement.org/issues/2003/04/NPC-p.htm

2   Andrew Scobell and Larry Wortzel, *Civil–Military Change in China: Elites, Institutes and Ideas after the Sixteenth Party Congress*, Carlisle, PA: US Army War College, Strategic Studies Institute, September 2004.
3   James C.F. Wang, *Contemporary Chinese Politics*, Upper Saddle River, NJ: Prentice Hall, 2002. A very useful outline, which I have used to check pre-2001 facts.

2   Mao Zedong

1   Tang Zongli et al., *Maoism and Chinese Culture*, New York: Nova Science Publishers, 1996.
2   Jung Chang and Jon Halliday, *Mao: The Unknown Story*, London: Jonathan Cape, 2005.

3   Central Government

1   This thesis has been further developed in 'The History of China until 1978', a paper delivered to HM Treasury in 2004 by Dr Hans van de Ven of the University of Cambridge, which he kindly supplied to me.
2   Yang Fengchun, *Chinese Government*, Peking: Foreign Languages Press, 2004, pp. 86–8.
3   Confusingly, there are two CMCs: the Party's, which is all-powerful, and the State's, which is of no importance. The PLA remains a Party force. David Shambaugh, *Modernizing China's Military*, Berkeley, CA: University of California Press, 2002, pp. 108–24.
4   The principal source for the procedural information in this section is Yang Fengchun, op. cit.
5   Carol Lee Hamrin, op. cit.
6   Susumu Yabuki and Stephen M. Harner, *China's New Political Economy*, Boulder, CO: Westview, 1999.
7   The problems posed by the bureaucracy itself that government has encountered and overcome in introducing its reforms can be seen to be quite astonishing, from a reading of Chapter 9, 'The Communist Cadre System', in Alan P. Liu, *How China is Ruled*, Upper Saddle River, NJ: Prentice Hall, 1986.
8   For example, David S. Goodman and Gerald Segal (eds), *China Deconstructs: Politics, Trade and Regionalism*, London: Routledge, 1995.
9   For example, Barry J. Naughton (ed.), *Holding China Together: Diversity and National Integration in the Post-Deng Era*, San Diego: University of California Press, 2004, p. 4.
10 Ibid., p. 7.
11 Ibid., p. 8.
12 Jude Howell, 'Governance: the Challenges', in de Burgh, 2005a, op. cit., p. 104.
13 Ibid.

4 Local Government

1 Michael Sheridan, 'Village Killings that China Concealed', *Sunday Times*, 18 December 2005.
2 Described in two major criticisms of Chinese government: He Qinglian, *China's Pitfall*, Hong Kong: Minjing Chubanshe, 1998, and Wu Chuntao and Chen Guidi, *An Investigation into China's Peasantry*, Zhingguo: Wenxue Chubanshe, 2004 (both in Chinese).
3 Jonathan Unger, 'Power, Patronage and Protest in Rural China', in White, op. cit. See pp. 80–81.
4 For example, *The Guardian*, 10 October 2005, p. 1.
5 Howell, op. cit., p. 104.
6 See Yia-Ling Liu, 'Reform from Below: the Private Economy and Local Politics in the Rural Industrialisation of Wenzhou', *The China Quarterly*, 130, 1992, pp. 53–64.
7 Howell, op. cit., p. 104.

5 Nationalism

1 Stanley Rosen, 'Chinese Media and Youth, Attitudes towards Nationalism and Internationalism', in Lee Chin-Chuan (ed.), *Chinese Media*, London: Routledge, 2003.
2 Edward Friedman, *National Identity and Democratic Prospects in Socialist China*, Armonk, NY: M.E. Sharpe, 1995.
3 Susan Daruvala, *Zhou Zuoren and an Alternative Chinese Response to Modernity*, Cambridge, MA: Harvard University Press, 2000, pp. 219–20. Also Wang Gungwu, 'Openness and Nationalism', in Jonathan Unger, *Chinese Nationalism*, Armonk, NY: M.E. Sharpe, 1996, pp. 113–25.
4 Chris Hughes's book describes this in some detail. See Christopher R. Hughes, *Chinese Nationalism in the Global Era*, London: Routledge, 2006, pp. 85–8.
5 Song Qiang et al., *China Can Say No*, Peking: Zhonghua Gongshang Lianhe Chubanshe, 1996; and Li Xiguang et al., *Behind the Demonisation of China*, Peking: Shehui Kexue Chubanshe, 1997 (both in Chinese).
6 Tucker, op. cit., pp. 264–6.
7 Acronym Institute, 'China Nuclear Spying Allegations: The Cox Report', *Disarmament Diplomacy*, Issue 37, May 1999.
8 Three expressions used by prominent US publications, cited in Peter Hays Gries, *China's New Nationalism: Pride, Politics and Diplomacy*, Berkeley, CA: University of California Press, 2004, Chapter 1.
9 Richard Bernstein and Ross H. Munro, *The Coming Conflict with China*, New York: Alfred A. Knopf, 1998; Edward Timperlake and William C. Triplett, *Red Dragon Rising: Communist China's Military Threat to America*, Washington, DC: Regnery, 1999; Humphrey Hawksley and Simon Holberton, *Dragonstrike*, London: Pan, 1997; Humphrey Hawksley, *Dragonfire*, London: Pan, 2001.

6 Armed Forces

1 Peng Guangqian, *China's National Defense*, Peking: Foreign Language Press, 2004.

2 Ellis Joffe, *The Chinese Army After Mao*, Cambridge, MA: Harvard University Press, 1987, and Srikanth Kondapalli, *China's Military: The PLA in Transition*, New Delhi: Knowledge World Press, 1999.

3 Shambaugh, op. cit., p. 7.

4 http://www.indianexpress.com/full_story.php?content_id=68342. Accessed 14 April 2005.

5 Ibid.

6 Shambaugh, op. cit., p. 276.

7 Ibid., p. 330.

8 Stephanie Donald and Robert Benewick, *The State of China Atlas*, Berkeley, CA: University of California Press, 2005, p. 19.

9 David Shambaugh, quoted in http://www.dailytimes.com.pk/default.asp?page=story_1-11-2002_pg4_4

10 US books dealing with these issues include: Timperlake and Triplett, op. cit.; and Bill Gertz, *The China Threat: How the People's Republic Targets America*, Washington, DC: Regnery, 2000.

11 Scobell and Wortzel, op. cit.

7 Softpower

1 Li Xiguang and Zhou Qingan, *Softpower and Global Media* (in Chinese), Peking: Tsinghua University, 2005.

2 'China View', at: http://www.xinhuanet.com/english/ or http://www.chinaview.cn. Accessed 31 July 2005.

3 'CCTV.com' (English), at: http://english.cctv.com/index.shtml. Accessed 31 July 2005.

4 Chin Yikchan, 'China's Regulatory Policies on Transborder TV Drama Flow', *Javnost/The Public*, Volume X, number 4 (Winter 2003), pp. 75–92.

8 Tibet and East Turkestan

1 This expression is used for convenience. To Tibetans there were simply a number of Tibets with different Tibetan administrations, all religious, Tibet being a theocracy, approximately equivalent to medieval abbots in Europe. Those in Eastern Tibet were nominally responsible to the Republic of China but saw themselves just as much as part of the Tibetan world, as did those under the pre-eminent abbot, the Dalai Lama.

2 Sources include: Melissa Harris et al., *Tibet Since 1950: Silence, Prison or Exile*, Denville, NJ: Aperture, 2000; Isabel Hilton, *The Search for the Panchen Lama*, New York and London: W.W. Norton, 2001; Ian Buruma, *Bad Elements*, London: Weidenfeld and Nicolson, 2001.

3 The proposals of the Dalai Lama amount to: (1) demilitarisation; (2) an end to

colonisation; (3) discussions on the future status of Tibet. See J. Wang, op. cit., pp. 181–6.

4   The most recent book in English to deal with the country under Chinese rule after 1949 is Christian Tyler, *Wild West China*, London: John Murray, 2005.

5   For the names of various writers persecuted, and notes on the denial of religious and cultural rights to the Turks in 2005, see Human Rights Watch, at: http://hrw.org/english/docs/2006/01/18china12270_txt.htm

6   C. I. E. Macartney, 'The Chinese as Rulers over an Alien Race', *Proceedings of the Central Asian Society*, London, 10 March 1909.

9   Economy

1   Luke Johnson, *Sunday Times*, 22 May 2005.

2   Fishman, op. cit., p. 194.

3   Linda Yueh, 'The Economy: Opportunities and Risks', in de Burgh, 2005a, op. cit.

4   Goldman Sachs, quoted by Stefan Stern in the *Financial Times*, 9 June 2005, p. A3.

5   'Economic Survey of China 2005', *OECD Economic Surveys*, Organisation for Economic Cooperation and Development, Volume 2005, number 13, pp. 1–208.

6   Lawrence E. Harrison and Samuel P. Huntington, *Culture Matters: How Values Shape Human Progress*, New York: Basic Books, 2000.

7   In 1980, the State sector accounted for 76 per cent of gross industrial output, and by 2001, 24 per cent; Paul E.M. Reynolds, 'The Chinese Economy – Hard Landing or Worse?', Global Economic Policy Institute, paper delivered at the China–Latin America workshop at the University of Westminster, 3 June 2005.

8   'Economic Survey of China 2005', op. cit.

9   The reforms began much earlier than 1992, but were paralysed by the 1989 Tiananmen massacre, one of the consequences of which was a return to power of the left. Deng's Progress to the South undermined the stasis that the leftists had forced upon China since June 1989.

10 Merryn Somerset Webb, 'Chinese Commodity Boom', *Sunday Times*, 6 July 2005.

11 'Economic Survey of China 2005', op. cit.; Wayne M. Morrison, 'China's Economic Conditions', Congressional Research Service, 2005; Yueh, in de Burgh, 2005a, op. cit.

12 Land is still all owned by the State. The owner of a property has, in effect, a lease on the land upon which it stands, protected by the as yet none-too-credible laws.

13 Al-Jazeera.Net, 'China's Congress: Key Topics', 5 March 2006.

10 Trade

1 'Beijing, not Washington, Increasingly Takes the Decisions that Affect Workers, Companies, Financial Markets and Economies Everywhere', *The Economist*, 28 July 2005.

2 'The Quiet Revolution', *Time Pacific Magazine*, 25 April 2005, at: http://www.time.com/time/pacific/magazine/article/0,13673,503050425-1051236-2,00.html

3 'Green Guise', *The Economist*, 26 March 2005.

4 Personal communication with the Chairman of Rio Tinto, Paul Skinner, at The Smith Institute seminar 'Valuing China', held at 11 Downing Street, 18 January 2006, by kind permission of the Chancellor of the Exchequer.

5 How China has overtaken the more advanced economies of the Latin American and Caribbean countries, and perhaps excluded them from opportunities in the emerging technology-based markets of the future, is interestingly argued in Sanjaya Lall, John Weiss et al., 'China's Competitive Threat to Latin America: An Analysis for 1990–2002' (QEH Working Paper Series – QEHWP120–WP120, January 2005), paper presented at the Asian Development Bank/Inter-American Development Bank conference, Peking, December 2004.

6 James Kynge, 'The World is Dancing to a Chinese Tune', *Financial Times*, 31 December 2004.

7 World Economic Outlook, *The Global Implications of the US Fiscal Deficit and of China's Growth*, Washington, DC: IMF Publication Services, April 2004, Chapter 2.

8 Elizabeth Croll, 'Consumption and Social Stability', in de Burgh, 2005a, op. cit.

9 The mechanics of this are spelled out in Chapter 7 of Fishman, op. cit.

10 *The Economist*, op. cit., 26 March 2005.

11 Robert Rowthorn and Ramana Ramaswamy, *Deindustrialization – Its Causes and Implications*, International Monetary Fund, 1997. The issue of whether the advanced countries are right to allow their manufacturing industries, and the associated skills, to die out, is a separate one. Rowthorn has started to address this in his more recent paper: Robert Rowthorn and Ken Coutts, 'De-Industrialisation and the Balance of Payments in Advanced Economies', *Cambridge Journal of Economics*, Volume 28, number 5, September 2004.

11 Money

1 For these figures, I am indebted to Mark Tucker, 'China and Britain', address by the CEO of Prudential plc at the seminar 'Valuing China', op. cit.

2 *Social Security White Paper of China*, Ministry of Labour and Social Security, 7 September 2004, at: http://www.China.org.cn

3 'A Great Big Banking Gamble', *The Economist*, 27 October 2005.

4 Full details of the financial services system are contained in the very useful *China Knowledge Financial Services in China*, Singapore: China Knowledge Press, 2005.

5 Ibid.
6 *China Business Weekly*, cited in Elizabeth M. Lloyd, 'China: Online Financial Services', Media Connection International, 9 August 2005, at: http://216.109.124.98/search/cche?ei=UTF-8&p=financial+servces+china&meta=vc
7 See Lance Blockley, 'Payment Cards in China: A Huge and Dynamic Market', *Insight*, London: Edgar, Dunn and Co., Volume 14, November 2004.
8 For details, see Stephen Green, *China's Stockmarket: A Guide to its Progress, Players and Prospects* (The Economist Series), London: Bloomberg Press, 2003.
9 Wang Shaoguang, 'China's 1994 Fiscal Reform: An Initial Assessment', *Asian Survey*, Yale University Department of Political Science, September 1997.

12 World Trade Organization

1 Yuezhi Zhao, '"Enter the World": Neo-liberal Globalisation, the Dream for [sic] a Strong Nation, and Chinese Discourses on the WTO', in Lee Chin-Chuan, op. cit., pp. 41–8.
2 'The Real Great Leap Forward', *The Economist*, 30 September 2004.
3 US Department of Commerce, Office of the United States Trade Representative, *Report to Congress on China's WTO Compliance*, 2003.
4 Colin Sparks and Hugo de Burgh, 'The Media: A Challenge to the Anglosphere?', in de Burgh, 2005a, op. cit.
5 Laurence J. Brahm (ed.), *China After WTO*, Peking: China Intercontinental Press, 2002.
6 Statistics from: US Department of Commerce, Office of the United States Trade Representative, *Report to Congress on China's WTO Compliance*, 2004; ibid.; *Report to Congress on China's WTO Compliance*, 2003; 'A Disorderly Heaven', *The Economist*, 18 March 2004; 'The Real Great Leap Forward', *The Economist*, 30 September 2004.
7 http://www.miamitodaynews.com/news/050324/story4.shtml
8 'Not Bashing Beijing', *The Economist*, 15 July 2004.
9 Tim Clissold, *Mr China*, London: Robinson, 2004.

13 Science and Technology

1 John Wilson Lewis and Xue Litai, cited in Susan Greenhalgh, 'Missile Science, Population Science: the Origins of China's One-child Policy', *The China Quarterly*, 182, 2005, pp. 253–76.
2 In 2001, Chinese R&D spending totalled $12.5 billion, or 1.1 per cent of GDP; the USA equivalent was $281 billion or 2.8 per cent of GDP. David Stipp, 'Can China Overtake the US in Science?', *Fortune*, 1 November 2004.
3 Ibid.
4 Yan Ke, *Science and Technology in China, Reform and Development*, Peking: Foreign Languages Press, 2004.
5 http://www.ucas.com/figures/ucasdata/subject/index.html#analyse

6   H. Lyman Miller, *Science and Dissent in Post-Mao China: The Politics of Knowledge*, Seattle, WA: University of Washington Press, 1996, pp. 96–7.
7   Lu Yongxiang, President of the Chinese Academy of Sciences, 'The Role and Contributions of the Chinese Academy of Sciences to China's Science and Technology Development', address to the Asia Society, Hong Kong, 4 January 2001, at: http://www.asiasociety.org/speeches/index.html
8   Ibid.
9   Melinda Liu, 'High-Tech Hunger', *Newsweek*, 16 January 2006.
10 'Report to Congress of the US–China Economic and Security Review Commission', November 2005, also available at www.uscc.gov, cited in ibid.
11 Craig Simons, 'The Huawei Way', *Newsweek*, 16 January 2006.
12 Roger Cliff, *The Military Potential of China's Commercial Technology*, Santa Monica, CA: Rand, 2001.
13 Liu, op. cit.
14 Greenhalgh, op. cit., p. 269.

14 Intellectual Property

1   'China's_Current_IPR_Environment', US Department of Commerce, International Trade Administration, 2003, at: http://www.mac.doc.gov/China/Docs/BusinessGuides/IntellectualPropertyRights.htm
2   'Drug Industry Concern as China Breaks Viagra Patent', DrugResearcher. com, 8 July 2004, at: http://www.drugresearcher.com/news/printNewsBis.asp?
3   Jonathan C. Spierer, 'Intellectual Property in China: Prospectus for New Market Entrants', at: http://www.fas.harvard.edu/~asiactr/haq/199903/9903a010.htm
4   'Have Patent, Will Travel: A New Generation of Chinese Companies Wants to Play by the Rules', *The Economist*, 28 June 2001.
5   US Department of Commerce, op. cit.

15 Jobs

1   Data from the 2000 census confirms that what Ling told me is typical – many employees work six or seven days a week.
2   See, for example, Isabel Hilton, 'Made in China', in *Granta*, 89, Spring 2005.
3   In 2002, 11–13 per cent of workers who are long-term urban residents were unemployed, according to Judith Banister, 'Manufacturing Earnings and Compensation in China', *Monthly Labor Review*, US Department of Labor, Bureau of Labor Statistics, Washington, DC, August 2005, pp. 20–42.
4   Ajit K. Ghose, 'Employment in China: Recent Trends and Future Challenges', *Employment Strategy Papers 2005/14*, Geneva: Employment Analysis Unit, Employment Strategy Department, International Labour Office, 2005.
5   Judith Banister goes into impressive detail to explain how she comes to these figures in 'Manufacturing Employment in China', *Monthly Labor Review*, US Department of Labor, Bureau of Labor Statistics, Washington, DC, July 2005, pp. 11–29.

6   Ibid.
7   See 'Five Groups to Join China's Middle Class Ranks', at http://www.china.
    org.cn/english/2002/Dec/50803.htm; and 'Economist Predicts Rise in Middle
    Class', at: http://www.china.org.cn/english/BAT/16771.htm
8   In 2000, I was in the company of a senior reporter of a national newspaper
    when we stopped to see the prices of some imported jackets. One cost fifteen
    times his annual salary.
9   Merryn Somerset Webb, 'Cash in on China Dolls', *Sunday Times Money*, 20
    November 2005.

16 Tourism

1   Leora Moldofsky et al., 'Lonely Planet Seeks to get China in its Orbit',
    Financial Times, 15 January 2006.
2   The most up-to-date and accessible description of this is in Chang and
    Halliday, op. cit.
3   The figures cited here are mainly taken from the National Bureau of Statistics,
    China Statistical Yearbook, Peking: Foreign Languages Press, 2004.
4   Li Hairui, *Le Tourisme en Chine*, Peking: China Intercontinental Press, 1998,
    p. 185.
5   Ibid., pp. 94–116.
6   Larry Yu and Ginger Smith, 'Tourism Takes Off', *The China Business Review*,
    March–April 2005.

17 History

1   C.H. Brewitt-Taylor (trans.), *San Kuo or Romance of the Three Kingdoms*
    (popular edition), Shanghai: Kelly and Walsh, 1929.
2   Jack Belden, *China Shakes the World*, New York: Harper, 1949.
3   W.J.F. Jenner, *The Tyranny of History: The Roots of China's Crisis*, London:
    Penguin, 1994, p. 11.
4   The temple is that of the tomb of Yue Fei, general commanding the troops of
    the Southern Song Dynasty. Yue Fei, who was executed in 1141, is a national
    hero with a popular novel, *Yue Fei Zhuan*, about him.

18 Arts and Literature

1   Ji Bo, 'Report Reveals Best-Selling Writers', *China Daily*, 14–15 January 2006.
2   Xiao Zhiwei, 'Chinese Cinema', in *Encyclopaedia of Chinese Film*, London:
    Routledge, 1998.

19 Culture of Food

1   On the culture of food, see Wang Renxiang, *Food and Chinese Culture* (in
    Chinese), Peking: Beijing People's Press, 1994, and K.C. Chang, *Food in
    Chinese Culture: Anthropological Perspectives*, New Haven, CT: Yale University
    Press, 1977.

2   Guo Yuhua, 'Food and Family Relations: The Generation Gap at the Table', in Jun Jing (ed.), *Feeding China's Little Emperors: Food, Children and Social Change*, Stanford, CA: Stanford University Press, 2000, p. 96.
3   Jun Jing, 'Introduction: Food, Children and Social Change in China', in Jun Jing, op. cit.
4   Ibid., p. 11.
5   Guo Yuhua, in Jun Jing, op. cit., p. 107.
6   James L. Watson, 'Food as a Lens: The Past, Present and Future of Family Life in China', in Jun Jing, op. cit., p. 203.
7   Jun Jing, op. cit., p. 19.

20 Religion

1   'The Present Conditions of Religion in China', in *Freedom of Religious Belief in China*, Office of the State Council of the PRC, 1997, at: http://www.china.org.cn/e-white/Freedom/
2   21 July 2005.
3   The story of one such, a grandmother, and of her daughter's vain quest for justice, is told in Ian Johnson, *Wild Grass: China's Revolution from Below*, London: Penguin, 2005. Many similar tales are publicised by the Falungong's newspaper, now available in English throughout the West.
4   Orvell Schell, 'Virtual Tibet', in Harris, op. cit., p. 175.
5   Donald and Benewick, op. cit., pp. 84–5.

21 Family Life

1   Yan Yuxiang, *Private Life under Socialism*, Stanford, CA: Stanford University Press, 2003, p. xii.
2   Nancy E. Riley, 'China's Population: New Trends and Challenges', *Population Bulletin*, June 2004, Population Reference Bureau, US.
3   'UCLA's Yunxiang Yan Receives Association for Asian Studies China Book Prize', at: http://www.international.ucla.edu/asia/print.asp?parentid=22811
4   'Chinese Women Changing Attitudes Toward Sexual Life: Survey', at: http://english.people.com.cn/200309/20/eng20030920_124593.shtml
5   Riley, op. cit.
6   Yan Yunxiang, referring to Francis L.K. Hsu's 1948 work, *Under the Ancestors' Shadow: Chinese Culture and Personality*, New York: Columbia University Press, p. 218.
7   G.E.M. Anscombe (trans.), *Wittgenstein's Philosophical Investigations*, New York: Macmillan, 1953.
8   I am summarising and simplifying the nuanced arguments of others, particularly Yan Yunxiang, whose wonderfully empathetic and scholarly study of one particular village should not necessarily be used to generalise.

22 Media

1 Figures variously from Baoguo Cui, *The Blue Book of China's Media* (in Chinese), Social Sciences Academic Press, 2005, and BBC Monitoring country profile, supplied 16 June 2005.
2 Ibid.
3 Alexander G. Flor, 'Social Capital and the Network Effect: Implications of China's E-learning and Rural ICT Initiatives', paper delivered at the Fourteenth Asian Media Information and Communication annual conference, Peking, 18–21 July 2005.
4 Hu Shuli, in interview, at: http://www.worldpress.org/asia/1510.cfm
5 The worlds of politics and business are not at all distinct, but complicit such that their interests may be the same. The Chinese expression *guanshang* gives a flavour: it means something like 'an official who is a businessman' or 'a businessman who is an official', and refers to those who used to be politicians or had connection with the topmost leadership. Decisions on content are made by such people, and reflect their priorities.
6 Matt Pottinger, 'China Restricts Media Coverage', *Wall Street Journal Europe*, 5–7 August 2005, p. A2.
7 Jane Macartney, 'Chinese Journalists Strike as Editor is Sacked', *The Times*, 31 December 2005.
8 Chin-Chuan Lee, 'The Conception of Chinese Journalists', in Hugo de Burgh (ed.), *Making Journalists: Diverse Models, Global Issues*, London: Routledge, 2005b.
9 See Sparks and de Burgh, in de Burgh, 2005a, op. cit.
10 Michael Curtin, 'Murdoch's Dilemma, or What's the Price of TV in China?', in *Media, Culture and Society*, Volume 27, number 2, March 2005, pp. 155–76.
11 Yik-chan Chin, 'From the Local to the Global: Television in China 1996–2003', doctoral dissertation, University of Westminster, 2005.
12 Breakingviews, 'Not a No-brainer', *Wall Street Journal Europe*, 5–7 August 2005, p. M8.

23 Sports

1 Taekwondo, a Korean version of a martial art (*wushu*), was admitted to the Sydney 2000 Olympic Games as an official event. Reportedly, the President of the International Wushu Federation (IWF) has applied to the International Olympic Committee to make *wushu* part of the 2008 Peking Games.
2 Hannah Beech, 'Turning the World Upside Down', *Time Asia Magazine*, Volume 164, number 9, 30 August 2004.
3 Susan Brownell, 'The Changing Relationship Between Sport and State in the Peoples' Republic of China', in Ferdinand Landry et al. (eds), *Sport: The Third Millennium, Proceedings of a National Symposium*, Sainte-Foy, Québec: Les Presses de l'Université Laval, 1991. See also, by the same author, *Training the Body for China*, Chicago: University of Chicago Press, 1995.

4   There are comprehensive descriptions of this history in Chapters 1, 3 and 4 of James Riordan and Robin Jones, *Sport and Physical Education in China*, London: Spon, 1999. Michael Speak of the University of Hong Kong is the best-known specialist in China's sports history.
5   Ren Hai, 'China and the Olympic Movement', in Riordan and Jones, op. cit., p. 206.
6   Tracey Holmes, 'China Takes the Olympic Limelight', CNN, 2004, at: http://edtion.cnn.com/2004/SPORT/08/30/athens.games
7   A full breakdown is provided by Shirley Reekie, 'Appendix: Administration of Sport', in Riordan and Jones, op. cit.
8   Dennis Whitby, 'Sports Science', in Riordan and Jones, op. cit., p. 229.
9   'Pinsent Shocked by China Training', BBC, 17 November 2005, at: http://news.bbc.co.uk/sport1/hi/other_sports/gymnastics/4445506.stm
10 Dennis Whitby, 'Elite Sport', in Riordan and Jones, op. cit., p. 139.

24 Geopolitics

1   Ross Terill, *The New Chinese Empire: And What it Means for the United States*, New York: Basic Books, 2003, discusses this in depth.
2   Steve Tsang, 'Geopolitics: China's Role', in de Burgh, 2005a, op. cit.
3   Joshua Ramo, *The Beijing Consensus*, London: The Foreign Policy Centre, 2004, p. 52.
4   'No Questions Asked', *The Economist*, 21 January 2006.
5   Joshua Kurlantzick, 'China's Challenge to US Softpower in Asia', *The New Republic*, 17 February 2005.
6   Nori Onishi, 'Tokyo–Beijing Ties Endure More Strain', *International Herald Tribune*, 23 December 2005.
7   Jo Johnson, 'Beijing Pressed on Arms to Nepal', *Financial Times*, 14 December 2005.
8   Herman Pirchner, 'The State of Sino-Russian Relations', statement before the US–China Economic and Security Review Commission, 22 July 2005.

25 Internet

1   'Better Use of the Internet', *China Daily*, 30 July 2005; Sandhya Rao et al., 'Gender and the Uses and Gratifications of the Internet in China', paper delivered at the Fourteenth Asian Media Information and Communication conference, op. cit.
2   http://www.opennetinitiative.net/studies/china/
3   Zhang Qiang, 'Analysis: New Media Mobilising China's Masses', BBC Monitoring, 23 June 2005.
4   In the story of the fireworks factory, the official interpretation first published by the media was undermined by more credible reports posted on the web, probably by journalists, until the Prime Minister had to admit the truth and have the story corrected. The well known case of Sun Zhigang, whose murder was

revealed on, and made into a major issue by, the internet, is a further illustration of this process.

5   Min Dahong, research fellow at the News and Communications Research Institute of the China Academy of Social Sciences, cited in BBC Monitoring, 16 June 2005.
6   http://www.opennetinitiative.net/studies/china/
7   Becky Hodge, 'The Great Firewall of China', 20 May 2005, at: http://www.opendemocracy.net/media-edemocracy/china_internet_2524.jsp
8   Zhang Qiang, op. cit.
9   http://www.rfa.org/english/news/technology/2004/08/01/142626/
10 Francis Harris, 'Yahoo Gave the Chinese Evidence to Help Jail Dissident', *Daily Telegraph*, 10 February 2006.
11 Cao Junwu, 'Suqian: Directing On-line Public Opinion: Suqian's On-line Propaganda Corps', *Southern Weekend*, 19 May 2005.
12 Social bookmarking is a way of locating, classifying, ranking, and sharing internet resources through shared lists, tagging, and inferences drawn from grouping and use of tags.
13 Hodge, op. cit.

26 Globalisation

1   Zhao Yang, 'State, Children and the Wahaha Group of Hangzhou', in Jun Jing, op. cit.
2   http://www.goasiapacific.com/specials/friendships/features_china_west.htm
3   Jun Jing, op. cit.; several of the contributors make similar points.
4   Peter Hessler, 'Letter from China', *New Yorker*, 13 and 20 February 2006, pp. 82–9.
5   Ibid., pp. 17, 20.
6   Watson, in Jun Jing, op. cit., p. 205.
7   Ibid., p. 205.
8   Peter Berger and Samuel P. Huntington, *Many Globalizations: Cultural Diversity in the Contemporary World*, Oxford: Oxford University Press, 2003.
9   Harrison and Huntington, op. cit.
10 M.H. Bond (ed.), *A Handbook of Chinese Psychology*, Hong Kong: Oxford University Press, 1996; and *The Psychology of the Chinese People*, Oxford: Oxford University Press, 1999.
11 See Charles Stafford, *The Roads of Chinese Childhood*, Cambridge: Cambridge University Press, 1995.

27 Population

1   Riley, op. cit.
2   Greenhalgh, op. cit. All references to Song Jian are derived from her; any interpretations may be my own.
3   Paul Ehrlich, *The Population Bomb*, New York: Balentine Books, 1968. For

an interesting contextualisation of the population control movement, see Jacqueline Kasun, *The War Against Population*, San Francisco: Ignatius, 1988.

4   Donatella Meadows, *The Limits to Growth: A Report for the Club of Rome's Project on the Predicament of Mankind*, New York: Universe, 1972.

5   Greenhalgh, op. cit., p. 264.

6   Riley, op. cit.

7   Susan Greenhalgh, 'Planned Births, Unplanned Persons: "Population" in the Making of Chinese Modernity', *American Ethnologist*, Volume 30, number 2, 2003, pp. 196, 215.

28 Agriculture

1   'Agricultural Reform Policy in China', policy briefing, Paris: Organisation for Economic Cooperation and Development, October 2005.

2   Kwan Chi Hung, 'How to Solve the Three Agriculture-related Problems – Labor Mobility Holds the Key', *China in Transition*, 25 August 2004, at: http://www.rieti.go.jp/en/china/04082501.html

3   Guanzhong James Wen, 'Challenges and Opportunities for China's Agriculture after its WTO Accession', in Ding Lu, Guanzhong James Wen, Huizhong Zhou et al., *China's Economic Globalization Through the WTO*, Aldershot: Ashgate, 2003.

4   Organisation for Economic Cooperation and Development, op. cit.

5   Mathew Shane and Fred Gale, 'China: A Study of Dynamic Growth', Washington, DC: Economic Research Service, US Department of Agriculture, *Outlook Report*, Number WRS-04-08, October 2004, also available at: www.ers.usda.gov/publications/wrs0408/

6   Richard Spencer, 'China's 800 Million Peasants to Escape Yoke of Farm Tax', *Daily Telegraph*, 21 December 2005.

7   Organisation for Economic Cooperation and Development, op. cit.

8   Ibid., p. 137.

9   Pieter Bottelier, *China's Economic Transition and the Significance of WTO Membership*, Stanford, CA: Center for Research on Economic Development and Policy Reform, 1999.

29 Environment

1   www.nujiang.ngo.cn

2   In 2004, the People's Bank of China criticised 'the blind expansion of seriously low-quality, duplicate projects' in steel, aluminium and cement; see Reynolds, op. cit.

3   Ralph Litzinger, 'Reflections on the Campaign to Halt the Nujiang Dam Project', paper at the symposium *Media and Citizenship in China, Oriental Institute*, University of Oxford, September 2004.

4   Judith Shapiro, *Mao's War Against Nature: Politics and the Environment in Revolutionary China*, Cambridge: Cambridge University Press, 2001.

5   Lynne O'Donnell, 'Thirst for Power', *The Ecologist*, 1 June 2004.

6   Crispin Tickell, 'Environmental Problems: How Big is the Footprint?' in de Burgh, 2005a, op. cit. See also 'Millennium Ecosystem Assessment Report', Washington World Watch Institute, 30 March 2005, at: http://www.millenium assessment.org/en/Products.BoardStatement

7   http://www.zhb.gov.cn/english/+sepa+china&hl=en

8   Chi Fulin, China, *The New Stage of Reform*, Peking: Foreign Languages Press, 2004.

9   Yves Engler, 'Red Road Rising', *The Ecologist*, 1 March 2005.

10 http://www.harbour.sfu.ca/dlam/newsletters/0103.html

11 http://www.china.org.cn/english/environment/119572.htm

12 http://www.sepa.gov.cn/eic/649094490434306048/20050914/11091.shtml

13 http://www.sepa.gov.cn/eic/649094490434306048/20050914/11091.shtml (in Chinese)

14 Christopher Flavin, 'Asia's Environmental Challenges', testimony at a US House of Representatives Committee on International Relations hearing, 22 September 2004, at: http://www.worldwatch.org/press/news/2004/09/22/

30 Three Gorges

1   See, for example, an editorial enthusiastically supporting the case: 'Asia Needs Dams: And Yes – There Are Ways to Minimize Ecological Damage', *Asiaweek*, 15 July 1996.

2   These issues are lucidly laid out in Allin S.R. Fishleigh, 'An Examination of China's Three Gorges Dam Project Based on the Framework Presented in the Report of the World Commission on Dams', Major paper, Master of Science in Urban Affairs and Planning, Virginia Polytechnic Institute and State University, Blacksburg, VA, 30 November 2004, upon which I have drawn.

3   For a clear argument as to why the project will not provide enough energy to justify the other outcomes, see Sandra Burton, 'Taming the River Wild', *Time*, 19 December 1994.

4   'The Great Flood Begins', *The Economist*, 7 June 2003, p. 35.

5   'Resettlement and Development: the Bankwide Review of Projects Involving Involuntary Resettlement, 1986–1993', Washington, DC: The World Bank Environment Department, 1996, Paper No. 032.

6   Dai Qing, Y*angtze! Yangtze!*, London: Earthscan, 1989, p. 6.

7   The paragraphs about her first appeared in Hugo de Burgh, *The Chinese Journalist*, London: Routledge, 2003.

8   Dai Qing, op. cit., p. xvi.

9   The difference, of course, is that UK journalists do from time to time draw our attention to such manipulation and falsification. See Channel 4 *Dispatches*, 'Cooking the Books', 1989; and, more recently, BBC *Panorama*, 'Politics of Spin', 2000.

31 Regions and Languages

1   For a fuller description of the development of the language, see Ping Chen (ed.), *Modern Chinese: History and Sociolinguistics* (excerpt), Cambridge: Cambridge University Press, at: http://www.cambridge.org/0521641977

2   *China – Overcoming Rural Poverty. A World Bank Country Study*, Washington, DC: The World Bank, 2001, p. 13, 'On Minorities and Poverty'.

32 Health

1   L. Chang, *Wall Street Journal*, 23 March 2001.

2   *HIV/AIDS: China's Titanic Peril. 2001 Update of the AIDS Situation and Needs Assessment Report*, UN Theme Group on HIV/AIDS in China for the UN Country Team, June 2002. Other journalism cited: Elisabeth Rosenthal, 'Deadly Shadow of AIDS Darkens Remote Chinese Village', *New York Times*, 28 May 2001; and Goran Lejonhuvud, 'Whole Villages on the Verge of Extinction', *Dagens Nyheter*, 9 June 2001.

3   Shengwang Li and Guijun Sun, 'Analysis on the Test Results of the Blood and its Products Tracked and Seized from the Illegal Blood Lairs', *Journal for China AIDS/STD Prevention and Control*, February 2000, Volume 6, number 1, pp. 12–13.

4   Riley, op. cit.

5   Marilyn Beach, 'China's Rural Health Care Gradually Worsens', *The Lancet*, Volume 358, number 9281, 2001, p. 567.

6   Criticisms of the health service are further detailed in: Bates Gill et al. (eds), *Defusing China's Time Bomb: Sustaining the Momentum of China's HIV/AIDS Response, A Report of the CSIS HIV/AIDS Delegation to China, April 13–18, 2004*, Washington, DC: Center for Strategic and International Studies, 2004.

7   UN Theme Group on HIV/AIDS, op. cit.

8   However, although it is a particularly distressing and now widespread way in which HIV is contracted, blood transfusion is not the main one. The worst affected areas of China are the drug-trafficking routes, particularly the southwest Asian border areas, but also the north-west frontiers with Pakistan, Afghanistan and Uzbekistan.

9   Janet Moore, 'A Billion Chinese, Growing Older', *Star Tribune*, 7 January 2006.

33 Law

1   Yang Fengchun, op. cit., p. 199.

2   Frank Dikotter, 'An Invisible Monument to Death and Despair', *Times Higher Education Supplement*, 23 September 2005, p. 25.

3   Described succinctly in Andrew Halper, 'A Long March to the Rule of Law?', in de Burgh, 2005a, op. cit., from which some of the following points are taken.

4   Joseph Kahn, 'Lawyer Takes on China's "Unwinnable" Cases', *International Herald Tribune*, 13 December 2005. See also Johnson, *Wild Grass*, op. cit.

34 Human Rights

1   Benjamin Joffe-Walt, 'They Beat Him Until He Was Lifeless', *The Guardian*, 10 October 2005.
2   An up-to-date survey of human rights in China is published annually by Human Rights Watch; see: http://hrw.org/english/docs/2006/01/18china12270 _txt.htm
3   The most accessible and recent compendium of these horrors is by Chang and Halliday, op. cit.
4   See Johnson, *Wild Grass*, op. cit.
5   James D. Seymour and Richard Anderson, *New Ghosts, Old Ghosts: Prisons and Labor Reform Camps in China*, New York: M. E. Sharpe, 1998, p. 197.
6   Philip F. Williams and Yenna Wu, *The Great Wall of Confinement: The Chinese Prison Camp Through Contemporary Fiction and Reportage*, Berkeley, CA: University of California Press, 2004, pp. 52–3.
7   Jean-Luc Domenach, *Chine: l'Archipel Oublié*, Paris: Editions Fayard, 1992.
8   Williams and Wu, op. cit., pp. 9–14, note that Foucault is wrong to find the origins of totalitarian oppression in the Enlightenment, arguing that they lie in the social interventionism of the 19th century, of which Marx was only the best-known exponent.
9   Williams and Wu, op. cit., p. 37.
10 Ibid., p. 41.
11 Ni Xiaoquan, *Sino-Russian Relations since the September 11 Incident*, Peking: Chinese Academy of Social Sciences, Institute of Russian, East European and Central Asian Studies, 2005.
12 The best guide to the world of Chinese dissidents is Buruma, *Bad Elements*, op. cit.

35 Civil Society

1   For an introduction to this, see David G. Green, *Civil Society: The Guiding Philosophy and Research Agenda of the Institute for the Study of Civil Society*, London: Civitas, 2000.
2   http://web.worldbank.org/WBSITE/EXTERNAL/COUNTRIES/EAST ASIAPACIFICEXT/CHINAEXTN/0,,contentMDK:20600360~pagePK: 1497618~piPK:217854~theSitePK:318950,00.html
3   Suzanne Ogden, *Inklings of Democracy in China*, Cambridge, MA: Harvard East Asia Center, 2002.
4   Jiang Ru, 'Environmental NGOs in China: Encouraging Action and Addressing Public Grievances', Washington, DC: statement at Congressional-Executive Commission on China, 7 February 2005, at: http://www.cecc.gov/ pages/roundtables/020705/Ru.php?mode=print&PHPSESSID=73bff362ab5 1d3bc99e04ff22f801288
5   Personal communication, Clare Lawrence, UK Consul General in Canton, 2005.
6   UN Theme Group on HIV/AIDS, op. cit.

36 Welfare

1 'Final' big act because it then allowed itself to be taken over by a French group, possibly to protect itself from government exploitation. All this is described in detail in Zhao Yang, 'State, Children and the Wahaha Group of Hangzhou', in Jun Jing, op. cit.

2 Data in this essay mainly come from *Beijing Youth Daily* (2004); *Modernization in China: The Effects on its People and Economic Development*, Peking: Foreign Languages Press, 2004; and the White Paper (see note 5 below).

3 Riley, op. cit.

4 Pete Engardio and Carol Matlack, 'Global Aging', *Businessweek Online*, 31 January 2005, at: http://www.businessweek.com/magazine/content/05_05/b3918011.htm

5 The following details come from the Ministry of Labour and Social Security, *Social Security White Paper of China*, 7 September 2004, at: China.org.cn

6 See James A. Dorn, 'A Fix for China's Pension', *The Asian Wall Street Journal*, 9 February 2004; and Pieter Bottelier, 'Where Is Pension Reform Going in China?', *Issues and Options Perspectives*, Volume 3, number 5, 2004, at: http://www.oycf.org/Perspectives/17_063002/Pension_China.htm

37 Intellectuals

1 Much extended discussion of these interests and themes is to be found in Ogden, op. cit., and in Joseph Fewsmith, *China Since Tiananmen*, Cambridge: Cambridge University Press, 2001.

2 Dai Qing, *Wang Shiwei and 'Wild Lilies': Rectification and Purges in the Chinese Communist Party 1942–44*, New York: M.E. Sharpe, 1994.

3 Chris Hughes details Wang's views in his *Chinese Nationalism in the Global Era*, op. cit., pp. 122–4.

4 He Qinglian, *China's Pitfall*, Hong Kong: Minjing Chubanshe, 1998, saw the new companies being set up simply as ways of stealing State assets, and described the process of selling of land as the equivalent of England's Enclosure Movement. See Fewsmith, op. cit., p. 171.

38 Universities

1 Parts of this section were first published in de Burgh, 2005a, op. cit., 'Introduction'.

2 Tuition paid by students at State institutions now accounts for 15–20 per cent of the total cost of their higher education. Bank loans are available.

3 Amelia Newcomb, 'China Goes to College – in a Big Way', *Christian Science Monitor*, 29 July 2005.

4 Michael Agelasto and Bob Adamson (eds), *Higher Education in Post-Mao China*, Hong Kong: Hong Kong University Press, 1998, p. 404.

5 Ibid., p. 413.

6   23 million, of whom 7 million are part-time. Figures provided by Professor Zhang Li, Director General, National Centre for Education Development Research, PRC Ministry of Education, 3 April 2006.
7   Adam Segal, 'Is America Losing its Edge?', *Foreign Affairs*, November/December 2004.
8   A US response to this can be found in *Rising Above the Gathering Storm: Energizing and Employing America for a Brighter Economic Future*, Washington, DC: National Academy of Sciences, 2005.

39 Schooling

1   Arthur H. Smith, *Chinese Characteristics*, New York: Fleming H. Revell, 1894, p. 29.
2   In such an enormous country, the variations and permutations are myriad; what is described here is the skeleton only. Essentials come from Su Xiaohuan, *Education in China: Reforms and Innovations*, Peking: China Intercontinental Press, 2002.
3   Ibid.
4   For descriptions of Chinese teaching methods in the late 1990s, and their influences on pupils, see Peter Hessler, *River Town: Two Years on the Yangtze*, London: John Murray, 2001.
5   Francesco Rampini describes this process in *Il Secolo Cinese, Mondadori*, 2005, pp. 100–02.

40 Rural China/Urban China

1   *The Economist*, op. cit., 30 September 2004.
2   Population statistics are notoriously unreliable. Officially, there are 1.3 billion Chinese, but many observers believe this underestimates the true number. See **Population**. For a discussion of PRC data, see Ghose, op. cit.
3   Sheridan, op. cit.
4   Wu Chuntao and Chen Guidi, *An Investigation into China's Peasantry*, Peking: People's Literature Press, 2004. Originally published in the literary magazine *Dangdai* in 2003, it was published as a book in 2004 by the Chinese Literature Press, but then withdrawn after the sale of some 250,000 copies a few weeks later. Since then, between 7 and 8 million copies are estimated to have been printed illegally. An English-language summary and evaluation can be found in Yang Lian, 'Dark Side of the Chinese Moon', *New Left Review*, Volume 32, March–April 2005, at: http://www.newleftreview.net/NLR26606.shtml
5   Johnson, op. cit.
6   US Embassy, *Hukou Reform Targets Urban–Rural Divide*, 2004, at: http://www.usembassy-china.org.cn/econ/hukou.html
7   'China Speeds up Healthy Urbanisation', State Development Planning Commission, press release, 13 August 2001.

8   'Argument: Urban Intervention Possibilities', available at IIASA (the Inter-national Institute of Applied Systems Analysis): http://www.iiasa.ac.at/Research/LUC/ChinaFood/argu/intposs/pos_34.htm

9   'Heating Up: Study Shows Rapid Urbanization in China Warming the Regional Climate Faster than Other Urban Areas', Atlanta, GA: Georgia Institute of Technology, press release (report of a NASA-funded study), 22 June 2004.

Exchange Rates

As this book went to press, traveller exchange rates were roughly as follows:

1 UK £ = 14.46 RMB (renminbi or yuan or Chinese dollar)
1 EURO = 9.75 RMB
1 US $ = 8.24 RMB
1 Australian $ = 6.06 RMB

Thus, 1,000 RMB are worth about:

UK £70
EURO 103
US $121
AUS $165

Glossary and Key Figures

Anti Spiritual Pollution Campaign
Campaign initiated by Deng Xiaoping in 1982 to counter Western-inspired 'decadence' in the arts; echoed by similar campaigns through the 1980s instituted by President Jiang Zemin.

Ba Jin (1904–2005)
Sichuanese novelist and chronicler of family life. Obtained positions in CCP government 1950. Purged 1968. Rehabilitated 1977.

Canton (Guangzhou, Kwang-chow)
An important trading city and capital of Canton Province since the Tang Dynasty. Centre of Cantonese culture, with its distinct language and customs.

CCP
Chinese Communist Party. Founded in 1921 in Shanghai as a satellite of the Comintern. Until the death of Sun Yatsen, the CCP, on Stalin's orders, worked with the KMT.

Chen Shui-bian
First non-KMT President of Taiwan, elected March 2000.

Chengdu
Capital of Sichuan Province. It was a capital of one of China's antecedent states, Shu, from 221–263 AD, and has been an important city ever since.

Civil War
Within months of the surrender of Japan in 1945, full civil war broke out and lasted until the KMT flight to Taiwan in 1949.

Communes, People's
Renmin Gongshe. Tens of thousands of families were organised into these economic and political units during the Great Leap Forward. They were re-emphasised during the Cultural Revolution, when traditional units of administration and distribution were abolished, as were, in some cases, families.

Confucianism

The way of life based upon the teachings of Confucius (551–479 BC) and his successors, particularly Mencius and Hsun-tzu. The Confucian classics, which principally dealt with social relationships and hierarchy as the bases for successful family and social life, were the key tenets of the State ideology until 1911, notwithstanding many other religious and philosophical currents in the Chinese world. A discussion of the relationship of Confucianism to China's modern political development is to be found in Edmund Fung, *In Search of Chinese Democracy*, Cambridge University Press, 2000.

(Great Proletarian) Cultural Revolution

Upheaval lasting from 1966 to 1976, but whose worst violence took place 1966–69. Ostensibly a movement for a final clearing out of old ideas and habits, it was more an attempt by Mao once again to re-establish his waning authority, as it was being marginalised by managers and experts more suited to guide a modern society than the ageing guerrilla and prophet. His prestige allowed him to call upon young people to first criticise and then attack those in authority, while commanding the forces of law and order to stand down. By the time those in authority realised what was happening they were beaten into submission, imprisoned or isolated. Most institutions ceased functioning as they were invaded and taken over by gangs of rebels and looters. The ruination of authority brought to local power cliques and thugs, who vaunted their loyalty to Mao while enjoying the fruits of power. Over this mess, the Gang of Four presided until 1976, although some of the old institutions and administrators gradually returned from around 1970.

Dai Qing (b. 1941)

Adopted daughter of Marshal Ye Jianying. Missile engineer and *Guangming Daily* journalist. Now freelance. Much web information available.

Democracy

Wherever a few intellectuals are gathered together, they will tend to agree that China is not ready for democracy. The politician will, even now that Taiwan is democratic, talk in Singaporean terms about 'Asian Values' which preclude democracy; businessmen will tell you sagely how unstable the workers will become, and warn of the chaos looming if society is not to go through a long period of preparation. This may not be so, as Andrew Nathan argues in his *Chinese Democracy*, Berkeley, University of California Press, 1986.

Democracy Wall

In 1978–79, posters were displayed on a stretch of the wall of the Forbidden City calling for democracy. The best known was that of Wei Jingsheng, who described democracy as the 'Fifth Modernisation'. In the subsequent clampdown, Wei was imprisoned for fifteen years.

Deng Xiaoping (1904–97)

Sichuanese. Active radical from 1919, in Sichuan, France, Jiangxi. Member of the Central Committee in 1945. Senior member of the central government by the early 1960s. Purged 1965. Recalled 1973; became third in the hierarchy. Purged 1976. Regained some positions 1977. Regained decision-making positions 1982–83. Implemented the Four Modernisations. Senior decision-maker at the time of the Tiananmen massacre.

East Turkestan (the Xinjiang Uighur Autonomous Region)

Large territory in Central Asia contiguous with Uzbekistan, Kazakhstan, Pakistan, Tibet and China. Under loose Qing Dynasty and Nationalist suzerainty until an independent state was declared in the 1930s. Culturally Turkic and Muslim, although there has been substantial Chinese immigration since the 1960s. Occupied by the Chinese army in 1950, and soon after incorporated into the PRC as an 'autonomous region'. Although up to the Cultural Revolution it appears that the indigenous population was generally not anti-Chinese, there is now considerable unrest.

Falungong

Banned in 1999 following peaceful demonstrations in Peking, the Falungong or Falundafa has been persecuted and vilified ever since. The movement claims to be a pacific organisation devoted to meditation and exercises to develop personal qualities; no evidence has yet surfaced that convinces otherwise, although many, perhaps thousands, of unlikely dissidents have been imprisoned and maltreated, some murdered. One possible explanation for the government's extreme reaction is that the movement too closely resembles that from which the Taiping and Boxer rebellions grew; another is that the government sees any nationwide organisation, however informal, as a threat to its monopoly. It claimed

100 million members; perhaps that was enough for it to be condemned, relentlessly, as an 'evil cult'.

Fang Lizhi (b. 1936)
Academic and scientist. Best known for his book *We Are Making History* and for his criticisms of government.

Fifth Modernisation
In a poster on Democracy Wall, Wei Jingsheng advocated democracy as the necessary next step and condition of further progress. He signed his name, for which he would be incarcerated for fifteen years. That he was not condemned to death may be due to the fact that a TV technician smuggled out a recording of the court transcripts, which were used by the international media to draw attention to his courage and his ideas.

Four Modernisations
In the last public speech of Prime Minister Zhou Enlai in 1975, he advanced the idea of four modernisations, implicitly acknowledging that China had stagnated. In late 1978, when Deng Xiaoping had regained power, he was able to draw upon them and selectively interpret them according to his own priorities. The first modernisation was to give peasants responsibility for production; the second was to revive urban private enterprise; the third was to decentralise decision-making in State Operated Enterprises, and the fourth was to reform prices. Together they amounted to a rejection of socialism, although this may not have been generally apparent at the time.

Gang of Four
The group of people most associated, aside from Marshal Lin Biao, with the carrying out of Mao's Cultural Revolution. It consisted of Jiang Qing (Mao's wife), Yao Wenyuan, Wang Hongwen, Zhang Chunqiao.

Great Leap Forward (1958–61)
The movement to raise productivity hugely and industrialise rapidly, which Mao instituted in order to circumvent the specialists and experts who denied the primacy of will in economic development. Agriculture was collectivised and industry decentralised, with the result of chaos and widespread starvation.

Greater China

China is much bigger than China proper. There are Hong Kong and Taiwan, but also Singapore and the diaspora. In every continent and most countries, Chinese communities have developed wealth and advanced skills that, if not repatriated to the motherland, provide resources and networks for domestic enterprise. They share many things, from the written language and poetry to martial arts novels, foods, household decorations, superstitions and music. Knowledge and habits in common can make people feel that even when they are not a political community, they are 'one family' and owe more loyalty to fellow Chinese than to the lands where they happen to work, or hold a passport. That is Greater China, with its cultural homogeneity and intra-group trust.

Guanxi

Usually translated as 'connections', *guanxi* refers to the networks that a person has, which, in Chinese society, tend to be infused with obligations. A person with good connections can get many things done more efficiently and more pleasantly than through impersonal systems, from finding an employee to getting tickets for a football match to arranging a bank loan. But entering into relationships of *guanxi* requires reciprocity; you have to acknowledge that you owe, as well as receive. A friendship or a business relationship with someone who operates according to the understandings of *guanxi* can be a rewarding and joyful relationship, but you need to know the rules if it is not to go badly sour in misunderstandings and recriminations.

Hong Kong

Until Taiwan became democratic, HK was the only place in the Chinese world where people could be free to express opinions, such that it has long been a haven for dissidents, an intellectual and artistic centre. After cosmopolitan Shanghai was closed down in 1949, HK became its muted successor, populated by innumerable refugees, many of whom became prosperous and then emigrated. Administered by Britain until 1997 with limited representation of local elites, it is now ruled by China under the 'one country, two systems' formula, by which the PRC agrees to allow HK to preserve its own institutions. To date, the vigilance of local lawyers and activists has helped preserve the freedoms and the minimally representative institutions that used also to be those of Singapore.

Hu Feng (1903–85)
Marxist writer who believed that freedom of artistic expression was compatible with communism. Disagreed with the conformist Zhou Yang and was purged in 1955.

Hu Jiwei (b. 1916)
Sichuanese journalist. Deputy Editor-in-Chief, the *People's Daily*. Purged 1967. Chief Editor 1977. Chairman, Journalists' Association 1980. Emerged in the 1980s as a champion of press freedoms. He was purged again in the summer of 1989 and held responsible for the involvement of many of his colleagues in the protest that led to the Tiananmen massacre. He has since been rehabilitated.

Hu Yaobang (1915–89)
CCP activist. Chairman of the Young Communist Youth League in the 1950s and General Secretary of the CCP in 1981. Dismissed in 1986 for sympathy for student protests. His death in 1989 inspired demonstrations which ended only with the Tiananmen massacre of 4 June 1989.

Hua Guofeng (b. 1921)
Political activist from age fifteen. Prime Minister 1976. Lost all senior posts in 1982.

Hundred Flowers
The phrase was used by Mao Zedong in a speech of 1956, when he called for freedom of expression, saying: 'Let a hundred flowers blossom, let a hundred schools of thought contend.' When he was taken at his word, he found the results unpalatable. Well-meaning people revealed the failures of the new government, the muddle and waste. They got their desserts. 300,000 were labelled 'Rightists', which ruined their careers, and many of the brightest intellectuals were jailed, exiled or driven to suicide.

Jiang Qing (1914–91)
Third wife of Mao Zedong, leading light of the Cultural Revolution.

Jiang Zemin (b. 1926)
Electrical engineer and CCP official. A Vice-Minister 1980. Mayor of Shanghai 1985. Politburo 1987. CCP Secretary General and Chairman of the Central Military Commission 1989. President of the PRC until 2003.

CHINA: FRIEND OR FOE?

Kang Youwei (1858–1927)
Scholar. Leader of the Hundred Days Reform Movement, aiming to modernise but retain Confucianism, repressed by the Empress Dowager in 1898.

Li Peng (b. 1928)
Adoptive son of Zhou Enlai. Engineer and Party functionary. Prime Minister 1988–98.

Liang Qichao (1873–1929)
Disciple of Kang Youwei. Journalist and leading intellectual of the reform movement of the early part of the century.

Liu Binyan (1925–2005)
Investigative journalist and CCP activist from the age of nineteen. Famous for his stories exposing corruption. Purged 1957. Rehabilitated 1979. In Paris during the period 4 June 1989, joins student fugitives in denouncing the government's action and in setting up a 'Front of Democratic China' 1989. Died in USA.

Liu Shaoqi (1900–74)
CCP activist from an early age. One of two Vice Presidents of the new PRC in 1949. Disagreed with Mao over the Great Leap Forward. Denounced in GPCR as a capitalist and vilified, probably badly maltreated. Lost all his positions 1968.

Long March
In autumn 1933, the CCP ruled an area of Jiangxi which was under threat from government troops. The decision was taken to flee to the far North-West. Nearly 100,000 followers started out, but barely 10,000 arrived in Yanan in autumn 1935, where the CCP made its new base, in Shanxi Province. The Long March is regarded as the great epic struggle of the CCP.

May 4th Movement
The demonstrations which took place all over China on 4 May 1919 against the Treaty of Versailles subsequentially came to symbolise the greater movement for reform of institutions, culture and language which is labelled the 'May 4th Movement'.

Meiji Restoration
The 1868 palace coup in Japan which abolished the Shogunate and

established in power a group of reformist nobles under the umbrella of the Meiji Emperor.

Nanjing (Nanking)
Capital of China under the Republic of China, 1928 to 1949.

Nationalist Party (Kuomintang or Guomindang, KMT)
Founded by Sun Yatsen in 1912 from various smaller reform parties as a democratic party, and elected to power in 1913. Outlawed by President Yuan Shikai 1914, it was recreated as the Keming Tang in exile in Japan. Re-established 1919 and then the ruling party until defeated in the Civil War, when party, government and the remnants of the army fled to Taiwan. Since democratic elections have been introduced into Taiwan, it has become the main opposition party.

One Country, Two Systems
The idea that you can have two or more varieties of political and economic arrangement in the same national entity was an ingenious formula, initially thought up by Deng Xiaoping when he wanted China to experiment with Special Economic Zones (SEZs). Here, capitalism was to flourish – by any other name – while the rest of China watched and waited. The idea was applied to Hong Kong when the British government persuaded the PRC that it would be in their interests to preserve the institutions that had made Hong Kong successful; it is probable that the PRC government was pleased to permit this, since the successful prosecution of such a policy would relax Taiwan's guard and make more realisable a peaceful reunion with Taiwan. Although, for other reasons, Taiwan does not seem likely to be enticed, nevertheless the plan has worked with Hong Kong. Development of the Chinese economy has moved so fast as to melt the distinctions between the SEZs and the rest of China. The areas of the PRC where the formula might have been most welcome, and just as useful, are Tibet and East Turkestan. It has not been on offer there, yet.

PLA (People's Liberation Army)
Originally founded as the Red Army, the PLA remains the armed force of the CCP, although it operates as if it were a State army.

Politburo
Powerful executive arm of the Central Committee, the central coordinat-

ing body of the CCP. From its members come the leading figures in Party and nation, the Standing Committee.

Rectification (*Zhengfeng*)
Between 1938 and 1942, the Party endeavoured to set its ideology and organisation straight under Mao Zedong. Disagreements over the direction of the revolution had evolved into a contest over the means and a power struggle among the top leadership. The public form of this contest was a long period of education and investigation of officials, beginning in 1938 but entering an intense stage in the Spring of 1942.

Red Flag
Theoretical journal of the CCP, renamed *Factseeker* in 1988.

River Elegy
A television series which provoked lengthy aknd virulent controversy as it lambasted Chinese traditional society and appeared to advocate sweeping Westernisation and rejection of the rest of Chinese culture. The dragon is attacked as symbol of power-worship, the Great Wall of xenophobia … China is unfavourably contrasted with the dynamic West and a 'brand-new civilisation' is called for.

Sichuan
South-westernmost province of China, bordering Tibet in the west. Its capital is Chengdu and it has a population of over 88 million, plus the 31 million in the metropolis of Chongqing.

Stars Group
After the sterile art of the Cultural Revolution, a group of artists got together a street exhibition, calling themselves the 'Stars' to emphasise that each one was an individual. Influenced by modern European art, particularly Picasso.

Sun Yatsen (1866–1925)
A Western-educated anti-Qing Dynasty activist, he founded several reform parties, some of which eventually merged to create the KMT. After the 1912 Revolution he became, briefly, first President of the Republic, ceding his position to General Yuan Shikai for reasons of realpolitik. Thereafter, he struggled for the remainder of his life to unite China. Allied with the Soviet Union. His wife would become a Vice President of the PRC, his sister-in-law married his successor as

President of the Republic of China, Chiang Kai-shek. An inspiration to all modernisers and anti-imperialists, Sun is hero to both left and right and regarded as the father of modern China.

Taiping

In the mid-19th century, Hong Xiuquan, claiming to be Jesus Christ's younger brother, established a sect called the Taiping Tienguo or Heavenly Kingdom of Great Peace, recalling the Yellow Turban sect of the 2nd century. He gathered armies of fanatical followers to overthrow the dynasty and, after several military successes, established his capital at Nanking in 1853. His edicts redistributed land, reformed the tax system and emancipated women. The movement failed to take Peking and was finally defeated in 1864.

Taiwan (Formosa)

A Chinese island off Fukien, which underwent a brief period of rule by Japan. In 1949, the government and army fled there under Chiang Kai-shek after defeats by the CCP. It remains the seat of the Republic of China, little recognised internationally. Both CCP and KMT have held similar views on 'reunification' of the province with China, regardless of the feelings of the local Taiwanese. Now that Taiwan is wealthy, and a democracy, public opinion on Taiwan is largely against unification, to the fury of the CCP. US policy under President Clinton was confused and suggested to China that he would abandon earlier pledges to respect Taiwan's right to self-determination. When he back-tracked, and the USA resumed helping Taiwan to modernise its military defences, the PRC regarded this as hostile. As the CCP has constantly maintained that it must 'regain' Taiwan and is prepared to use force, this is the issue most likely to lead to hostilities between the USA and PRC.

Three Representations

In 2000, Jiang Zemin claimed that the Party represented the most advanced productive forces, the most advanced culture and the fundamental interests of the people. This was a considerable deviation from even Deng Xiaoping, who, while dumping 'class struggle' and other socialist shibboleths, had nevertheless upheld 'socialism with Chinese characteristics', which, whatever else it might mean, had not appeared to presage replacement of the proletariat by the business class. And that is what Jiang was held to be advocating, for the 'most advanced productive forces' could not but be them. Left critics were right to be suspicious, for very soon afterwards, businesspeople were admitted to membership of the CCP.

Three Worlds Theory
In the 1970s, Mao Zedong declared that all countries belonged to one of three worlds. The first was that of exploiters and imperialists, led by the USSR. The second was the intermediate countries – Japan and Europe, for example – and the third world consisted of the poor countries and the exploited. He argued for the unity of the second and third worlds against 'Soviet social-imperialism'. A profound and enthralling transcript of Mao discussing these matters with Kenneth Kaunda can be found in *Mao Zedong on Diplomacy*, Peking: Foreign Languages Press, 1998, p. 454, or at: http://www.revolutionarydemocracy.org/rdv10n1/mao.htm

Tiananmen Incident
On 5 April 1976, demonstrations ostensibly expressing regret at the death of Zhou Enlai took place in Peking and were interpreted as criticism of Mao and the Cultural Revolution.

Tiananmen Massacre
1989. After many months of demonstrations in favour of democracy all over China, but in particular in Peking, the government sent the troops in. Several thousand students and others were encamped in Tiananmen Square, the symbolic centre of CCP power in the capital, and had been asked repeatedly to withdraw when, after much debate among the Party leaders, the decision was taken. On 4 June 1989, the Square was cleared and many hundreds killed and wounded. This is not admitted by the government. It is still not permissible publicly to discuss the full story in China.

Tiananmen Mothers
A movement to find out the truth about the murdered innocents of the Tiananmen massacre of 1989. Founded in 1991 by Professor Ding Zilin, whose seventeen-year-old son was shot in the back while running away. In 1994, she and her associates began to publish a record giving the circumstances of their children's deaths. Like the parents of other 'disappeared' people in other societies, they want to know rather than to hold the killers to account.

Tiananmen Papers

The most extraordinary collection of documents ever to come out of the PRC, as edited and published by Andrew Nathan and others, these are minutes and other records of the discussions held by the leaders over the 1989 student demonstrations. Smuggled out by a senior official, the papers allow us to hear how the leaders reasoned as they debated whether to force the students out of Tiananmen Square, why they were reluctant to impose martial law, how they tried to avert it, and who voted for what. The papers also show how Jiang Zemin came to power. (Andrew J. Nathan et al., *The Tiananmen Papers*, London: Little, Brown, 2001.)

Tibet

Country on China's south-west, bordering India and China's Qinghai Province. Nominally part of the Manchu Qing Empire, it remained ethnically homogenous and distinct both culturally and linguistically until quite recently. Invaded by China in the 1950s, its government overthrown, it has been subjected to some harsh colonial measures but may also have benefited from modernisation. Its traditional government is in exile and there is an active liberation movement.

Wang Ruoshi (1926–2002)

Journalist and sometime Deputy Editor-in-Chief of *The People's Daily*. Writer on humanism. Criticised Mao in 1972 and sent for rectification. Reinstated 1976. Member of the official commission on interpretation of the Cultural Revolution. Dismissed 1983. Died in the USA.

Wei Jingsheng (b. 1949)

Editor of *Exploration*, activist in Democracy Movement of 1978–79, imprisoned 1979, exiled 1997.

Wu Han (1909–69)

Scholar and administrator. Author of the oblique criticism of Mao's purging of Peng Dehuai, *The Dismissal of Hai Rui from Office*, which stimulated responses from the left and so started the Cultural Revolution.

Yanan (also Yenan)

Shaanxi Province, small town in a mountainous area which was capital of the CCP 'State' from 1936 to 1947, when it was captured by government forces.

Yao Wenyuan (1931–2005)

Shanghai journalist and associate of Jiang Qing who became one of the Gang of Four. He was author of the article which attacked Wu Han's *The Dismissal of Hai Rui from Office*, regarded as the start of the Cultural Revolution.

Zhang Ailing (b. 1921)

Writer Zhang Ailing (also known as Eileen Chang) was born in Shanghai in 1921, a descendant of the great Qing statesman Li Hongzhang. She spent her childhood in Peking and Tientsin, but returned to Shanghai in 1929. She emigrated to the USA in 1955. Her best-known novels are *The Rice Sprout Song* (1955), *Bare Earth* (1956) and *The Golden Cangue* (1943).

Zhang Chunqiao (1917–91)

Member of the Gang of Four. Journalist and leading Shanghai radical. Convicted in 1980.

Zhao Ziyang (1919–2005)

Official of Canton CCP when denounced and publicly humiliated in 1967. Rehabilitated 1971. Minister of the Commission for the restructuring of the Economic System 1982. Prime Minister from 1980 to 1987, CCP General Secretary to 1989. His apparent sympathy for student demonstrators in 1989 and opposition to their military suppression earned him house arrest for the remainder of his life.

Table of Dynasties

Dates	Dynasty	
c. 2000–1700 BC	Xia	
1700–1027 BC	Shang	
1027–771 BC	Western Zhou	
770–221 BC	Eastern Zhou	
	770–476 BC – Spring and Autumn period	
	475–221 BC – Warring States period	
221–207 BC	Qin	
206 BC–AD 9	Western Han	
AD 9–24	Xin (Wang Mang interregnum)	
AD 25–220	Eastern Han	
AD 220–280	Three Kingdoms	
	220–265 – Wei	
	221–263 – Shu	
	229–280 – Wu	
AD 265–316	Western Jin	
AD 317–420	Eastern Jin	
AD 420–588	Southern and Northern Dynasties	
	420–588	Southern Dynasties
		420–478 – Song
		479–501 – Qi
		502–556 – Liang
		557–588 – Chen
	386–588	Northern Dynasties
		386–533 – Northern Wei
		534–549 – Eastern Wei
		535–557 – Western Wei
		550–577 – Northern Qi
		557–588 – Northern Zhou

Table of Dynasties (continued)

Dates	Dynasty
AD 581–617	Sui
AD 618–907	Tang
AD 907–960	Five Dynasties
	907–923 – Later Liang
	923–936 – Later Tang
	936–946 – Later Jin
	947–950 – Later Han
	951–960 – Later Zhou
AD 907–979	Ten Kingdoms
AD 960–1279	Song
	960–1127 – Northern Song
	1127–1279 – Southern Song
AD 916–1125	Liao
AD 1038–1227	Western Xia
AD 1115–1234	Jin
AD 1279–1368	Yuan
AD 1368–1644	Ming
AD 1644–1911	Qing
AD 1911–1949	Republic of China (in mainland China)
AD 1949–	Republic of China (in Taiwan)
AD 1949–	People's Republic of China

Chronology

1895

The Sino-Japanese War ends; Taiwan ceded to Japan.

1898

The Hundred Days Reform: attempted inauguration of a modern system of government and administration, emulating the Meiji Restoration in Japan; aborted in a conservative backlash.

1900–01

Eight allied powers invade China to suppress the anti-foreign Boxer Rebellion. Russia invades Manchuria.

1908

Empress Dowager Cixi dies.

1911

Xinghai Revolution. Overthrow of Qing Dynasty and collapse of Manchu power throughout China. Republic of China established.

1912

The Nationalist Party (KMT) is formed in Peking. Sun Yatsen, Provisional President, cedes to General Yuan Shikai, who becomes President of the Republic of China.

1913

Sun Yatsen flees to Japan following the failure of his putsch against Yuan.

1916

The death of Yuan Shikai marks the beginning of the 'warlord era' of political instability and regional military rule. The Republic continues to exist in name, but China is in fact parcelled out among a succession of warlords.

1919

May 4th Movement. Demonstrations against Japan and the Versailles Treaty. Language reform.

1920
Sun Yatsen establishes a new Republican government at Canton.

1921
First Congress of the CCP.

1923
Soviet advisers in China help to negotiate a united front between the Nationalist and Communist forces.

1924
First Congress of Nationalist Party.

1925
Sun Yatsen, leader of the Chinese revolution, dies aged 58.

1926
The National Revolutionary Forces, under the leadership of General Chiang Kai-shek, launch the Northern Expedition to defeat the warlords and unify China.

1927
KMT launches Anti-Communist Campaign and the united front between the Nationalists and Communists collapses.
The National Government is established by the Nationalist Party, with its capital in Nanking.
The Red Army is founded.

1928
Mao Zedong and Zhu De found a guerrilla base in Jiangxi, on Jing-gangshan.

1930
First KMT campaign of extermination against CCP.

1931–32
Chinese Soviet Republic proclaimed, capital at Ruijin.
Japanese invade and occupy Manchuria, creating the puppet state of Manchukuo under the nominal reign of the last Qing Emperor.

1934–35
The CCP makes the 6,000-mile Long March from Jiangxi Province to Yanan, which becomes the new Party headquarters.

At the Zuiyi Party Conference of 1935, Mao Zedong becomes Chairman of the CCP.

1937

CCP and KMT agree to cooperate against the Japanese invaders.

1938

The government of the Republic is transferred to Chunking (Chongqing), Sichuan.

1941

Hostilities break out between CCP and KMT.

After the Japanese attack on Pearl Harbor, the US enters the Second World War and works closely with the Nationalist government in China.

1942

At Yanan, Mao Zedong launches a Rectification Campaign, to liquidate opposition.

1945

Japan surrenders to the Allies after atomic bombs are dropped on Hiroshima and Nagasaki in August. US forces in China provide support to the Nationalists, Soviet troops help the CCP in Manchuria.

1949

KMT flees to Taiwan, where it establishes the 'temporary' seat of the Republic of China.

CCP proclaims People's Republic of China in Peking.

Media nationalised.

1950

Occupation of (Eastern) Tibet and East Turkestan, existing governments overthrown. Sino-Soviet Agreement. Land reform.

1956

Hundred Flowers (ends 1957).

1958

Great Leap Forward. Creation of Rural Communes.

1959

Mao Zedong resigns as Head of State to Liu Shaoqi, but remains CCP Chairman.

Dalai Lama flees to India after Tibetan government overthrown.

CHINA: FRIEND OR FOE?

1960
Sino-Soviet split.

1962
Famine. President Liu blames the Rural Communes.

1966–76
The Cultural Revolution starts with an article by Yao Wenyuan in *Wenhuibao*.

1968
Millions of urban young people are sent to the countryside to learn through physical labour and help in rural development. The USSR invades Czechoslovakia and issues the Brezhnev Doctrine, claiming the right to interfere in the affairs of other socialist states in order to protect the international socialist cause.

1969
Ninth Party Congress. Marshal Lin Biao announced as Mao Zedong's heir.

1971–72
Attempted coup d'état by Lin Biao is foiled. He dies in a plane crash while attempting to flee to the Soviet Union.
PRC takes the China seat on the United Nations Security Council.

1972
US President Nixon visits the PRC.

1976
January, death of Zhou Enlai.
The first Tiananmen demonstrations against the Cultural Revolution take place during the Qingming Festival in April.
September, Mao Zedong dies. Hua Guofeng succeeds.
October, Gang of Four arrested.

1978
December, resumption of US–China diplomatic relations (from 1 January 1979) announced.
December, Third Plenum of the Eleventh Party Central Committee endorses modernisation and agriculture reforms. Household Production Responsibility System introduced.
The Deng Xiaoping faction dominant.

1979

Advertising introduced onto Chinese television.

28 January–5 February, Deng Xiaoping makes a State visit to the US.

April, suppression of 'Democracy Wall' Movement in Peking. Wei Jingsheng arrested.

China attacks Vietnam to punish it for border incursions and for its treatment of ethnic Chinese minority.

1980

26 August, the fifteenth session of the Standing Committee of the Fifth National People's Congress approves 'Regulations for the Special Economic Zones of Guangdong Province'.

Zhao Ziyang replaces Hua Guofeng.

China admitted to IMF and World Bank.

1980–84

Abolition of the People's Communes. Town and township governments are established in their place.

1982

Population reaches 1 billion.

Prime Minister Margaret Thatcher of Great Britain visits Peking to discuss the future status of Hong Kong.

1983

Special Economic Zones are announced for the Pearl River area.

Campaign against spiritual pollution from the West.

Regulations on Chinese–Western Joint Stock Ventures are promulgated.

1984

Zhao Ziyang to US.

President Ronald Reagan to China.

The Sino-British Joint Declaration on Hong Kong is signed, inaugurating a fifteen-year process for Hong Kong's return to Chinese rule. The announcement of 'One Country, Two Systems' policy.

The Third Plenum of the Twelfth Central Committee endorses urban reforms.

1985

Zhao calls for freeing up of wages and prices as essential for the economy.

First public demonstrations against nuclear testing take place.

1986

Sino–Soviet border fighting.

Shanghai Stock Market opens (closed 1949).

Sino–British Declaration on Hong Kong.

The media attack bourgeois liberalisation.

Fang Lizhi makes a speech calling for openness and students demonstrate for democracy in many cities.

Bankruptcy Law promulgated.

1987

The People's Daily attacks bourgeois liberalisation and hails the Four Cardinal Principles (CCP leadership; Marx–Lenin–Mao Thought; People's Democratic Dictatorship and The Socialist Road).

CCP admits that there is widespread corruption in the Party.

Independence demonstrations in Tibet.

CCP General Secretary Hu Yaobang is blamed for the student demonstrations and forced to step down. An anti-bourgeois liberalisation campaign stifles pressures for political reform and further protests.

1988

CCP sends condolences to KMT on death of Chiang Ching-kuo.

Li Peng encourages Taiwan businesses to invest in the mainland.

Most commodity prices to be deregulated and allowed to move according to the market.

Lee Teng-hui, a Taiwanese, becomes the President of the Republic of China after the death of Chiang Ching-kuo.

1989

The first Soviet minister visits China since 1959.

President George Bush visits China.

Anti-Chinese demonstrations in Tibet.

22 April, a major demonstration in Peking calls for the rehabilitation of Hu Yaobang, just deceased, and for democracy.

Zhao Ziyang is dismissed as General Secretary and replaced by Jiang Zemin of Shanghai.

Demonstrations increase in size and number through May; university students swear to remain in Tiananmen Square until democracy be granted.

Soviet President Gorbachev visits the PRC and normalisation of Sino–Soviet relations is declared.

20 May, martial law declared; students call for overthrow of Prime Minister Li Peng.

4 June, Tiananmen massacre in Peking.

9 November, Deng Xiaoping announces that he will resign as Chairman of Military Affairs Commission. Jiang Zemin to succeed him.

November, Berlin Wall falls.

December, the Communist government of Romania is overthrown.

1990

Martial law lifted from Peking, many student demonstrators released.

1991

GDP growth is predicted to be 11 per cent, fastest of any economy.

August, in the former Soviet Union a coup d'état by the conservative faction fails; the Soviet Communist Party is disbanded.

December, Deng Xiaoping starts his 'Southern Progress'.

1992

Foreign investment to be permitted in major Southern cities.

1 March, Communist Party Central Document No. 2 (1992), Deng Xiaoping's Southern Progress Talks, is disseminated.

12–18 October, convening of the Chinese Communist Party's Fourteenth Party Congress. The theory of 'the socialist market economy' introduced. Jiang Zemin is elected General Secretary.

1993

Wei Jingsheng released from prison as a goodwill gesture.

GDP grows by 14 per cent.

1995

Wei Jingsheng re-arrested and sentenced to a further fourteen years.

5–10 May, the Standing Committee of the National People's Congress adopts the Commercial Bank Law and the Commercial Bills Law.

6–12 June, ROC President Lee Teng-hui visits Washington, DC; Peking protests.

1996

12 January, China's first shareholding bank, China Minsheng Bank, established.

23 March, Lee Teng-hui re-elected President of the Republic of China by popular vote.

8–25 March, missile exercises in the Taiwan Strait.

CHINA: FRIEND OR FOE?

1997

19 February, death of Deng Xiaoping in Peking, aged 92.

The National People's Congress passes revisions to the Chinese criminal code, eliminating the category of counter-revolutionary crimes.

Forty per cent of the delegates to the National People's Congress register their protest over rising crime and corruption by voting against or abstaining from approval of the work of the Supreme Court by the chief prosecutor.

CCP issues a code of conduct prohibiting officials from personally engaging in profit-seeking activities.

China resumes control of Hong Kong, ending 156 years of British rule.

The Taiwan National Assembly approves constitutional changes to end Taiwan's status as a province of China.

28 October–11 November, President Jiang Zemin visits the USA. President Clinton and Jiang agree to establish a hot-line.

16 November, dissident Wei Jingsheng released, arrives in USA.

1998

Rupert Murdoch, the owner of HarperCollins publishers, denies trying to censor a book critical of China by former Hong Kong governor Christopher Patten.

Former Peking Party head Chen Xitong sentenced to sixteen years in prison in July for corruption; the highest-level Communist leader to be tried for dishonesty.

1999

More than 10,000 followers of Falungong demonstrate around Zhongnan-hai in Peking, protesting at a recent article in an academic journal.

Huge popular protests in China against the NATO missile attack on the Chinese embassy in Belgrade.

President Lee Teng-hui of Taiwan endorses state-to-state relations with mainland China, abandoning the 'one-China' policy.

In a telephone conversation with President Clinton, President Jiang Zemin says that China will not rule out the use of force to crush the independence of Taiwan.

Following the police detention of some 70 leaders of the Falungong, demonstrations erupt in more than 30 cities.

Liu Xianbin, organiser of the China Democracy Party, sentenced to thirteen years in prison for subversion of State power.

Macau returned to the PRC by Portugal.

2000

Sydney Olympics: China wins 28 gold medals and a total of 59 medals, third behind Russia and the USA.

2001

Collision between a US spy plane and a Chinese fighter jet. Diplomatic crisis.

Shanghai Cooperation Organisation (SCO) launched by China, Russia and the Central Asian states to fight ethnic and religious militancy while promoting trade and investment.

China carries out military exercises simulating an invasion of Taiwan.

Peking elected Host City for the XXIX Olympiad in 2008.

China joins the World Trade Organization.

PRC granted permanent normal trade status with the US.

2002

Taiwan officially joins the World Trade Organization, as Chinese Taipei.

Sixteenth Congress of the CCP. Hu Jintao becomes General Secretary.

Vice President Hu Jintao replaces Jiang Zemin, the outgoing President.

2003

Attempted cover-up of the SARS outbreak in China by the Health Minister is foiled when surgeon Jiang Yanyong exposes the true situation to the US media.

Launch of China's first manned spacecraft; astronaut Yang Liwei is sent into space by a Long March 2F rocket.

2004

Athens Olympics; China's final medal tally of 63 medals puts it in third place behind Russia (92) and the United States (103). China is in second place in gold medal count (32), behind the United States (35).

2005

NPC passes law requiring force should Taiwan declare independence.

Relations with Japan deteriorate amid sometimes violent anti-Japanese protests.

China and Russia conduct their first joint military exercises.

China conducts its second manned space flight, with two astronauts circling Earth in the Shenzhou VI space capsule.

Further Reading

Jung Chang, *Wild Swans: Three Daughters of China*, Glasgow: HarperCollins, 1991

Jung Chang and Jon Halliday, *Mao: The Unknown Story*, London: Jonathan Cape, 2005

June Dreyer Teufel, *China's Political System: Modernisation and Tradition* (4th edn), London: Pearson Longman, 2004

Stephanie Hemelryk Donald and Robert Benewick, *The State of China Atlas: Mapping the World's Fastest Growing Economy*, Berkeley, CA: University of California Press, 2005

Christopher R. Hughes, *Chinese Nationalism in the Global Era*, London: Routledge, 2006

Ann Paludan, *Chronicle of the Chinese Emperors: The Reign-by-Reign Record of the Rulers of Imperial China*, London: Thames and Hudson, 1998

Jonathan D. Spence, *The Search for Modern China*, London: Hutchinson, 1990

John Bryan Starr, *Understanding China: A Guide to China's Economy, History, and Political Culture*, London: Profile, 2001

Totem CCE Trust Ltd, *China: The Dragon's Ascent* (eight hour-length films on video or DVD), 2000. Obtainable from Auric, 51 Whitehall Park, London N19 3TW, 00 44 (0) 2075 619730.

Tyrene White, China Briefing 2000: *The Continuing Transformation*, Armonk, NY: M.E. Sharpe, 2000

Susumu Yabuki and M. Stephen Harner, *China's New Political Economy* (revised edn), Boulder, CO: Westview Press, 1999

Index

Why Do People Hate America?

Ziauddin Sardar and Merryl Wyn Davies

The economic power of US corporations and the virus-like power of American popular culture affect the lives and infect the indigenous cultures of millions around the world. The foreign policy of the US government, backed by its military strength, has unprecedented global influence now that the USA is the world's only superpower – its first 'hyperpower'. America also exports its value systems, defining what it means to be civilised, rational, developed and democratic – indeed, what it is to be human. Meanwhile, the US itself is impervious to outside influence, and if most Americans think of the rest of the world at all, it is in terms of deeply ingrained cultural stereotypes.

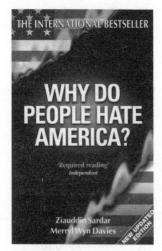

This best-selling book explains exactly why America is so hated. It is an important contribution to a debate which needs to be addressed by people of all nations, cultures, religions and political persuasions.

Paperback £7.99

ISBN: 1 84046 525 5

50 Facts that Should Change the World

Jessica Williams

- A third of the world is at war

- Cars kill two people every minute

- America spends more on pornography than it does on foreign aid

- More than 150 countries use torture

A third of the world is at war
30 million people in Africa are HIV-positive
The US owes the UN $1 billion in unpaid dues
One in five people live on less than $1 a day

facts that should change the world
Jessica Williams

'A research handbook for the *No Logo* generation'
Guardian

'Fearless and compelling. You need to know what's in this book.'
Monica Ali

Think you know what's going on in the world?

Jessica Williams will make you think again.

Read about hunger, poverty, human rights abuses, unimaginable wealth, the drugs trade, corruption, gun culture, the abuse of our environment and much more in this shocking bestseller.

'A research handbook for the No Logo generation'
Guardian

'Fearless and compelling. You need to know what's in this book.' Monica Ali

Paperback £9.99

ISBN: 1 84046 547 6

Iran: Everything You Need to Know

John Farndon

- Could Iran build and use nuclear weapons?

- Might London become the target of an Iranian nuclear attack?

- How would we be affected if Iran cut off oil supplies?

- Does the West's attitude drive young Iranians to extremism?

Iran's President shocked the West when he described the Holocaust as a myth and called for Israel to be 'wiped off the map'. No wonder then that some Western leaders are terrified at the prospect of Iran resuming its nuclear programme – and perhaps building nuclear weapons.

Many argue that Iran is a huge danger. But are the doomsayers right? Is Iran the rabid Islamic dog that some paint it? Is it in fact, as others say, the most prosperous, sophisticated, cultured nation in the Middle East?

Iran: Everything You Need to Know gives you the facts and lets you form your own opinion on this crucial world issue.

Paperback £5.99

ISBN 10: 1 84046 776 2 ISBN 13: 978 1840467 76 5